SAPPHIC CROSSINGS

PECULIAR BODIES: STORIES AND HISTORIES

Carolyn Day, Chris Mounsey, and Wendy J. Turner, Editors

SAPPHIC CROSSINGS

Cross-Dressing Women in Eighteenth-
Century British Literature

ULA LUKSZO KLEIN

UNIVERSITY OF VIRGINIA PRESS

Charlottesville and London

University of Virginia Press

© 2021 by the Rector and Visitors of the University of Virginia

All rights reserved

Printed in the United States of America on acid-free paper

First published 2021

1 3 5 7 9 8 6 4 2

Library of Congress Cataloging-in-Publication Data

Names: Klein, Ula Lukszo, author.
Title: Sapphic crossings : cross-dressing women in eighteenth-century British literature /
Ula Lukszo Klein.
Description: Charlottesville : University of Virginia Press, 2020. | Series: Peculiar bodies :
stories and histories | Includes bibliographical references and index.
Identifiers: LCCN 2020035739 (print) | LCCN 2020035740 (ebook) | ISBN 9780813945507
(hardcover ; acid-free paper) | ISBN 9780813945514 (paperback ; acid-free paper) |
ISBN 9780813945521 (ebook)
Subjects: LCSH: English literature—18th century—History and criticism. | Cross-dressers
in literature. | Male impersonators in literature. | Desire in literature. | Gender identity
in literature.
Classification: LCC PR448.C77 K57 2020 (print) | LCC PR448.C77 (ebook) |
DDC 820.9/3526643—dc23
LC record available at https://lccn.loc.gov/2020035739
LC ebook record available at https://lccn.loc.gov/2020035740

Cover art: "Hannah Snell, a woman who passed as a soldier," mezzotint by J. Young, 1789,
after Richard Phelps. (Wellcome Collection; CC BY 4.0)

To Kathryn

That she might execute her Designs with the better Grace, and the more Success, she boldly commenced a Man, at least in her Dress, and no doubt she had a Right to do so, since she had the real Soul of a Man in her Breast.

—*The Female Soldier; or, The Surprising Life and Adventures of Hannah Snell*, 1750

Notwithstanding my Distresses, the want of Cloaths was not amongst the Number. I appeared as Mr. *Brown* . . . in a very genteel Manner; and, not making the least Discovery of my Sex by my Behaviour, ever endeavouring to keep up to the well-bred gentleman, I became, as I may most properly term it, the unhappy Object of Love in a young Lady.

—Charlotte Charke, *A Narrative of the Life of Mrs. Charlotte Charke*, 1755

The whole truth having been disclosed before the Justice, and something of too vile, wicked and scandalous a nature, which was found in the Doctor's trunk, having been produced in evidence against her, she was committed to Bridewell, and Mr. Gold, an eminent and learned counselor at law, who lives in those parts, was consulted with upon the occasion, who gave his advice that she should be prosecuted at the next sessions, on a clause in the vagrant act, *for having by false and deceitful practices endeavoured to impose on some of his Majesty's subjects.*

—Henry Fielding, *The Female Husband*, 1746

CONTENTS

ACKNOWLEDGMENTS

This project has been a formative one in my academic and writing career, both enjoyable and frustrating at times, but ultimately incredibly satisfying. It could not have happened, however, without the tireless support, imaginative suggestions, and detailed feedback of many friends, readers, and fellow researchers and scholars.

First, I thank the mentors, readers, and peers who encouraged this project when it was in the dissertation stage. Kimberly Cox, Nicole Garret, Margaret Kennedy, and Anthony Teets provided invaluable support, hot meals, and helpful feedback at all stages of the writing process, while the committee members Heidi Hutner, Peter Manning, and Adrienne Munich offered their expertise and advice throughout the process. Kristina Straub served as outside reader on the project, and her support and detailed feedback truly made me feel that I could contribute something of value to eighteenth-century studies and the history of sexuality very early in this project. For that, and her continued support, friendship, and mentorship, I cannot thank her enough. Similarly, Kathleen Wilson's enthusiasm and collaboration shaped an important stage of my early career, both as a graduate student and as an early career researcher; her amity and scholarly pursuits continue to motivate and inspire me. Other professors and mentors at Stony Brook University included Eugene Hammond, Izabela Kalinowska-Blackwood, and Celia Marshik, all of whom helped me develop into the scholar I am today.

As this project continued to change and develop from dissertation to book, the tireless dedication of my writing group helped me find my way.

Kasia Bartoszyńska, Nicole Garret, Emily Kugler, and Amanda L. Johnson have been fierce supporters and compassionate critics of my work, and I could not have developed and improved my project and related articles without their incisive commentary and helpful suggestions. I also thank the writing group at Tennessee Technological University that helped me develop my arguments about female beards for the article that became the foundation for the first chapter of *Sapphic Crossings,* as well as parts of the introduction. These kind people include Paulina Bounds, Martin Sheehan, and Brian Williams.

Beyond the readers who helped shape the arguments of my book project, I thank the many scholars at the American Society for Eighteenth-Century Studies (ASECS) whose presentations and conversations continue to inspire my work, especially Katherine Binhammer, Fiona Brideoake, Jason Farr, Caroline Gonda, George Haggerty, Declan Kavanagh, Paul Kelleher, Sue Lanser, Travis Lau, Devoney Looser, Kathy Lubey, Lisa Moore, Chris Mounsey, Jared Richman, Chris Roulston, Jarred Wiehe, and Eugenia Zuroski, among many others. The work of these scholars and others, such as Terry Castle, Emma Donoghue, and Lillian Faderman, have been foundational to how I think about women in literature, the history of sexuality, queerness, lesbianism, and the stakes of these conversations for the world in which we live. The Gay and Lesbian Caucus, the Disability Studies Caucus, and the Women's Caucus at ASECS have worked tirelessly to make eighteenth-century studies an inclusive space for discussions of queerness and lesbianism, and for that I thank them as well.

This book would not have been possible without several grants from my former institution, Texas A&M International University (TAMIU), in Laredo, Texas. The project was funded by a Texas A&M International University Research Grant, a Texas A&M International University Creative Projects Grant, and a Texas A&M International University Travel Grant. Several University Travel Grants allowed me to visit the Folger Shakespeare Library in Washington, DC, and the National Library of Ireland, as well as the British Library in London, so I could gather sources for this book. The Grants Office at TAMIU was a wonderful resource for me during my time there, and I thank Celeste Kidd and John Kilburn especially for their help in preparing materials and guiding me during the application processes. In addition to the Grants Office, I thank the public relations team both past and present at TAMIU, especially Melissa Barrientos-Whitfield, Ana Clamont, and Steve Harmon, who together helped me promote and publicize my research while at the university and who showed unending enthusiasm and support for my research and service endeavors. I thank the colleagues at TAMIU who were consistently supportive of my work in gender and sexuality, including Malena Charur, Stephen Duffy, Puneet Gill, Jeannette Hatcher, Andrew Hazelton, Hanna Lainas, and Jonathan Murphy. A very special thank you to Deborah Blackwell and Lola Orellano Norris, whose mentorship, encouragement, and good humor sustained me emotionally as well as intellectually. I also thank the members of the TAMIU Knit and Wit Society, TAMIU Philosophy Society, League of Empowered Women, Department of Humanities, and College of Arts and Sciences for support throughout the process of researching and writing this book.

A huge thanks to Sabina Cardenas, Antonia Flores, and Kathryn Wayne who, as students at TAMIU, helped with the research for this project and particularly with finding the images for the book. An especially warm thank you to Antonia for her tireless work as the grant-funded research assistant who helped with so much of the bibliographic work on this project, in addition to helping research and collect sources for this and other projects. These students and many others also contributed to the completion of this project through class discussions of texts that inspired and encouraged me to keep writing.

I thank the team at the University of Virginia Press, especially Angie Hogan, whose commitment to and enthusiasm for this project have helped me navigate the writing and publishing of a first book. Thank you also to the two anonymous manuscript readers whose suggestions overwhelmingly improved the scope of this project and its arguments.

I thank the writing community on Twitter that has supported me in this journey, as well as the writing accountability group on Facebook that has helped keep me going. Thanks to Tita Chico for keeping us all accountable and enthusiastic to write another day.

Portions of some chapters previously appeared elsewhere. A section of the introduction and chapter 1 originally appeared as "Eighteenth-Century

Female Cross-Dressers and Their Beards," *Journal for Early Modern Cultural Studies* 16, no. 4 (2016): 119–43. The section on *Belinda* in chapter 2 appeared in a slightly modified form in "Bosom Friends and the Sapphic Breasts of *Belinda*," *ABO: Interactive Journal for Women in the Arts, 1640–1830* 3, no. 2, art. 1 (2013). A portion of chapter 3 appeared in modified form as "Dildos and Material Sapphism in the Eighteenth Century," *Eighteenth-Century Fiction* 31, no. 2 (2019): 395–412.

Finally, I thank my family for their immense support of my work and scholarship, especially my parents, Jan and Ewa Lukszo; my in-laws, Jo-Anne and Ken Klein; and my brother and sister-in-law, Adam and Casey Lukszo. Most important, I thank my wife, Kathryn Klein, for her love and support throughout this long process; for her feedback on my writing; for the time spent talking through ideas over the dinner table; for her patience when my career took us to places that were not accommodating or comfortable for us; and for her commitment to our relationship and our lives as writers, thinkers, and academics. She inspires me every day with her commitment to her creative writing, to her students, and to building a life together that can sustain our personal and professional goals.

SAPPHIC CROSSINGS

INTRODUCTION

►◄

IMAGINING SAPPHIC POSSIBILITY

First published in London in 1746, *The Female Husband; or, The Surprising Adventures of Mrs. Mary, Alias Mr. George Hamilton, Who Was Convicted of Having Married a Young Woman of Wells and Lived with Her as Her Husband* recounted the story of the cross-dressing lady-killer and convicted fraud Mary Hamilton.[1] Although much of her story—in which she dresses as a man, poses as the physician named George Hamilton, and marries several women while pretending, still, to be a man—was likely highly fictionalized by Henry Fielding, Hamilton's story is only one of many in the eighteenth century in which a woman dresses in men's clothing and successfully seduces willing young women who may or may not realize she is actually a woman. Narratives of cross-dressing women proliferated in Britain throughout the century, and the figure of the female cross-dresser attracted the interest of the eighteenth-century reading public in a variety of literary genres. From the "breeches roles" of the stage and popular novels such as Daniel Defoe's *Moll Flanders* (1722) and Elizabeth Inchbald's *A Simple Story* (1791) to the biographies of female soldiers and female husbands, these narratives focus on how the cross-dresser manages her female body within a masculine gender performance and why she appeals to the women she meets.

Sapphic Crossings: Cross-Dressing Women in Eighteenth-Century British Literature explores how the figure of the cross-dresser comes to take on a central role in the defining and negotiating of gendered and sexual categories in the long eighteenth century. Specifically, this book argues for a reconsideration of the female cross-dresser in eighteenth-century Britain as a central figure who teaches readers how to recognize the realistic, pleasurable, and serious possibility of female same-sex desires that are not apparitional but, rather, tangible, visible, and embodied. While many scholars have indeed discussed the queer resonances of cross-dressing on the stage and among working-class women of the eighteenth century, queer readings of novelistic cross-dressing remain undertheorized. Therefore, among its many goals, this project aims to problematize the notion of generic difference in representations of female cross-dressers. The cross-dresser unites disparate texts, and her representations in these texts indicate the changing and often ambivalent representation and understanding of gender categories at this time and their tenuous, troubling relationship to desire. Further, the female cross-dresser brings the body itself to our attention and urges us to reconsider how desires are not bounded by the gendered body. Instead, the cross-dresser, with her cross-gender appearance and behaviors, and the inability of textual representations to contain her within traditional gender norms, demonstrates for readers the fluidity of desires not predicated on embodied sex and the conflicting eighteenth-century attitudes toward these possibilities. The cross-dressing narrative queers desire and transes categories of embodied gender in the eighteenth century while implicating cisgendered and apparently heterosexual women of all classes as deeply attracted to nonnormative gender performances. Finally, the female cross-dresser becomes a figure that disrupts the attempts of hegemonic eighteenth-century discourses to define and rigidly maintain concepts such as masculinity, whiteness, heterosexuality, and able-bodiedness.

The female cross-dresser of the past is and remains a figure of cultural fascination for the ways in which she is represented as able to negotiate categories of gender and sex, as well as her ability to attract both men and women in her guise as a man. In many ways, when we look closely at the cross-dresser and her irresistible attractiveness to both men and women, her ingenuity and individuality, as well as her ability to cross categories of masculinity and femininity, we can discern a conversation on the nature of gender and desire with important reverberations for our own time. We live in a world with increasing visibility and even acceptance of gender-variant persons, nonheteronormative desires and relationships, and gender fluidity more generally—but only in some parts of the world. In other communities, these people and discourses are brutally repressed and monitored, if not punished or criminalized. The fraught issue of gender, its boundaries, and its relation to sexuality and desire encourages and necessitates further investigation. Looking to the past, we may indeed find preexisting structures of meaning and interpretation, as well as forgotten or discarded methods for thinking about sex and the body. The female cross-dresser and her rise in popularity in the eighteenth century is a cultural motif that encourages reexamination both for how her representation reflected and influenced eighteenth-century debates on gender and sexuality and for how she might change our understanding of these categories even today. As Marjorie Garber points out in *Vested Interests,* cross-dressing is a way to disrupt the male-female binary, and the cross-dresser functions as a "third sex" or "third term" that "questions binary thinking and introduces a crisis."[2] She emphasizes that the "third category" is a crisis of the idea of category itself, and *Sapphic Crossings* argues for giving our close attention to the eighteenth-century female cross-dresser as a third category of gender representation that challenges our understanding of gender and its relationships to desire and the body. Such a new perspective is necessary not only for its implications for the study of eighteenth-century notions of embodiment, desire, and identity, but also for our understanding of these categories in our world today and how they intersect with discourses of nationality, race, and ethnicity.

There has been some disagreement among scholars as to whether historical female cross-dressers were genuinely attracted to the women they courted in disguise, whether the other women recognized them as women, and whether or not these women engaged in sexual acts together.[3] This book is less concerned with sex acts between historical persons than it is interested in how bodies and desires are represented and perceived within narratives, as well as how readers learn to recognize such sapphic possibilities. The stories of cross-dressers present readers with a character who is nominally a woman, even when other characters treat her as a man or as something in-between; thus, readers of these narratives, whether of the eighteenth century or today, are able to perceive the possibilities for same-sex desires and acts in the relationships between the cross-dresser and her female admirers, as well as the possibilities for reading gender fluidity and transgender subjects. Other studies have begun outlining how the female cross-dresser puts gender categories into question. Theresa Braunschneider, Dianne Dugaw, Lynne Friedli, and Kristina Straub, among others, have examined the representation of gender and the female cross-dresser and her ability to "disconnect masculinity (and, with it, sexual orientation towards women) from biological maleness."[4] The representation of the cross-dresser's body and specific body parts, however, has been undertheorized in these discussions, even as the cross-dresser specifically draws attention to the functioning and representation of the body in narrative. In focusing specifically on representation, this project seeks to understand how gender and sexuality functioned in the creative imaginations of eighteenth-century authors and what kinds of ideas were disseminated among readers of the time.

Earlier discussions of female cross-dressers have paid little to no attention to the representation of her body in texts, and this investigation seeks to establish the centrality of the body to our understanding of discursive iterations of female same-sex desires and gender performance. The study thus draws inspiration from performance theories of gender, as well as phenomenological approaches to the body in feminist and disability studies discourses, to examine how body parts function in both physical and metaphorical registers, how bodies are represented, and how they are perceived or "read." Specifically, this book proposes four distinct body parts that draw attention to how bodily appendages function simultaneously in material and metaphorical registers that, taken together, illustrate eighteenth-century attitudes toward women, gender, female desire, cross-gender performance, and mobility. The beard, the breast, the penis, and the legs each play a role in constructing or deconstructing a masculine persona for the cross-dressing woman while also implicating her and her body in the construction of female same-sex desires. Though many of these narratives explicitly deny that the cross-dresser is attracted to the women she courts, the desires of the other women are represented far more ambiguously.[5] Further, these body parts connect the enterprise of cross-dressing to other categories of humanness that were being negotiated via the body in the eighteenth century, such as race, nation, and disability, as well as the question of who could be termed "human" at all.

Unlike other studies of the female cross-dresser, *Sapphic Crossings* considers her in all her forms: as female husband, female pirate, or female soldier; cross-dressing actresses and cross-dressing novel characters; in working-class narratives and in texts coded as genteel or middlebrow. Similarly, this book avoids taking a chronological view of the development of the history of sexuality. Rather than describing a straightforward teleology of the body or female sexuality in literature, I focus on how the image of the cross-dresser complicates such narratives, crossing genre and time, and becomes an indicator of the epistemological dramas of gender and sexuality throughout the century. The fluctuating, ambivalent, and complex gender performances of the female cross-dresser, as represented textually throughout the eighteenth century, complicate the history of sex and the narrative of movement from a one-sex to a two-sex model of gender.[6] Representations of female cross-dressers in the long eighteenth century deconstruct binary understandings of gender difference and, instead, indicate the profound confusion eighteenth-century writers betray with regard to categories of gender and desire. If we regard the texts containing female cross-dressers as constituting a loose literary canon, united by this exciting figure who inhabits the discursive space between the transgressive and the normative, it is no longer possible to distinguish so easily between the laudatory, working-class female cross-dresser who appropriates masculine garb to follow a sweetheart into war or access the independence associated with men and the middle- or upper-class novel characters who must be punished for their frivolous cross-dressing freaks.[7] Instead, the metaphors of the body that emerge from these texts suggest that female same-sex desire and gender fluidity are legible throughout the eighteenth century. It is the cross-dresser who overtly, and with some panache, illustrates the exciting possibility of female same-sex desire and nonbinary gender expressions.

Sapphic Crossings calls attention to the constitutive role of the representations of female cross-dressers to categories of gender and sexuality in the eighteenth century even as they upset the linear development of these categories. Excellent existing studies have investigated how female cross-dressers form part of a larger discussion on female same-sex desire in eighteenth-century texts and how the trope of cross-dressing resonated differently for working-class, plebeian women and middle- and upper-class women, and this book would not be possible without them. Bringing these two intersecting conversations together with queer, trans, and material histories of the body ultimately demonstrates how representations of female cross-dressing serve as large-scale indicators of social fascination with lesbianism and lesbian desires, as well as gender fluidity and cross-gender representation. Further, this study illuminates how non-cross-dressed women who were attracted to the cross-dresser contribute to the growing recognition of lesbian desire and relationships in the eighteenth century.

Eighteenth-century texts represent the cross-dresser's body as ambiguously gendered, or possibly transgendered, but also attractive to other women in large part due to her feminine qualities. These texts are often adamant that the cross-dresser's body can never be biologically male and thus her performance of masculinity is always imperfect. The cross-dresser and her body draw attention to the sapphic or queer possibilities between the cross-dresser and her non-cross-dressed female admirers, in many ways positing explicitly the notion of butch-femme lesbian relations of the mid-twentieth century. Through the representation of the cross-dresser and her body, these texts demonstrate sapphic possibilities despite attempts to ignore, ridicule, or trivialize same-sex desires by the society of the time. By looking at a variety of genres—the novel, the actress memoir, the scandalous criminal biography, popular poetry, and news clippings—*Sapphic Crossings* describes a pattern of representation that indicates the importance of sapphic desires to the stories of female cross-dressers across the eighteenth century. Further, these texts implicitly propose that transgendered representations of bodies were crucial ways of negotiating and representing same-sex desires. The narratives of female cross-dressers explicitly link gender and sexuality in ways that challenge attempts to reincorporate the cross-dresser into a heteropatriarchal narrative while forming a central paradigm for the understanding and acknowledging of a lesbian identity, as well as transgendered embodiment in the eighteenth century. At the same time, these narratives problematically rely on categories of racial and national legitimacy that were becoming increasingly ossified across the eighteenth century.

Histories of Sexuality, the Sapphic, and the Eighteenth-Century Cross-Dresser

Despite the interest in the development of the history of sexuality and other major works on female same-sex desires, there is no book-length study to date on the role of the female cross-dresser in British literature of this time period—or any other time period. The female cross-dresser is both celebrated and reviled in the eighteenth century, and her popularity in works of fiction demonstrates the centrality of her figure to the developing discourses on the modern conceptions of gender, sexuality, and embodiment. Such an undertaking is necessary not only because many scholars currently working in the field focus on only one "type" of female cross-dresser, such as the female husband or the female soldier, thus limiting their purview, but also because such a work exposes the workings of gender and sexuality more broadly in the eighteenth century. Vern Bullough and Bonnie Bullough, for example, focus almost exclusively on real life cross-dressers, while Dianne Dugaw and Julie Wheelwright focus entirely on the figure of the female warrior or soldier. By contrast, Susan S. Lanser and Catherine Craft-Fairchild focus most closely on cross-dressed women in fiction. Rudolph Dekker and Lotte Van de Pol combine a cultural reading of cross-dressing across the centuries with the stories of real-life cross-dressers. They spend little to no time examining the sapphic undertones of many of these stories. Likewise, the figure of the cross-dressed actress is often discussed separately in other studies, such as in Pat Roger's essay "The Breeches Role." Like Lisa L. Moore in *Dangerous Intimacies*, however, I believe that certain nuances and patterns of representation can be understood only when texts are "read together."[8]

The figure of the sapphic subject has recently taken on greater prominence in both literary and cultural studies of the eighteenth century. Lanser persuasively argues in *The Sexuality of History* that the seventeenth and eighteenth centuries saw a rising interest in lesbianism in Europe, where authors, "writing in multiple discursive spheres, conjure female same-sex desire a feature of modern life that calls for consideration or comment."[9] Although narratives of cross-dressing rarely represent sex acts between women, they allude to the titillating possibility of such acts and their pleasurableness in ways that play a constitutive role in eighteenth-century discourses on female same-sex desire and female sexual desires more generally. The female cross-dresser's appeal to other women and "the unquestioned success with which the protagonists not only fool but magnetically attract other women testifies to the fluidity of both gender and desire."[10] Another recent intervention into the history of sexuality is *Thinking Sex with the Early Moderns,* by Valerie Traub, who notes that the study of sex is crucial to knowledge production, and yet "sex is an experience of the body (and hence fleeting) and . . . individual sex acts are likewise local and ephemeral."[11] Textually, the body of the cross-dresser may seem at times to be fleeting and ephemeral, with a breast revealed here, a missing beard alluded to elsewhere. Lanser and Traub illustrate the difficulties as well as the potential rewards of looking at both the discursive effects of sexuality and material histories of the body and sex acts. In considering textual representations of the female cross-dresser's body, her female admirers, and their erotic attractions toward one another, this book draws on studies of the sapphic as a discursive feature of modernity and on material history approaches to the body and sex as an important methodology for scholars of female sexuality in the past.

Like many projects of lesbian literary history, this one has likewise had to grapple with the argument that calling women in the eighteenth century "lesbians" is anachronistic. Terry Castle, Emma Donoghue, Lisa Moore, and Susan Lanser have all made persuasive arguments, however, as to the critical value of looking at lesbian desire and proto-lesbian identities of women in the eighteenth century. The issue of historical accuracy is often a precarious one for the scholar of queer historiography, and this project approaches the topic of lesbian desire in the past with an eye toward both historical accuracy and theoretical rigor. For much of the project, therefore, I focus on the idea of sapphic or same-sex desires, referring to the textual apertures within which we can read female same-sex desires, where they are either represented or perceived, as sapphic possibilities. Lanser similarly calls on the term "sapphic" in her project "for its very vagueness, for its emergence but not overdetermination in the eighteenth century," as well as for its ability "to encompass 'lesbian-like' discourses and representations like those sometimes signaled by 'romantic friendship' that are plausibly if not provably sexual: desire and habits that give primacy to same-sex bonds through words amenable to an erotic rendering."[12] The term "sapphic" allows for a certain amount of flexibility when discussing the female cross-dresser, her body, and her interactions with other women, as well as both her representation in a text and how she was perceived by others in the eighteenth century. Further, "sapphic" was a term used in the eighteenth century much more readily than "lesbian" and signaled specific desires between women that went beyond friendship. For this study in particular, the term "sapphic" is apt as I focus on the different ways in which female same-sex desire manifested on the page, on the stage, and to the readers of these various texts. Rather than searching for material "proof" of lesbian sexual relations between women of the past, this study focuses on the places where such relationships could be imagined and thus made possible.

In attending to the development of lesbian relationships and sapphic possibilities, *Sapphic Crossings* also looks to scholars working in other time periods whose interventions into lesbian literary studies have been formative to the field. Carolyn Dinshaw's study of queer temporalities in medieval texts uses the notion of possibility to articulate a framework for her analysis, writing that "these forms of being show, in fact, that time itself is wondrous, marvelous, full of queer potential. The interrelations between desires, bodies, and the *now* create a broad framework."[13] The importance of "queer potential" highlights the role of the reader and thus the interpreter of a text. The potential pleasures of reading texts this way echo Louise Fradenburg and Carla Freccero's assertion that queer studies may intervene productively in historicist studies of past sexualities by "recognizing pleasure's role in the production of historical discourse."[14] Pleasure and desire mingle in the narratives of female cross-dressers, whose bodies and gender performance offer various pleasures to her interlocutors, while these narratives offer readerly pleasures, as well. Like Martha

Vicinus's *Intimate Friends: Women Who Loved Women, 1778–1928*, *Sapphic Crossings* "reveals a more embodied history" of relationships between women, taking up Vicinus's idea on cross-dressing as "symboliz[ing] sexual fluidity, an assertion that what is seemingly natural and immutable is socially constructed. By highlighting the disjunction between the body and clothing, a woman can draw attention to the rigidities of both female and male sex roles."[15] In this study, it is the texts themselves that work to "draw attention" to these "rigidities" of desires and gender roles. Therefore, *Sapphic Crossings* works within existing strands of thought on how to read same-sex desires in the past while building on these ideas to posit a way of connecting the body and sexuality and revealing the radical potential for reading sapphic desires in the past. The representations of female cross-dressers open up the possibility for reading lesbian desires, but they also thematize eighteenth-century struggles to understand, define, and categorize gender and sex identities more broadly.

Recent interventions into eighteenth-century studies from a trans studies perspective can help shed light on how the female cross-dresser challenges both gender and sexual hierarchies. As characters who cross gender boundaries, in the broadest sense, the cross-dressing characters under study here are necessarily trans, as they are, in the words of Susan Stryker, "people who cross over (*trans-*) the boundaries constructed by their culture to define and contain [their] gender."[16] Thus, the trans perspective informs this study of these women or "women" who cross this binary designation, even as this designation stems from the very texts in which they appear. Scholars working in trans literary studies have put increasing pressure on scholars working on queer, lesbian, and feminist approaches to gender nonconformity and queer sexualities to acknowledge the workings of transness in these texts. As Stryker notes in her foreword to the collection *TransGothic in Literature and Culture,* "'trans-' has additional interpretive capacity in that it can accommodate and account for representations of bodily transformations rooted in desire."[17] According to Jolene Zigarovich, "While the term *queer* opened up a wider space for sexual non-normativity, *trans* captures a range of gendered embodiments, practices, and movements."[18] The work of *Sapphic Crossings* takes place at the intersection, at the *crossing,* of queer and trans, where bodies and desires hold out multiple interpretive possibilities. Relatively recently, the HBO show *Gentleman Jack* (2019), about the Regency era landowner Anne Lister, foregrounded the debates about gender nonconformity and same-sex desire. Was Lister trans? Gender nonconforming? Or was she, as she is frequently touted, "the first modern lesbian"? Questions such as these reveal how high the stakes can be for identity politics in society, as well as in the classroom. In her discussion of the cross-dressing American Revolutionary War soldier Deborah Sampson, alias Robert Shurtliff, Greta LaFleur "refuse[s] to weigh in on the question of whether Sampson/Shurtliff was a feminist, a queer person, or a trans person," preferring instead to recognize that Sampson/Shurtliff and her/his textual representation are crucial to "feminist, queer, and trans political histories" rather than to only one of these interpretive threads.[19] Importantly, this project emphasizes that by placing trans and lesbian in binary opposition, we fall into the same trap that trans studies and queer studies themselves have sought to elucidate and evade. Lister's and Sampson's stories, like those of many eighteenth-century cross-dressing women, potently suggest the pleasures and perils in identifying with historical figures, identifications that have important resonances for classroom teaching, as well.

As texts frequently taught in the university classroom, the narratives I examine here have been taught in what Kirsten T. Saxton, Ajuan Maria Mance, and Rebekah Edwards rename the "transgendered classroom."[20] Thus, the potentialities for reading these texts beyond male-female, man-woman, and masculine-feminine binaries must be acknowledged and explored. Even as this project focuses primarily on how these texts produce and disseminate knowledge about sapphic desires, it is also committed to examining how these texts attempt and fail to sustain coherent concepts of sex and gender that neatly fall into binary notions of either. As Saxton and her colleagues note, often same-sex desires and genderqueer performances become conflated: "Trans-aware inquiry reveals what might be at stake in eighteenth-century representations of crossdressing in the disciplining and binding not only of the femininity of women—by sex or text—but also in eighteenth-century representations of anything 'reading' as feminine (body or text), even elements identified or experienced as 'male.'"[21] I argue that this conflation of embodied sex, perceived gender(s), and possible desires is precisely how these texts reveal the possibilities for *both* same-sex desires *and* transgendered bodies/identities. Nowell Marshall has argued that the term "transtextuality," which he coins, is a "narrative strategy" that "occurs when authors transition characters from one sex to another to safely evoke same-sex desire within their work."[22] Importantly, however, the narratives representing women who cross-dress as men see nothing "safe" at all about this transition; instead, the transition to and performance of masculine gender are, by definition, unsafe, not unlike the often-precarious lives of many trans people or butch/androgynous lesbians in our world today. Even the desires of the non-trans, non-cross-dressed women for the cross-dresser are not "safe." They can "beard" the cross-dresser, as I discuss at length in chapter 1, but they are no guarantee of continued safety, and they manifest in patently unplanned, apparently spontaneous ways in each text. It is this apparent, presupposed spontaneity, and yet simultaneously *expected* element of the genre (a transgenre if there ever was one) that creates pleasurable tensions for the reader, proposing a readerly *jouissance* in the loss of self that is the moment in which the equivalence between "to be a man" and "to love a woman" is overtly exploded.

Studying the inherent nonbinarism of gender is part of the project of this book, even as gender itself is often thought to be crucial to our understanding of same-sex desire. In *Undoing Gender,* Judith Butler expands her previous conversations on the performativity of gender and the social norms that undergird our understanding of ourselves as gendered subjects. She argues that "to keep the term 'gender' apart from both masculinity and femininity is to safeguard a theoretical perspective by which one might offer an account of how the binary of masculine and feminine comes to exhaust the semantic field of gender. Whether one refers to 'gender trouble' or 'gender blending,' 'transgender' or 'cross-gender,' one is already suggesting that gender has a way of moving beyond that naturalized binary."[23] *Sapphic Crossings* works to foreground how the crossing of gender in the narratives of female cross-dressing draw on both masculinity and femininity while also crossing beyond both, denaturalizing the binary and, in Garber's term, introducing a "third sex" or "third term" that "questions binary thinking and introduces a crisis."[24] The destabilization of gender or gender binaries, however, does not negate the reading of sapphic desires in the texts under discussion here. In her study of the "Ladies of Llagollen," Eleanor Butler and Sarah Ponsonby, Fiona Brideoake explicitly argues that "the queerness of their lives and legacy points still further to the instability of all constructions of female same-sex desires, which remain, like Butler and Ponsonby, stabilized only conditionally and to particular cultural and political ends."[25] Thus, Brideoake's project is to uncover the "queerness of lesbian subjectivity itself" through the after-lives of the "Ladies," a perspective that dovetails with my readings of the female cross-dresser, the queerness of lesbian desire, and the transness of the cross-dresser's body.[26] In doing so, this project acknowledges the critical ambivalence of such texts and their disruptive role within the eighteenth-century literary canon, as well as of dominant, teleological understandings of the history of sexuality. Further, this project asserts that eighteenth-century texts often link transgender performances with lesbian desires in ways that question the naturalness of gender binaries while exploiting the sexually provocative nature of trans embodiment and sapphic possibility.

The reading of trans people and proto-lesbians in the past is, of ne-cessity, linked to issues of identity politics of today—as the debates sur-rounding *Gentleman Jack* potently and colorfully illustrate.[27] In tracing an alternative history of same-sex desires between women through the figure of the female cross-dresser, *Sapphic Crossings* engages in the project of tracing queer histories, the form and content of which are increasingly up for debate in queer scholarship. In their introduction to *Premodern Sexualities*, Fradenburg and Freccero ask scholars to acknowledge their own identifications with their historical objects of study in an attempt to go beyond the notion of sexuality as difference and excavate the his-tories of pleasure and the pleasures of history.[28] They push against the dominant discussions of sexuality in history, rooted as they are in Michel Foucault's initial and important theorization of modern sexual categories that cohered around persons rather than acts in *The History of Sexuality, Volume 1*, to consider the pleasurable investments of history and histo-rians.[29] For the proponents of unhistoricism, however, the Foucauldian paradigm focuses too much on difference as the structuring framework for sexuality in the past, which, they argue, works only to confirm history as heteronormative. In their essay "Queering History," Jonathan Goldberg and Madhavi Menon argue that "unhistoricism would acknowledge that history as it is hegemonically understood today is inadequate to housing the project of queering. In opposition to a history based on hetero difference, we propose homohistory. Instead of being the history of homos, this history would be invested in suspending determinate sexual and chronological differences while expanding the possibilities of the nonhetero."[30] *Sapphic Crossings* situates itself as part of the project of homohistory, as I argue that the representations of the female cross-dresser disrupt the neat teleological account of sex and gender categories as entrenched or set by the end of the eighteenth century. Further, the narratives and representations under discussion here cannot be read properly without an understanding of the pleasures inherent in their narratives, the narrative *jouissance* that revels in disjointed storytelling, gender bending, and same-sex juxtapositions of bodies and gazes.

At the same time, I am mindful that unhistoricism and homohistory are themselves problematic and incomplete concepts that cannot fully encompass the current work being done in queer historiography and literary studies. In *Effeminate Years,* Declan Kavanagh points out that "in recent debates on modes of historical inquiry, historicist and unhistoricist alike, the mutually constitutive relationship that exists between queer history and the history of heterosexuality has not been considered." He argues that, regardless of our point of entry, queer scholarship must engage with "the forceful unsettling of the ahistoricism that underwrites heterosexuality and serves to naturalize its universalizing tendencies."[31] The history of heterosexuality is at work in the narratives of female cross-dressers; thus, *Sapphic Crossings* works to unsettle its naturalness by looking at how heterosexual configurations are constantly undercut by the presence of queer desires and trans bodies. Valerie Traub has also critiqued the idea of unhistoricism, a critique that Emily Kugler and I discuss in our introduction to the special issue, "Eighteenth-Century Camp," of *ABO: Interactive Journal for Women in the Arts, 1640–1830.* As we note there, "In Traub's analysis, however, the rejection of purely identitarian queer politics then results in queer readings emptied of historicist and empiricist rigor."[32] Instead, Traub advocates "practic[ing] a queer historicism dedicated to showing how categories however mythic, phantasmatic, and incoherent, came to be."[33] Chris Roulston sums up, "The debate still comes down to the difference between finding *queers in* history and the act of *queering* history, between an investment in identity formation . . . and a questioning of the grounds both of historical practice and queer practice" which, despite outward differences, "the two strands are mutually determining."[34] This project situates itself as part of both of these discussions, foregrounding the "queer vision" with which we must view history—especially, in this case, literary history—while situating this vision within the context of queer people in the past. Thus, the larger stakes of *Sapphic Crossings* are to reveal how eighteenth-century narratives functioned to construct a lesbian-themed canon of literature and propagated lesbian representations that constructed lesbian desire as between women, for the pleasure of women—even as such representations contain important moments for reading gender fluidity and transness in the past. In many ways, lesbian desire can be read in these texts as mediated and enabled through trans histories and bodies. Further, this project hopes to show just how fragile the concepts of masculinity and heterosexuality were for eighteenth-century authors and how writers attempted to reinscribe those categories through the bodies and desires of cross-dressing women.

The case of the "passing" female cross-dresser highlights most clearly the issues of embodiment and desire and the entangled categories of gender and sexuality, trans bodies, and lesbian desires.[35] The women who pass as men are often described as attractive youths whose impeccable imitation of masculinity and maleness seduce unsuspecting young women. For example, the female soldier Hannah Snell "learned her military Exercise, which she now performs with as much Skill and Dexterity as any Serjeant or Corporal in his Majesty's Service,"[36] and in Henry Fielding's *The Female Husband,* the narrator notes, "As [Mary Hamilton] was a very pretty woman, she now appeared a most beautiful youth."[37] When we look more closely at these representations, we begin to see the notion of "impeccable maleness" fall apart in the stories of cross-dressers, whether in print culture or in novels. Hannah Snell fears discovery when her fellow sailors begin to "damn her, calling her Miss Molly Gray" because she does not have a beard to shave.[38] Meanwhile, Mary Hamilton is, at various points, exposed as not manly enough through her high voice; her lack of sexual "wherewithal," or penis; and her breasts, which, when exposed by accident during a bar brawl, "tho' beyond expression beautiful in a woman, were of so different a kind from the bosom of a man, that the married women there set up a great titter."[39] Even in this last example, though, the notion that Fielding singles out the "married" women, as opposed to anyone else male or female, as being singularly able to recognize female breasts suggests a fascinating set of interpretive possibilities for scholars of gender and sexuality.

As these examples illustrate, the representations of female cross-dressers often bring our attention to issues of the body and its role in the representation of same-sex desire. Across the literary genres of the eighteenth century, we see how gender is tied to certain body parts. Breasts are the mark of a woman; facial hair is the mark of a man, and so forth. Yet the representations of female cross-dressers inevitably question such facile determiners of sex and gender. Hannah Snell is mocked by her fellow sailors for her lack of beard, yet her youthful good looks, as well as her knowledge of what women want, render her extremely attractive to a variety of women around Europe. The female soldier Christian Davies is finally exposed as a woman when a surgeon sees her breasts and the embodied markers of motherhood and breastfeeding—yet the female husband Mary Hamilton has her breasts exposed at a public dance hall and no one is the wiser. Despite the "great titter" on this occasion, when Hamilton is finally brought before a justice of the peace and exposed as a woman, the narrator tells us, it was "to the great shock and astonishment of every body."[40] Thus, perception is exposed as faulty, bound up as it is with our own point of view, personal desires, and expectations. The other characters in the text are never completely sure of the cross-dresser's gender: they understand her to be a man, even as she herself fears exposure as a woman. As readers, it becomes difficult for us to separate the contrary visions of the cross-dresser: we are to understand her fear of exposure because she is a woman at the same time as we are to see her as performing maleness and successfully enacting heterosexual courtships. The two versions of the cross-dresser and her appeal to other women become blurred and ambivalent, suggesting both the mutability of the body and the problem of how to "read" it, as well as the irrepressible and irresistible possibility of sapphic desire between these women. These ambiguities also highlight the role of reading and the reader and the way that the cross-dresser's body and desires are effects of perception. If, as Sara Ahmed writes, "it is the ordinary work of perception that straightens the queer effect," then the female cross-dresser invites us to consider the queer effect, the "slant" perception that becomes evident when we read her stories.[41] Further, we can apply this slant or queer perception to many different kinds of texts once we see how even quite disparate texts often focus on the same body parts of the cross-dressing woman.

Indeed, if we read across or aslant various texts, putting criminals' biographies, actresses' memoirs, and satirical poems into conversation with novels, we begin to see certain patterns emerge. Catherine Craft-Fairchild, Dianne Dugaw, and Fraser Easton, each in different ways, have suggested that plebian or working-class women who passed as men for economic advantage were perhaps more "acceptable" to eighteenth-century readers and moralists than upper- and middle-class women who cross-dress in novels, suggesting a fascinating aperture within which to read trans acceptance in these narratives.[42] By contrast, upper-class women's stories rarely represent passing women and instead suggest that their cross-dressing is an occasional whim or a "freak." I argue that the popular narratives of passing women are in conversation with novel representations and therefore must inform our reading of more middle-class, bourgeois texts—texts that often have been deemed heteronormative in their representations of the cross-dresser and female desires. The narratives of passing women such as Hannah Snell and Mary Hamilton were undoubtedly available to and consumed by middle-class readers, who were also reading the popular triple-decker novels, as I explore in more detail in chapter 1.[43] It becomes more difficult to hold on to the argument that bourgeois literary products such as novels were devoid of the same nuances as the stories of passing women when we consider the cross-period, cross-genre connections of these texts and representations. The cross-dressing Leonora in Sarah Scott's tale of Louisa and Leonora in *A Journey through Every Stage of Life* (1754), the gender-neutral costume of Elizabeth Inchbald's Miss Milner in

A Simple Story, and the masculine virago Mrs. Freke in Maria Edgeworth's *Belinda* (1801) each rely on common tropes and received ideas about female cross-dressing in the eighteenth century—ideas that appeared in and were distributed through newspaper stories of passing women, as well as through the stories of female soldiers and female husbands. The way novel characters use their bodies to display, hide, or confuse gender categories, and the manner in which their bodies are seen, understood, and even desired by other women, emphasize the dependent relationship of discourses of sexuality on discourses of gender even within the genre of the novel. Often both become inadequate when speaking about individuals who do not fit any one category of identity.

It may seem contradictory for a study of desire and relationships between women to suggest that the female cross-dresser shows us how contingent bodies and gender can be. Rather than focus on lesbian desire as rigid and identitarian, however, this study urges us to use a more capacious, flexible, and critically aware understanding of the lesbian through the notion of sapphic possibility and sapphic crossing. The body as an object that is subject to interpretation, that is never just one thing, opens up rather than forecloses the possibilities for sapphic desire. If, as Butler has theorized, gender is performative rather than given or inborn, and "the performance of drag plays upon the distinction between the anatomy of the performer and the gender that is being performed," then the cross-dressing woman's performance of maleness illustrates to readers the problem of defining gender.[44] The cross-dresser's ability to put categories into question takes place in parallel with textual representations that emphasize the cross-dresser as a woman whose performance of masculinity is impressive but always imperfect. She is woman and not-woman, and the emphasis on the femaleness of the cross-dresser suggests her potent ability to open up texts to reading sapphic possibilities—even, or perhaps *especially,* in the moments when she also appears masculine or male or androgynous. Further, as this project showcases, the desires of the "femme" women *for* the cross-dresser may in fact more potently suggest sapphic desires and lesbian identifications than the gender-bending performance of the cross-dresser herself. The butch, in this case, makes the notoriously invisible femme visible and identifiable.

In *The Renaissance of Lesbianism,* Traub theorizes the notion of "cycles of salience," a phrase she coins to explain "why certain figures of eroticism (and gender) become culturally salient at certain moments"[45] The female cross-dresser is one such figure whose cycle of salience is at a high in the eighteenth century. In many ways, the cross-dresser is, to use Traub's words, an "explanatory logi[c]" that "seem[s] to underlie the organization and reorganization of erotic life."[46] Further, Traub, drawing on the work of Gayle Rubin and Jeffrey Weeks, suggests that "cycles of salience may be linked temporally and conceptually to moments of social crisis which have their sources in anxieties peripheral to eroticism (such as fears about changing gender roles, nationalist or racist fears of contamination, and broad concerns about morality or social discipline)."[47] If we accept the arguments of scholars of the eighteenth century that this was a time period in which categories of race, nationality, gender, disability and even sexuality emerged, ossified, or were codified into their modern iterations, then the cross-dresser may be, in fact, one erotic figure through whom such anxieties manifested or were (temporarily) alleviated. More specifically, though, Traub notes that the passing woman and the female friend were two particularly popular and well-known ways, throughout Western European history, to represent lesbianism and female same-sex desires, and these are the erotic figures that she uses to theorize the idea of cycles of salience. In this book, I focus primarily on the idea of the passing woman, and yet, her story crosses over into the story of the female friend. It is my argument that the cross-dressing woman, the "passing woman" who is both masculine and feminine, makes lesbian sexuality visible through her relationships to other, non-cross-dressed women. In this way, the relationships under consideration here may form another kind of erotic category, the double category of the butch-femme relationship, which, in the words of Joan Nestle, is "one of the oldest [traditions] in lesbian culture."[48]

In today's twenty-first-century moment, the butch-femme lesbian tradition appears to have receded in the West, and even when it appears, it is often subject to criticism. Since the 1970s, skepticism, disapproval, and overt criticism have denigrated butch-femme relationships and identities, and, as Nestle notes, such negative attitudes and labeling "forgets two women who have developed their styles for specific erotic, emotional, and social reasons."[49] And while Nestle is thinking more specifically here of twentieth-century categories of lesbian identity, she nods to the history of passing women and their "wives," the femme women who desire them: "to others, the femme woman has been the most ambiguous figure in lesbian history; she is often described as the nonlesbian lesbian, the duped wife of the passing woman."[50] *Sapphic Crossings* attempts to resituate the history of the butch-femme relationship, looking at its representation in the eighteenth century, even if such terminology is not historically appropriate or accurate. As Traub notes, the erotic formations that cycle through culture periodically are most fruitfully considered not in terms of "identifications" but, rather, through consideration of "discrete yet recurring moments when certain definitional elements crop up as particularly meaningful to understandings of eroticism."[51] This project therefore does not locate meaning through one-to-one connections between modern-day lesbians and cross-dressing women—and their femme admirers or lovers. Instead, it seeks to identify how same-sex desires implicated these femme women in sapphic relations and how both butch and femme women of the past made lesbian desires visible to readers of these narratives. At the same time, such a reading does not intend to, nor should it be read to, negate the possibility of reading a trans man loving ciswomen and ciswomen attracted to a trans man. The fascination that eighteenth-century authors and readers had for women who crossed gender and sexual binaries and boundaries is not self-evidently tied to only gender crossing or only sexual crossing. The desire for sexual as well as gender fluidity, therefore, allows for multiple readings at once while also potently suggesting cross-gender representations of women as "definitional elements" that tell us something about eighteenth-century eroticism.

The stories of women who passed as men, stories that often appear in popular and cheap broadsides, most overtly illustrate the gender-bending possibilities of desire between women. Their stories suggest new ways of understanding other forms of gender transgression and female same-sex desire in texts that purport to be about heterosexual desires or even those that explicitly seem to disavow female same-sex desires. These texts read differently when we keep in mind the complex, complicated intermingling of vision and knowledge, expectation and desire, gender and sexuality. Eliza Haywood's briefly cross-dressing Violetta in *Love in Excess* (1719) reads differently when we consider that Count D'Elmont perceives her as a credible rival for his beloved Melliora's affections because the reader knows that Violetta is a woman. The actress Charlotte Charke's mournful apologies for inadvertently seducing young women while she appeared onstage *en cavalier* make us reconsider how appealing the female cross-dresser's female masculinity appears to be to women everywhere. Scott's Leonora similarly apologizes for how well she inadvertently seduces young women who think she is a man, yet her feminine beauty and impeccable knowledge of "what women want" suggest other possibilities. In Inchbald's *A Simple Story*, Miss Milner's scandalous, androgynous masquerade costume and her friend Miss Woodley's admiration of it take on a new meaning when we consider the eighteenth-century preoccupation with vision and desire, while the shared site of Lady Delacour's breast between Belinda and the cross-dressing Mrs. Freke reveals the potential for reading a sapphic love triangle. The textual representations of the cross-dresser and the women who fall for, admire, or befriend her reveal lesbian connections and desires.

Even as this project focuses on the ways in which texts create sapphic possibilities between women, it is a part of a larger project of lesbian historiography. The power of the term "lesbian" is derived in part from the notion of difference: a lesbian is different from other women; she desires differently; she sees the world differently; she is Other. But what if she is also everywhere? The female cross-dresser suggests this radical possibility as her presence in a text challenges the boundaries of sex, gender, and the body and their tenuous links to desire, while also suggesting the importance of same-sex desire to female eroticism writ large. She makes bodies alternately visible and invisible, male and female, masculine and feminine and asks us to question these rigid binaries while demonstrating further possibilities for reading across the spectrum of desires and sexual identities. The appeal of the female cross-dresser to other women—women *not* coded overtly as gender non-normative—opens up the possibility that there may be many women in the world who desire their own sex, or that it might be possible for any or every woman to be attracted to another woman at some point in her life, thus invoking Adrienne Rich's nuanced concept of the "lesbian continuum."[52]

Scholars of the lesbian have struggled against heterosexist biases in historicist and literary studies that often argue against even the possibility of the lesbian in the past. This problem has been addressed notably by Terry Castle, whose essay collection *The Apparitional Lesbian* asserted in its titular essay that lesbians of the past were consisted ghosted or marginalized, despite being implicated in all areas of life and creative endeavor. More recently, Lanser's argument about sapphism as being constitutive of modernity has worked to reassert the important role of the oft-marginalized lesbian figure. Scholars such as Castle and Lanser, as well as Fiona Brideoake, Sharon Marcus, Valerie Rohy, and Martha Vicinus, have worked diligently to recenter the lesbian and reveal her influence on our society and literary output, as well as to challenge heterosexist biases in these areas of scholarship.[53] Like these previous works, *Sapphic Crossings* argues that to reject the lesbian as a vital figure in the understanding of the world is just another kind of blindness, another kind of desire to not see. The representations of the female cross-dressers in the eighteenth century in some ways foreground these debates by putting issues of knowledge, sight, desire, and disguise at the forefront, forcing us to confront our biases even as she holds out the possibility of multiple interpretations not just of herself or her desires, but of all bodies and all desires. Finally, she encourages us to question how we read and interpret, what we choose to see or not see as readers, as critics, and as people.

Overview of the Project

The body parts under consideration here are not chosen at random; instead, they are appendages that feature prominently in the narratives of eighteenth-century female cross-dressers in ways that function to question gender binaries and triangulate desire between women. In addition to functioning as physical parts, they also function within these narratives in important metaphorical registers. Each chapter considers a single body part and its representation in narratives containing female cross-dressing while also juxtaposing texts of different genres and from different decades of the eighteenth century. At least one novel features in each chapter to reveal how these works are affected by and in conversation with theatrical performances, criminal biographies, actress memoirs, female husband narratives, and female soldier biographies. Together, these chapters consider how eighteenth-century texts negotiated the boundaries of gender and female desire through the body of the cross-dresser and the women who desire her.

Chapter 1, "Eighteenth-Century Female Cross-Dressers and Their Beards," focuses on situating the concept of the beard as an important tool of critical inquiry when it comes to representing gender and desire. The facial beard is often represented as the most prominent, visible indicator of masculinity, and various cross-dressing heroines must compensate for the missing facial beard when other characters draw attention to their hairless faces. The cross-dresser courts other women whose desires will then take the place of the missing facial hair. In this way, the beard functions physically and metaphorically, as the women who come to desire the cross-dresser function as her "beards." The beard first and foremost, as a conceptual tool, demonstrates the importance of the cisgendered, "femme" women who desire the cross-dresser, and thus how both the cross-dresser and her admirers reflect eighteenth-century curiosity and interest in female same-sex desires. Further, the idea of the beard challenges eighteenth-century ideas about masculinity and definitions of manliness. This chapter establishes the term "beard" as a critical tool of inquiry that will then engage with the remaining appendages. In the chapter I explore the stories of Mary Hamilton in Henry Fielding's *The Female Husband;* Hannah Snell in *The Female Soldier; or, The Surprising Life and Adventures of Hannah Snell* (1750); and the fictional Leonora in Scott's *A Journey through Every Stage of Life,* all of which explicitly link the facial beard to the project of passing successfully as a man and avoiding discovery, rape, or loss of work. Consequently, these texts work to "beard" the cross-dresser in some other way—frequently by having her solicit and gain the desires of other women, who often respond positively to the cross-dresser and her gender nonbinary embodiment. The women who desire the cross-dresser in her disguise, her "beards," and their (purported) collective failure to see the cross-dresser as something other than a male-sexed object of desire opens the space for sapphic possibilities in the text, as the reader always knows that the cross-dresser is a woman. Though other critics have read these courtships in a more negative light, arguing that the female cross-dresser uses these women in a rakish and irresponsible way, upon closer examination these representations appear much more nuanced. The desires of the cross-dresser are frequently as ambiguous as her own gender performance, while the admiration and desire of the other women *for* the cross-dresser are clear to the reader, who, in turn, knows that the cross-dresser is a woman. Thus, the notion of the beard makes lesbian desires visible in part through the metaphorical beards themselves, bringing femme women's desires for butch women (or trans men) into stark relief.

Chapter 2, "The Sapphic Breasts and Bosom Friends," considers the breast as both a physical marker of femaleness and as a metaphorical term for the seat of human emotions, revealing the desirableness of the cross-dresser to men and women. Narratives of female cross-dressers often emphasize that the presence of breasts, like the missing facial beard, is a hazard for her gender performance, and many of these narratives focus on the moment in which other characters, both male and female, see the breast or breasts exposed. The moments in which the cross-dresser reveals her breasts to other women demonstrate to readers the moments in which desire might be elicited through vision. In both cases, the beard and the breast are represented textually as undeniably male or female, respectively, before those assumptions become suddenly untenable. This chapter focuses on the moments in which the female cross-dressers' breasts are revealed, whether intentionally or inadvertently, and how other characters respond to these breasts in texts such as Captain Charles Johnson's *A General History of the Robberies and Murders of the Most Notorious Pyrates* (1724); *The Life and Adventures of Mrs. Christian Davies, the British Amazon, Commonly Called Mother Ross* (1741); and *The Female Husband*. The implied viewing of body parts indicates the erotic potential of the breast as it is visually consumed by women. The inability of some to correctly identify the exposed breast as female also transes the breast by suggesting that breasts are not always female. By the end of the century, in Maria Edgeworth's novel *Belinda,* the breast denotes femaleness through maternity, yet its power to elicit female same-sex desire is stronger than ever. Looking at breasts, we must reconsider current discussions of female sexuality in the eighteenth century and acknowledge the power of the visual to both confound and enlighten. The exposed breast complicates ideas of gender difference while also suggesting the erotic potential of shared bodies and emotions as a part of the physical intimacy that is often a consequence of female cross-dressing. The representations of the body always exceed narratorial attempts to contain the body within the traditional confines of male and female, masculine and feminine; instead, the reader is privy to the ways that, taken together, these various texts allow for the fluidity of both gender and desire. At the same time, the racialized qualities attributed to the breast point to how fluidity of gender and sexuality functioned in contrast to the entrenched ideas about racial difference in the eighteenth century. The chapter considers how the project of defining racial hierarchies in the eighteenth century intersected with the rising interest in sapphic possibilities and transgender embodiments.

Chapter 3, "Penetrating Discourse and Sapphic Dildos," takes up the appendage of the penis, arguably the most gendered body part under consideration here. However delicately or indelicately, many narratives allude to the missing male appendage as a problematic inadequacy of the cross-dresser, only to then contradict themselves and show that despite the missing marker of maleness, cross-dressers can still pass as men and perform masculinity—and, in so doing, fulfill other women's desires. In some of these stories, the penis is replaced materially through a prosthetic phallus—that is, the dildo. The chapter explores the roles of the penis and the dildo in the stories of female husbands and female soldiers, as well as in John Cleland's erotic novel *Fanny Hill; or The Memoirs of a Woman of Pleasure* (1749). The stories of female soldiers and female husbands construct the cross-dresser's missing male genitalia as an important signifier of maleness without which she is exposed to danger and discovery while also suggesting she is incapable of fully satisfying female desires. As with the beard, however, these texts ultimately question the importance of being in possession of a penis by suggesting that female cross-dressers can please women in other ways, including through the use of a dildo.

Eighteenth-century discourses portray the dildo as superior in function to the penis, even as it is always inferior because it is fraudulent, as depicted in early eighteenth-century dildo poems. It is never a "real" penis, even as it performs better and more dependably than the penis. I return to the stories of Christian Davies and *The Female Husband* and add to this chapter the narrative of Italian female husband Catherine Vizzani in Giovanni Bianchi's *An Historical and Physical Dissertation on the Case of Catherine Vizzani* (1751). Together, these texts reveal how the dildo becomes a way for the female husband to access male power while enjoying same-sex desires that the narrators of these texts cannot completely account for or completely condemn. In *Fanny Hill* we see how entwined heteronormative desires are with same-sex ones and how the penis itself comes to function, discursively, like a dildo. The dildo draws our attention to the ambiguity of the body and gender while also functioning as an appendage that allows explicitly for the fulfillment of lesbian desires. Thus, the penis is and is not a marker of maleness in these texts, and the dildo is a penis replacement as well as an appendage of female desire. The chapter therefore also interrogates histories of heterosexuality and cisgenderedness as the case studies focus on just how aggressively these normative concepts must be defended, therefore revealing their fragility as a social construct constantly in need of reifying and protecting.

Chapter 4, "Putting on Gender, One Leg at a Time," considers legs, an appendage not defined by a single gender and yet intimately bound up with gendered expectations and desires. The final chapter explores how legs and their presence as visible or not become associated with different genders and function as important parts of the cross-dresser's erotic performance of female masculinity. In the metaphorical register, legs are also linked to masculine prerogatives, including independence and mobility, as well as materially linked clothes metaphors: the breeches and the petticoats. The chapter considers the role of actresses' legs in breeches parts on the eighteenth-century stage through a reading of Charke's autobiography, as well as stage biographies of the Irish actress Margaret "Peg" Woffington. Both actresses often bragged about their ability to seduce women in the audience through their beautiful legs, revealing how sapphic desires were triangulated through actresses' legs. The performative aspect of the body and the role of legs in soliciting same-sex desires and giving women access to enhanced mobility is then also visible in the legs of cross-dressing novel characters in Inchbald's *A Simple Story* and Edgeworth's *Belinda*. The legs of Miss Milner and Mrs. Freke symbolize their desire for freedom while also potently alluding to female same-sex relationships in the novels. Finally, the legs of the cross-dresser powerfully highlight the importance of able-bodiedness, mobility, and movement in the late eighteenth century, representations that intersect with the growing discourses of disability, challenging the notion of a modern subject as one who is, by default, cisgender, heterosexual, and able-bodied.

The representations of female cross-dressers depict them exposing their body parts to other women; seducing other women; and spending intimate moments together, sometimes caring for a sick or ailing friend. Each of these scenarios suggests a moment in which women are seeing the bodies of other women in intimate situations, while the texts themselves are ambiguous as to whether these women "know" each other to be women and whether they experience same-sex desires. When we read how Hannah Snell gives "ocular demonstration" of her femaleness to another woman, or when Lady Delacour exposes her diseased breast to Belinda's view, we are reading intimate, embodied moments that foreground sapphic possibilities between characters. These characters see the exposed bodies, but their desires are not described, though they are sometimes implied. The possibility of desire is there for the reader to imagine, as narrators and authors of these texts frequently call on the readers of the texts and reference their presence, explicitly rendering the intelligibility of these texts as triangulated through an interested reader. These texts maintain that such bodily sightings exist for the purposes of plot or function as conduits for female friendship, yet the vision of the exposed body parts alludes to bodily intimacies and same-sex desires.

The cross-dressed woman is often represented as puzzling and perplexing, or even as delighting in the process of confusing others' vision. The process of looking and vision itself is exposed in these texts as partial, doubled, obscured, and unclear, at best. The ability of other women to fall in love with the beautiful cross-dresser, to look at her feminine face and body and "see" something attractive but *not* see the woman under the clothes, further reveals that vision is selective, incomplete, and very often faulty. Despite the cross-dresser's often obvious femininity—or perhaps because of it—other women fall in love with her. The women who desire a feminine-looking man (who is actually a woman in disguise) demonstrate both the ease with which misreadings are possible and how quickly female desires become queer in these texts. Sapphic possibilities are often predicated on these other women's misreading of the female cross-dresser as male, yet the female cross-dresser herself, while appearing male within the context of the narrative, has a body whose representation, whose very embodiment, exceeds the confines of gender binaries and heteronormative structures of desire. By the same token, the desires of the women who respond to the female cross-dresser's performance of maleness suggest the malleability of desire and its only ever-tenuous connection to embodied sex. These women become the metaphorical beards whose role in the female cross-dressing narrative is crucial both to the suggestion of sapphic desires and to the cross-dresser's performance of masculinity.

Sapphic Crossings explores how cross-gender performances become coded as opportunities for exploring, enjoying, or even eliciting same-sex desires. This study takes into consideration not just the body of the cross-dresser, but also how women who cross paths with the cross-dresser come to love, admire, and desire her—not for her superb performance of masculinity, but precisely for what a woman can bring to the concept of masculinity. Both the cross-dresser and the women who desire her cross boundaries of desire, social codes, and even gender, as represented in eighteenth-century British literature. Further, this study crosses and connects various genres to posit that the stories of cross-dressing women form their own narrative subgenre, one that connects what might otherwise appear to be disparate texts. It is only when we understand the exposed breasts of the female soldier Christian Davies and those of the female pirate Mary Read as discursively linked that we understand more completely how the exposed breast of Lady Delacour in *Belinda* might be more than a marker of inadequate mothering: it may also be the marker of sapphic possibility. Similarly, the stories of the female husbands Mary Hamilton and Catherine Vizzani and their allusions to and euphemisms for the women's dildos cause us to pause and rethink the boundaries of gender and desire as they are represented in Cleland's *Fanny Hill*. This cross-genre, cross-time, and cross-body approach seeks to bring about a new way of thinking about the history of sexuality—as a history that relies not just on what was, but also on what was imagined, and what might be possible to imagine. Finally, *Sapphic Crossings* takes seriously the role of the reader, both in the eighteenth century and today, to consider how the past crosses over into the present and what interventions past knowledge might make in our world today.

1

▸◂

EIGHTEENTH-CENTURY FEMALE CROSS-DRESSERS AND THEIR BEARDS

In eighteenth-century narratives of cross-dressing women, the facial beard is a marker of maleness and masculinity, and its lack can be disguised by successful courtship of other women.[1] In the female soldier Hannah Snell's history, *The Female Soldier; or, The Surprising Life and Adventures of Hannah Snell* (1750), the narrator reports that her fellow sailors "began to declare her to be a Woman on account of her smooth Face, seeing she had no Beard."[2] Sarah Scott's narrator in "The Story of Leonora and Louisa," in the novel *A Journey through Every Stage of Life* (1754), explains that the older ladies who see Leonora in her disguise as a young clergyman "would frequently ridicule her want of Beard."[3] Even Daniel Defoe's Moll Flanders (*The History and Misfortunes of the Famous Moll Flanders*, 1722), who disguises herself as a man only briefly, worries about her ability to portray a masculine character successfully, as she believes she is "a little too smooth-faced for a man."[4] In these examples, narratives emphasize the facial beard as an important component of masculinity, one whose absence draws attention to the cross-dresser's femaleness. These texts clearly draw on eighteenth-century expectations for embodied masculinity and visible markers of maleness via facial hair at a time when beards were unfashionable. At the same time, the cross-dresser's feminine features are often what makes her so attractive to other women. Thus, female cross-dressing narratives in the eighteenth-century link gender and desire, only to disrupt this connection by suggesting that other women desire the cross-dresser for her feminine qualities as much as for her masculine ones. The women who desire the female cross-dresser become her "beards," metaphorically taking the place of the facial beard and supplementing the missing marker of masculinity. The textual emphasis on the facial beard builds on constructions of maleness and masculinity, suggesting how masculinity might be troubled in the eighteenth-century imaginary. The ambiguous gender presentation of the cross-dresser in these texts, their emphasis on embodied markers of maleness, and their final rejection of these embodied markers, also suggests a trans reading of these texts that highlights the in-betweenness of the cross-dresser's body.

Today's readers may be familiar with the term "beard" as one that references a woman who appears with a gay man to disguise his homosexuality or refute allegations of it. In this sense, "beard" is an apt term for the women who desire the female cross-dresser.[5] These women camouflage the female cross-dresser's perceived dearth of masculinity or maleness, just as homosexual men who acquire a beard do so partly because of a perceived lack of (normative) masculinity that they wish to disguise. The person in the position of beard becomes a marker of masculinity and heterosexuality. The idea of the beard, in its many meanings and its cultural attachment to erotic discourses—masculinity, homosexual hiding, sexual virility, female pubic hair, and rampant female sexuality—emerges as a term whose meaning may vacillate, yet its historically-constructed genealogy indicates its persistence. The term "beard," therefore, can be read through Valerie Traub's idea of the "cycles of salience," as one whose ideological functioning asserts itself over and over in discourses of sexuality, marking it as a site of sexual difference and gender performance throughout Western culture.[6] The notion of the metaphorical beard— the woman who desires the cross-dresser—suggests that gender is defined through an array of different, at times contradictory, components that can be manipulated by an individual. The women who function as beards also function as indicators of the possibility of same-sex desires that are legible to eighteenth-century readers of these texts, regardless of the cross-dresser's purported intentions. These narratives allude to the titillating possibility of lesbian sex acts and sapphic possibilities by representing women attracted to the cross-dresser for her androgynous/ feminine qualities as much as for her masculine ones. Readers of these narratives, whether of the eighteenth century or today, are made aware of

the possibilities for same-sex desires and acts in the relationships between
the cross-dresser and her beards, even as trans identities are also made
legible in the text.[7] Though many of these narratives explicitly deny that
the cross-dresser is attracted to the women she courts, the desires of the
other women are ambiguous.[8] The focus on the beard therefore demonstrates how textual representations make female same-sex desires legible
to readers as not only possible, but also as pleasurable and even preferable
to heterosexual couplings.

Indeed, Theresa Braunschneider posits that a more nuanced reading of
the cross-dresser and her female admirers might focus on the "question of
how these texts construct knowledge. . . . Each of these narratives establishes an epistemological drama in which the narrator and readers 'know'
that the body in question is really female while the characters within
the narrative 'know' it is really male."[9] In other words, even if female
soldiers, for example, were historically and uncritically accepted as male
by their female companions, a reader's knowledge actively shapes his or
her interpretations of a cross-dressing heroine in a text. The narratives
often emphasize that the cross-dressing woman is female, and the text
represents her as such: the texts consistently place the femaleness of her
body at the forefront of the narratives, often alluding to her sex in the
title, such as *The Female Soldier* or *The Female Husband.* These texts portray
the female cross-dresser's ability to solicit female desires, not as a man
but, rather, as a woman, and the reader inhabits the privileged position
of being able to see the metaphorical beards in the context of same-sex
desires: women who desire women. Cross-dressing narratives scrutinize
the cross-dresser's physical body, often portraying lack of facial hair as a
flaw in these women's performance of maleness and masculinity. Thus,
in literary texts the absence of beard comes to represent a weakness in
the cross-dresser's disguise for which the metaphorical "beard" of feminine desire compensates. Yet these beards who are meant to establish the
cross-dresser's appropriated masculine gender, in turn, demonstrate to
eighteenth-century readers the exciting possibility of same-sex desire, as
readers are privy to the fact that the cross-dresser is a woman desired by
other women. The attraction the cross-dresser holds for other women, her
beards, as well as for the reading public of the eighteenth century marks

her as a figure that emblematizes eighteenth-century debates about the boundaries of bodies, gender, sexuality, and desire.

More recent scholarship has indeed examined the homoerotic tensions in the stories of female cross-dressers, emphasizing how the cross-dresser embodies "a provocatively fluid, performative and transgendered construction of human sensibility" in which "the ongoing play of homoeroticism within the story's frame constitutes a vivid, characteristic feature of the female hero's cultural power."[10] Similarly, in her discussion of the breasts of the female pirates Anne Bonny and Mary Read, Sally O'Driscoll has argued that the women's "ability to pass could be interpreted as an acknowledgment that gender is malleable and performative, rather than essential and naturalized."[11] The notion of the beard as a marker of masculinity that is inadequate yet replaceable suggests the fluidity of gender that both Dianne Dugaw and O'Driscoll identify in the representations of female cross-dressers. The metaphorical beard disrupts notions of binary sex and gender, as the beard, whether literal or figurative, never fully defines maleness or femaleness. Similarly, the focus on the beard and representations of embodiment complicate previous arguments about the progressive "desexualization of fictional heroines" in eighteenth-century literature.[12] The beard keeps gender and desire linked to the body, demonstrating how eighteenth-century representations of lesbian desires function in discursive, affective, and embodied modes. By looking at the attraction of other women for the cross-dresser, the metaphorical beards who come to take the place of the facial beard, we render a larger picture of how cross-dressing narratives responded to and shaped eighteenth-century discourses of gender, desire, and sexuality. Further, the gender fluidity of the cross-dresser also opens the possibility for reading transgender identities and bodies in eighteenth-century texts. The desires of the "beards" for the cross-dressed character disrupt binary notions of gender and desire, even as these relationships thematize a "butch-femme" paradigm.

Cross-dressers and their beards in popular texts are also indicators of how female same-sex relations and sex acts, as well as gender fluidity, became of interest to eighteenth-century readers and makers of culture. If indeed, as Susan Lanser argues in *The Sexuality of History*, female same-sex desire took on a greater cultural prominence in this time, it can be said to have happened only in tandem with a broader interest in defining and defying gender roles.[13] The narratives of female cross-dressers thus reflect eighteenth-century writers' interests in both female same-sex desires and gender fluidity and the body. As a tool of critical inquiry, the term "beard" is one that acknowledges the indeterminacy and ephemerality of sexual pasts, as suggested by Traub, as well as the fluidity and possibility of textual representation. In looking at representations of the female cross-dresser's body, her beards, and their erotic attractions toward one another, this chapter, like this larger project, seeks to bridge studies of the sapphic as a discursive feature of modernity with material, historical approaches to the body and sex. The narratives about beards thus also intersected with the growing discourses on masculinity in the eighteenth century, which were, in turn, also discourses that helped define and categorize humanity through embodied notions of civilization, as we shall see.

This chapter on the beard and female cross-dressing considers, first, how facial beards helped define masculinity and, by extension, "civilized" humanity before turning to three narrative case studies that specifically link the problem of the missing facial beard to passing as a man and courting women's affections. These three texts clearly illustrate the importance, as well as the ambiguity, of the beard in its many meanings, and they each represent different genres in which the female cross-dresser often features: the woman warrior story, the novel, and the criminal biography. The texts are, respectively, *The Female Soldier;* "The History of Leonora and Louisa," in Scott's *A Journey through Every Stage of Life;* and Henry Fielding's *The Female Husband* (1746). Together, these texts reveal a pattern of representation regarding female cross-dressing and same-sex desire: they emphasize that female cross-dressers need other women to complete their masculine performance and represent the positive reaction of other women to the cross-dresser. The last section widens the purview of this analysis by adding texts that do not specifically mention a missing facial beard yet clearly contain metaphorical beards who help the cross-dresser pass as a man. The previous texts, as well as the popular memoirs of the female soldier Christian Davies, *The Life and Adventures of Mrs. Christian Davies, the British Amazon, Commonly Called Mother Ross* (1741), and the actress Charlotte Charke, *A Narrative of the Life of Mrs. Charlotte*

Charke (1755), present the cross-dresser's masculine performance as superior to actual maleness. The depictions of female cross-dressing in the narratives of Davies and Charke demonstrate metaphorical bearding and further possibilities for representing the reality and pleasurableness of same-sex desire.

Although the intended audience for these works may seem disparate—*The Female Soldier* draws on lower-class balladry traditions and archetypes while Scott's novel presents a middle-class heroine for a middle-class readership—this variety of representation and genre underscores the degree to which the concept of bearding contributed to the discourses of desire and embodiment in the eighteenth century while also intersecting with discourses of masculinity and effeminacy. Working-class women often cross-dressed "in order to secure some of the economic and social advantages accorded to men," while "plays and novels depicted cross-dressing as either a whimsical or a vicious activity," but it is also likely that bourgeois readers and consumers of plays and novels had access to more positive representations of lower-class female cross-dressing.[14] The narratives of Christian Davies and Hannah Snell were reprinted several times in popular publications such as the *London Magazine,* the *Gentlemen's Magazine,* the *Daily Advertiser,* and the *Scots Magazine.* Fielding's *The Female Husband* also appeared in those three publications.[15] Many of these publications regularly published smaller notices of instances of female cross-dressing throughout the eighteenth century. As Fraser Easton explains, "These press reports draw on a variety of generic modes, including romance, melodrama, rogue narrative, jestbook anecdote, the picaresque, and patriotic adventure."[16] Such various modes clearly intersect and influence novelistic representations and further, as popular and regularly featured news items they would have reached a large number of eighteenth-century readers.[17] *The Female Soldier* and *The Female Husband,* with their middle-class audience and influence from the novel genre, represent a new type of ephemeral literature—the "middling class texts"—that O'Driscoll identifies as crucial to the evolving attitudes toward women's sexuality in the middle of the century.[18] Thus, while narratives of working-class heroines often contain archetypal representations of the cross-dresser and her struggles, her body exceeds these representations in fascinating and exciting ways that, like novels, demonstrate the struggles of eighteenth-century writers to maintain control over their unruly subjects.[19]

The concept of the beard reveals the erotic potentialities of these texts, highlighting the difficulty of narrating the body, and thus the transing of gender, while also drawing our attention to the queer desires of the non-cross-dressed women who desire the cross-dresser. For the cross-dresser, the facial beard is something that exists only in its absence, and it becomes material through the involvement of other women and their desires with those of the cross-dresser, however witting or unwitting. The metaphorical and linguistic slippage of the beard as a term for interrogating sexuality in a text illustrates the tension inherent to reading the history of sexuality in discourse: the body is notoriously difficult to represent, yet it is crucial to desire and the bodily acts that define sexuality. The ambiguousness of the term "beard," its very capaciousness, is what lends it power as an interpretive tool: it allows for the simultaneous analysis of several different representations of bodies and desires while also acknowledging explicitly the constructed nature of gender binaries rooted in the body. In the analysis that follows, we see how the beard functions as an indicator of the fluidity of gender representation and the possibility of lesbian desire.

Beards and Masculinity in the Eighteenth-Century Imaginary

Facial hair, like other gendered accessories such as clothes, hair, and makeup, has gone through various fashions. In the early modern or Renaissance period, beards were de rigueur for almost all men past a certain age. Will Fisher argues that in Renaissance portraiture and stage performance, beards are "made to matter" in the sense that they do more work than signify straightforward masculinity. The Renaissance beard denotes age and maturity in addition to "confer[ing] masculinity: the beard made the man," and the beard and genitals are part of an "array of features and prosthetic parts" that create a readable sex in this time period.[20] For Fisher, the preponderance of beards in the Renaissance suggests something about the ideal male body in a historically situated time and place.[21] Beardlessness in the early modern era demarcated not just youthfulness, but apprenticeship. Having a beard signaled that a young man had completed his term as apprentice and could now marry.[22] Beardlessness could also function in the register of androgyny, a prized aesthetic category in the early modern period. Laurence Senelick notes that androgyny was popular in the Renaissance, and "for both Horace and Montaigne, this absolute beauty, confusing rather than differentiating the sexes, is bestowed on the male adolescent, who can pass as female. The perfect universe of poetic illusion is best configured by a youth in women's garb, rather than a girl in men's clothes."[23] The emphasis on a beard acquired with age, the different fashions for beards, and the near-ubiquity of beards in early modern England point to that time period's fascination with facial hair as an outward symbol of age, wisdom, and masculinity. While the eighteenth century associated many of the same qualities with facial beards, fashions of the time turned away from the actual wearing of beards.

In the eighteenth century, as many scholars have noted, "fashion dictated that the face of the male *beau monde* was clean-shaven."[24] Overall, beards were unpopular in the eighteenth century, especially in contrast to their popularity in the Renaissance and late Victorian periods. Well-known portraits of Jonathan Swift, Alexander Pope, Samuel Johnson, Samuel Richardson, and all three King Georges represent clean-shaven men.[25] There is little indication that the eighteenth-century male found it incumbent upon himself to grow any kind of facial hair in the way that was the fashion in the Renaissance.[26] In fact, the eighteenth century represents perhaps the longest period in English history in which a shaved face was a requirement for men of all classes, despite the fact that the beard was viewed as an undeniable symbol of masculinity, virility, and wisdom.[27] The eighteenth century saw a dearth of beards, with only a couple exceptions, such as artists or military men, though all men were encouraged or required to shave regardless of occupation.[28] While men were pressured to shave—or even, as in the case of Peter the Great's Russia, monetarily penalized with a beard tax if they chose not to shave—ideologically the beard was an important marker of white male privilege.[29]

At the same time, the ability to grow a beard was crucial to conceptions of maleness and masculinity in this time period. Eighteenth-century naturalists believed that the beard was an embodied sign of masculinity and virility, as they believed it resulted, according to humoral theory, due to "reabsorbed semen."[30] Importantly, according to Angela Rosenthal, the beard was a cultural marker of racial and gender difference, even as Enlightenment principles emphasized that a clean-shaven face was necessary for one's "true face" to be "visible and legible," thus constructing the practice of shaving as "a sign of Western civilization."[31] Similarly, Alun Withey explains that "the removal of facial hair implied control, discipline, and self-mastery," while "to be facially hirsute spoke of savagery and wildness."[32] As modern categories of race were theorized by eighteenth-century writers, many of them focused on "the relative growth of beard [as], therefore, a touchstone for proving physical masculinity; in this line of reasoning, beards signified superior rights, while the presumed sparsely-haired chins of Native American men or those from East Asia were thought to align these peoples . . . with beardless eunuchs or castrato performers in terms of a deficiency of those humors producing full virility."[33] The ability to grow a beard was a sign of European superiority, and "the presence or absence of a beard not only drew a sharp line between men and women, it also served to differentiate the varieties of men."[34] Eighteenth-century naturalists such as François Bernier and Richard Bradley used the relative beardedness of different peoples to identify and classify races. While not all naturalists assigned a negative value to beardlessness, there were many who did, believing in the humoral explanation of the beard.[35] Similarly, the beardlessness of women was thought to indicate their "less noble character."[36] Despite the importance of the beard, however, shaving it was also a part of a larger cultural discussion of Western masculinity and privilege.[37]

Thus, while beards are unfashionable, the ability to *grow* a beard was of central concern to many European naturalists of the time, many of whom believed that beardedness indicated not only sexual but also racial difference. The ability to grow a beard was thought to be a sign of white, male European intelligence and exalted position. By contrast, the *missing* beard, the *smooth* face, were, by implication, signs of effeminacy. As Declan Kavanagh has argued in *Effeminate Years,* discourses of and about effeminacy were heightened "across the domains of eighteenth-century political life, literary culture, and the aesthetic" during the years 1756–74, a time during which several popular narratives of cross-dressing women were published.[38] Thus, these narratives, and their focus on missing markers of masculinity, figure as part of the larger discussion that determined acceptable masculinity and pointed out laughable effeminacy.

Erotic and pseudo-medical texts of the eighteenth century also indicate that beards were parts of a system that established sexual difference, although their status was constantly undercut. Karen Harvey argues that in the eighteenth century, beards were considered secondary sexual characteristics that suggested maleness but could not completely confirm it. She notes that "breasts could signal both the construction and the disruption of sexual differences, and beards had the same potential. Beards were deemed markers of bodily distinction."[39] At the same time, in some erotic texts the beard is not enough to "convince" other characters of someone else's maleness. In erotic texts such as *The Genuine Memoirs of the Celebrated Miss Maria Brown* (1766) and *The Fruit-Shop, A Tale in Two Volumes* (1765), the beard does not signify maleness beyond a doubt. In *The Genuine Memoirs*, "The man's beard aroused suspicions of sex difference, but these were satisfied only when he revealed his genitals."[40] What is perhaps more significant is Harvey's conclusion that beards and breasts "could be ascribed incorrectly, but heterosexual women and men who behaved in an appropriately gendered manner possessed the correct accoutrements."[41] The female cross-dresser, especially the passing woman, directly challenges this assertion. She is explicitly constructed as beardless but in possession of breasts and "normal" genitalia—that is, she is physically a woman—yet she does not behave in an "appropriately gendered manner." Thus, while the beard's ability to gender a person is established nominally in cross-dressing narrative, the body of the cross-dresser confounds the beard's meaning. However, as in *The Fruit-shop*, which vilifies "manlike females, [who are] odiously remarkable for beards or great-whiskers," many passing women's tales mention explicitly or implicitly the possibility of bearded women.[42] In this case, concepts of both age and gender come under scrutiny.

The symbolic equivalence of beards with strength, intelligence, maturity, and masculinity are visible in the stories of bearded women. Some of the most prominent examples of bearded women come from earlier time periods, as in the case of bearded female saints in the middle ages, or portraits of bearded women in the Renaissance.[43] In the case of the latter, these women were often reincorporated into a patriarchal system of subordination through portraits that depicted bearded women alongside their husbands, often holding a male child or even nursing it.[44] In the early modern and Enlightenment periods, a woman who exhibited strong opinions or intellectual capacities beyond what was thought proper for women could also be deemed "bearded," as "the female beard was imagined to exist in manifestations other than literal, facial beardedness. An overtly sexual or economically independent woman could, as we shall see, be allusively or metaphorically rather than literally bearded."[45] Immanuel Kant invoked the beard in his attack on learned women such as the classicist Madame Dacier and the physicist Emilie du Châtelet, citing that women like them "might just as well have a beard, for that expresses in a more recognizable form the profundity for which she strives."[46] This association between beards and intelligence and wisdom is evident in eighteenth-century naturalists' discussion of the "philosopher's beard" and was used to rationalize European men's rank above women as well as men of other, "beardless" races. Interestingly, animals that appeared to have a beard were thought to have increased intelligence beyond their beardless equivalents.[47] Bearded women, however, were dismissed as unfeminine, while the whiskers of postmenopausal women were explained through the Galenic model of reabsorbed bodily fluid—the fluids no longer expelled through menstruation re-formed into facial hair.[48]

Thus, the beard is a fraught symbol in the eighteenth-century imaginary. It is a sign of racial and sexual status, but it must be contained, cut off, and regulated. To be a "man," one needs a beard; yet the gender performance of the female cross-dresser appears to put this requirement into question. In contrast, a smooth face was an attractive trait in the eighteenth century, and a certain amount of androgynous beauty was fashionable. The attractiveness of such an androgynous look may also have stemmed from eighteenth-century neoclassicism and interest in Renaissance humanism, though with a new focus on the woman in men's clothes rather than the young man in drag.[49] Androgynous appearance was coveted and suspect at the same time, as moralists struggled against the prevailing fashion for castrati singers, cross-dressed heroines, macaronis and fops, and excesses in clothes and wig fashions for both men and women. The beard existed in the minds of eighteenth-century writers as a mark of physical maleness with connotations of power and sex. While the standards of masculinity may have been low, as Lynn Friedli suggests, the concern of these cross-dressers for their "smooth faces" indicates that facial roughness was a male quality that was noticeable in the eighteenth century even as wearing a beard was unpopular.[50]

Therefore, the figure of the female cross-dresser must navigate the expectations of beardedness when passing, even as many women she meets respond positively to her smooth face. These texts often depict the cross-dresser compensating for the absence of facial beard with the performance of certain male behaviors: enthusiastic drinking, feats of strength, and the successful courtship of other women. At the same time, the beard is rejected by each text as an unvarying sign of maleness, exposing it as an ambiguously gendered and only ever a prosthetic, rather than inherent, marker of gender. In fact, the ambiguity created by the lack of a beard that espouses a kind of androgynous beauty also suggests the possibility of both sexes having a desire for the cross-dressed woman as a result of a pleasurable failure of vision. As Kristina Straub has already argued in regard to breeches and travesty roles, "Some of the pleasure afforded by the spectacle of the cross-dressed actress arose, then, out of the doubling of sexual attraction. The actress in men's clothes appeals to both men and women—at least as a specular commodity."[51] Her ability to confuse or trans gender and, as Marjorie Garber argues, to occupy a third category that puts the idea of category in flux, renders her fascinating and attractive.[52] The spectacle of feminine masculinity becomes an opening for sapphic pleasures and desires, among the other queer desires enabled by this ambiguity. The beardlessness of the female cross-dresser is significant precisely because it engenders desire in women who desire a feminine man or a trans man or a woman masquerading as a man, with the slippage between those categories part of what adds to the cross-dresser's allure.

In this context the discussion of facial hair, facial smoothness, and beards cannot be overlooked. The way that facial hair combines elements of masculinity, sexuality, and sexual maturity and viability, as well as power and desire, makes it an important signifier of gender. Its prosthetic quality becomes evident when we consider how the beard is displaced by female same-sex desires. The move from "beard" to "bearding" stretches the concept of the facial beard to encompass these prosthetic qualities while also connoting the beard's ornamental value, as well as its disguising powers. To go back to Judith Butler, we might reconceptualize the performance of the female cross-dresser as exemplifying "the distinctness of those aspects of gendered experience which are falsely naturalized as a unity through the regulatory fiction of heterosexual coherence."[53] Notably, the female cross-dresser's gender performance emphasizes idealized masculinity: female cross-dressers make "better" men than (biological) men. The beard functions as the fissure in this idealized performance, drawing attention to the "falsely naturalized" experience of eighteenth-century masculinity. The women who are courted by the cross-dresser, her beards, appear to accept this performance even when they are able to "read" the dissonances in it. On top of this layer of ambiguity is the layer of the reader's knowledge. The reader is constructed as always able to read this "gendered experience" as a performance, yet he or she is asked to accept it as part of the cross-dresser's survival skills. Of all the people who see the cross-dresser, the reader is the one least able to accept her unquestioningly as a biological male. The cross-dresser's body performs masculinity while, at the same time, being carefully framed as female—that is, missing a beard. This contradiction in her performance leads to the sapphic possibilities of the texts while also potently alluding to the transing of gender.

Cross-Dressing and the Need for a Beard

The narratives of female cross-dressers often present the lack of beard as a problem for the cross-dresser's performance of masculinity. The lack of physical beard provides the cross-dresser with the narrative impetus to pursue other women, the metaphorical beards, even as beards and facial hair were not fashionable for men in the eighteenth century. The presence of a five o'clock shadow or facial stubble, however, and the need to shave were still considered determining factors in establishing maleness.[54] In his *Pogonologia* (1786), Jacques-Antoine Dulaure declares that the facial beard is a "symbol of [man's] sovereignty." He acknowledges that there are also bearded women, though he characterizes them as freaks: bearded women are "one of those extraordinary deviations with which nature presents us every day."[55] He lists examples of bearded women from ancient times through the eighteenth century not to normalize such women but, instead, to highlight their exceptional status: "It is as ridiculous for a man to look like a woman, as for a woman to look like a man."[56] His pronouncements reiterate the idea that throughout the eighteenth century the facial beard symbolizes masculinity and virility. Reginald Reynolds has noted that "*to beard* has always expressed offer of insult with an implication of courage, e.g. in bearding the lion in his den."[57] In different ways, the beard is etymologically linked to insult and ridicule, as well as European notions of masculinity and its adjunct qualities of courage, intelligence, and reason.

Female cross-dressers are depicted as beardless and beautiful, and the texts eschew any suggestion of masculinity in their looks, though many of these narratives reiterate that the cross-dresser can imitate masculinity in other significant ways. Nevertheless, the missing facial beard is emphasized as one of the "tells" that alerts others in the text to her gender nonconformity. The cross-dresser's lack of beard renders her body ambiguous, and the narratives highlight her female difference, only then to suggest the appeal of her gender ambiguity to other women. Some of these texts seek to convince readers that romantic pursuit of a woman is necessary for the cross-dresser to pass as a man; other texts report that the female cross-dresser attracts other women without actively trying to do so. The stories of Hannah Snell and Sarah Scott's Leonora, while differing in genre (one is a partially fictionalized biography and the other is a novel) portray women who must beard themselves as a part of their male disguise. These two texts explicitly demonstrate how female desires can successfully dissimulate the lack of a facial beard.

Published in two London editions in 1750, *The Female Soldier* recounts the adventures of Hannah Snell, who disguises herself as a man to search for her husband after he abandons her.[58] Snell travels to Portsmouth and joins the marines, with whom she sails to Lisbon, eventually taking part in the Battle of Pondicherry, India, where she is wounded. She maintains her disguise throughout her voyages until she returns to England, claims her pension, and reveals her true sex. Early on, the narrator explains that aboard ship, Snell observes the "horrible Oaths, and many lewd Actions and Gestures" of the other sailors and notes that "she saw too much not to be afflicted lest her Sex should by their impudent, and unlimited Behaviour, be discovered, and her Virtue sacrificed to their rapacious, boundless and lustful Appetites."[59] The lustful appetites of the men become the greatest danger from which she must preserve herself. *The Female Soldier* portrays Snell's bearding as born out of necessity, therefore exculpating her from any possible accusation that she was purposefully trying to deceive other women. Still, the desires of these other women read queerly, as the reader is constantly reminded that Snell is female-bodied, performing masculinity only ever imperfectly.

In *A Journey through Every Stage of Life,* the cross-dressing character Leonora has similar reasons for searching out metaphorical beards, even though the threat to her virtue is not nearly as violent as Snell's. Scott's novel consists of a series of stories within a story; the very first of these tales, "The History of Leonora and Louisa," recounts the adventures of two cousins who must run away from their home, where Leonora's stepmother mistreats them. To avoid being recognized, they alter their appearance. Leonora, the stronger and more extroverted of the two, decides to cross-dress as a clergyman, while Louisa, the more fragile and introverted cousin, remains in women's clothing; the two women pose as brother and sister.[60] Together they journey to the spa town of Buxton, where close to half of their narrative takes place. Leonora knows that, if her identity is revealed, she will be sent home, where she will be married off to "a Gentleman in the Neighbourhood; a Man of above fifty Years of Age, odious both in Person and Heart, and despicable in Understanding."[61] Scott's narrator presents the reader with a young woman who is motivated to disguise herself and make use of the unsolicited female desires that will help keep her bearded. The appearance of heterosexual desire between the cross-dresser and her beards is crucial to the cross-dresser's bearding; the narrative makes it clear that posing as brother and sister is not enough to establish Leonora's masculine disguise.

Both narratives raise the issue of a missing facial beard early on. Having established the threat of discovery, they create tension by emphasizing the tenuousness of Snell's and Leonora's disguises and the implicit peril they face if they should be discovered. For example, although the narrator of *The Female Soldier* reiterates Snell's abilities to take on the toils of a life at sea, for the other sailors her physical prowess is not sufficient proof to establish her masculinity and, consequently, her maleness. The sailors tease Snell so relentlessly about her smooth face that she begins to fear for her virtue: "They [the sailors] began to declare her to be a Woman on account of her smooth Face, seeing she had no Beard. . . . She could not prevent their calling her by the name of *Molly Gray*."[62] If put to the challenge, of course, Snell cannot provide any corporeal markers of maleness, so the narrator tells us that she was "plunged" into "Disorders, Terrors and

Hannah Snell, The Female Soldier, drawing by L. P. Boitard, engraving by B. Cole, 1750. (Reprinted with permission from the Anne S. K. Brown Military Collection, Brown University Library)

Hannah Snell, John
Faber, mezzotint after
a painting by Richard
Phelps, 1750. (© Trustees
of the British Museum)

Distractions."[63] Similarly, "The Story of Leonora and Louisa" emphasizes
the beauty of Leonora's face and her femininity. The text constructs this
perfection as problematic for her *and* Louisa's successfully remaining disguised. As Leonora's lack of beard initially thwarts her performance of
masculinity in Buxton, she takes "as much care to shade the Resplendency
of her own Complexion as to improve her cousin's [Louisa's], in order to
lessen in some Degree the Effeminacy of her Countenance, which before
made her not appear Man enough even for a Lady's Page."[64] How Leonora
achieves this alteration is left to the reader's imagination. Dugaw notes
that ballads about female soldiers often emphasized the use of pitch and
tar that women used to darken their faces, perhaps to simulate a beard
or disguise the lack of one.[65] The beauty of Leonora's features, however,
remains untouched, and her attempt to look less feminine is only with
regard to her cousin's unfeminine pallor.[66] Her feminine beauty, when in
disguise, becomes a form of androgynous beauty that many of the other
women in the novel find extremely attractive.

Lack of facial hair becomes problematic for Leonora due in part to the older women in Buxton who draw attention to it: "The Widows indeed, and some of the more experienced Matrons, looked with a Mixture of Scorn upon her, the antient Ladies especially, to whose Chins Age had given an ornament that even Leonora's Manhood could not boast, proud of their hoary Honours would frequently ridicule her want of Beard, and elated with their Abundance, despite her Poverty."[67] Although the text satirizes these "antient Ladies" for the apparent superiority they feel from considering their own hairy chins, Leonora takes their dissatisfaction with her performance of masculinity seriously.[68] The threat of exposure as a woman, whether it comes from the attention of men or women, is a constant source of fear for Leonora, just as it is for Snell. Scott's narrator tells us that Leonora "would have been glad, if she could have borrowed what they might so well have spared, but as that could not be, she was obliged to beat the Jests which were half whispered among them, with the best Assurance she could summon."[69] The texts emphasize the lack of beard as significant to the performance of maleness; the fear of being exposed as not bearded, and thus female, equates the facial beard with maleness and forces the cross-dresser to consider other ways of becoming bearded, often by courting the women who desire her in her male persona.

The narratives of Snell and Leonora overtly suggest that the two heroines court other women to prove to onlookers that they are truly male. For example, the narrator of *The Female Soldier* emphasizes that Snell undertakes to imitate the other tars' behavior to "pass" more successfully: "She often went on Shore in Company with the Ships Crew, upon Parties of Pleasure. . . . This Part she acted, not out of Choice, but for wise Ends. . . . Therefore, she pointed out this Method as the most effectual, to prevent any further suspicious *Reflections for the future*."[70] Part of her act is to flirt with women in Lisbon, revealing how those young ladies function metaphorically as her beards. Those women replace Snell's missing beard—her missing marker of masculinity—with their interest and desire. The narrative suggests that her beards function as indicators of sexuality, as well as sex: if Snell attracts women, then she appears to be a heterosexual male in possession of male genitals. The irony is, of course, that this metaphorical beard uses the guise of heterosexual romance to attract same-sex desires. Similarly, the "best Assurance" Leonora can find against discovery are the young women who desire her in her clergyman's disguise. Leonora and her sister immediately claim the attention of all the young ladies and gentlemen of Buxton: Louisa for her feminine delicacy, and Leonora for her dashing charm in the guise of a young clergyman. It turns out that "Leonora's Beauty charms many of the young Ladies, [and] she soon found by the forward Advances of the Coquets, and the sly Glances of the Prudes, that an effeminate Delicacy in a Man is not disagreeable to a Sex to whom it should more peculiarly belong."[71] Many women in these narratives are not averse to the sight of a feminine-looking young man; in fact, they are quite attracted to such beardless youths.[72] These narratives may deny or be silent about the cross-dresser's potential desire for other women, yet they reveal how the cross-dresser's ambiguous gender performance is attractive to other women. The narratives of female cross-dressers present female desire as necessary additions to or inevitable consequences of masquerading as a man, whether they represent the cross-dresser in a favorable, condemnatory, or ambiguous light. For the reader, who has a privileged view of the cross-dresser within the narrative, the positive reactions of these other women hint at the possibility of female same-sex desires even as the texts emphasize that the women desire the cross-dresser because she appears to them as a (feminine) man, teasing readers simultaneously with lesbian desires and transmasculine appeal.

The stories of Snell and Leonora illustrate the appeal of the female cross-dresser to other women, though their narratives present their search for a beard as stemming from a virtuous necessity: these women access same-sex desires, but they are motivated nominally by the need to preserve their virtue. The issues of the missing beard and bearding are also apparent in representations of less virtuous female cross-dressers, as in Henry Fielding's criminal biography of Mary Hamilton, *The Female Husband*.[73] The narrative is based on the story of the real-life cross-dresser Mary Hamilton, whom Fielding likely heard about from his cousin Henry Gould, a lawyer consulted by the magistrate who heard her case.[74] *The Female Husband* recounts Hamilton's adventures as she successfully marries several women, swindles some of them, and happily lives with two of them for a while. Like Leonora, Hamilton has a feminine appearance that explicitly appeals to other women in the narrative; unlike Leonora or Snell, she is represented as seeking out metaphorical beards not only to further her disguise but also to fulfill her financial and sexual needs. The negative language surrounding Hamilton and her "monstrous and unnatural" appetites marks her story as different from that of Snell and Leonora, and yet we see parallels in these narratives in the cross-dressers' erotic appeal to other women.[75] The text portrays Hamilton as extremely attractive to other women, declaring that because she is "a very pretty woman, she now [in men's clothing] appeared a most beautiful youth."[76] These good looks are, as they are for Leonora, a double-edged sword: feminine good looks appeal to some women while making others overly suspicious of Hamilton's sex. Fielding's text elaborates on the issue more overtly by drawing attention to the problematic and often fluid definitions of gender boundaries and how they affect sexual desire, and the narrative depicts Hamilton's successes as well as her failures when wooing other women.

Initially Hamilton meets with resistance from her paramours because of her feminine appearance. An early conquest, a "brisk widow of nearly 40 years of age," rejects Hamilton for her feminine appearance, citing that "for certain reasons, when your cold is gone, you might sing as well as [the castrato] Farinelli, from the great resemblance there is between your persons."[77] Another conquest, a younger woman, tells Hamilton when she realizes she is a woman, "I always wondered that you had not the least bit of beard; but I thought you had been a man for all that."[78] These earlier encounters illustrate to readers the precariousness of Hamilton's situation and the difficulty of managing her masculine performance. Eventually, Hamilton finds women to whom her feminine aspects are attractive, and she meets with success when she manages to marry an older widow, Mrs. Rushford. Unlike the "antient ladies" in Scott's novel who are suspicious of Leonora's smooth-faced masculinity, the Widow Rushford is captivated by her female husband. She takes no notice when, during their wedding, a guest "jested on the bridegroom [Hamilton] because he had no beard."[79] The sixty-eight-year-old widow is described as being "proud of the beauty of her new husband" and calls him "the best man in Ireland."[80] The widow's age and experience do not make her suspicious of Hamilton; her desire for Hamilton beards Hamilton entirely. The women who desire Hamilton (or reject her)—the metaphorical beards—do so both because of and despite her feminine appearance. Thus, *The Female Husband,* like *The Female Soldier* and "The History of Leonora and Louisa," illustrates the tension between being exposed as female and being desired for one's femininity or gender fluidity.

Through the trope of the beard, *The Female Husband* demonstrates that sapphic possibilities and sexual desires more generally are neither predicated on nor limited by certain appearances or circumstances—they are predicated on or limited only by individual tastes, allowing the female reader to judge for herself how appealing a female husband might really be. Indeed, in Scott's novel the women who admire and desire Leonora beard her by comparing her to other "imaginary Heroes who had been celebrated for effeminate Beauty," demonstrating how female masculinity exists on a spectrum of masculine types in Western culture.[81] The literary heroes who sport feminine beauty demonstrate that male femininity is both heroic and attractive and masculine; further, this admiration beards the disguised Leonora, equating her with other men and compensating for her absence of the obvious masculine signifier—that is, a facial beard.[82] Just as Snell feels safer while soliciting flirtation from other women, so Leonora "had . . . the Gratification of over-hearing very different Observations made by the younger Part of the Company" who would "praise her Features, another her Complexion, a third sigh out, as smooth as Hebe's unrazored Lips."[83] Leonora's face, quintessentially feminine while in women's clothes, is extremely attractive in her canonical habit, just as Mary Hamilton appears as an attractive youth in Fielding's text. It is evident here that masculinity (i.e., beardedness) is not necessarily what young women desire.[84] The stories of female cross-dressers reveal there are many women who desire other women or women-like men, illustrating potent cultural fantasies about the mutability of gender and female same-sex desire in the eighteenth century.

Ideal Beards: The Female Cross-Dresser as the Perfect (Wo)man

The performance of maleness and masculinity become linked to representations of female same-sex desires and relationships in the stories of female cross-dressers. Further, these narratives suggest that female cross-dressers use their knowledge to offer women what they most desire: men who are actually women. The female cross-dresser's appearance and body, as well as her knowledge of and behavior toward her would-be lovers, appeal to these women. The performance of a heteronormative courtship script in the text reveals to the reader the possibility of authentic female same-sex desires that go beyond playacting. The beards respond positively to the advances of the female cross-dresser wherever she goes, and in many of these narratives, female cross-dressers surpass men in their appeal to women because the cross-dressers are women themselves. The stories of female cross-dressers frequently imply that the cross-dresser is a superlative man; the corollary to this suggestion is that the *performance* of masculinity by a woman is just as desirable as, if not preferable to, actual maleness.

In *The Female Soldier,* the narrative demonstrates how Snell is able to ingratiate herself with other women and how these women respond to her positively. Snell's narrative depends on her fear of and her imperviousness to overtures by men, which her narrative emphasizes as necessary to preserving her feminine virtue. It is difficult, however, not to read her virtuous preservation queerly: Snell has no desire to couple with men; instead, she is primarily interested in creating emotional bonds with other women.[85] Likewise, the text represents the female beards as having no desire to couple with physical males; instead, they are overwhelmingly attracted to the cross-dresser's ambiguous performance of (female) masculinity. One of the scenes where we see quite clearly how strongly the "beards" respond to Snell's performance of masculinity is when she returns to Portsmouth. There, she looks up her inamorata: "This young Woman knew *Hannah* to be the young Soldier that had enlisted and been sent abroad. . . . Then entering into this Conversation, introduced a farther Intimacy, and *Hannah,* rather than sit to drink with her Shipmates, spent most of her Time with this young Woman. . . . Sometimes they conversed upon Love; and *Hannah* finding this young Woman had no dislike to her, she endeavoured to try if she could not act the Lover as well as the Soldier."[86] This passage implies that the other woman's interest in Snell encourages her to "act the Lover," and the phrase "farther Intimacy" connotes both friendship and, possibly, other, more passionate feelings.[87] The reader, knowing Snell is a woman, may read this section in at least two ways: Snell is so adept at mimicking a man that she attracts other women, or Snell's disguise enables her to act on same-sex desires—hers, the other woman's, or both. Regardless, there is an intimation of female same-sex desire in this scene made available by the reader's knowledge of Snell's gender and the text's own ambiguity.

Scott's Leonora similarly illustrates ideals of masculinity and masculine behavior, especially regarding the eighteenth-century ideal of the man of feeling. When she preaches a sermon, the "Warmth of her Heart soon took off her Attention to her Audience, and left her only just Modesty enough to grace her Words; and give her Doctrine the Air of Advice and Entreaty, rather than of commanding Injunctions; a Method to make it most availing as Preacher then has not both the Pride and Inclinations of his Audience to combat."[88] The women in the audience respond enthusiastically to her preaching—as enthusiastically as they do to her appearance. The text indicates that her appeal arises not only from her youthful, attractive androgyny, but also from the fact that as a preacher, she does not "command" like a man but, rather, gives "advice" like a woman. In addition to the admiration of many women, Leonora has a more devoted admirer who falls passionately in love with her.[89] This young lady, Laetitia, "endeavoured by all the Arts of Reserve and Modesty, to hide her Passion from all Eyes, and most of all from Leonora's; but it is very difficult for Woman to conceal from Woman the Situation of her Heart."[90] The text implies that because she is passing as a man, Leonora can become the love object of another woman. As a woman herself, though, Leonora can read Laetitia's passion without hearing about it from Laetitia herself. The texts construct the female cross-dresser as the ideal mate for other women, and those other women, the beards, desire this particular performance of feminine masculinity for how it prioritizes feminine affects and expectations in courtship.

The narrator of *The Female Husband* explicitly mentions that Hamilton's being a woman facilitates her amours with other women and may, in fact, make her a better lover—even when it comes to matters of the bedroom. Hamilton promises one of her "wives" that a marriage to her will include "all the pleasures of marriage without the inconveniences"—that is, sexual satisfaction without pregnancy.[91] Hamilton's final relationship in the narrative is with a young, inexperienced girl, Mary (Molly) Price, who, after their wedding, tells such stories of her "husband's" prowess in the bedroom, that "poor Molly . . . was received as a great fibber."[92] When questioned by a court of law, the young woman asserts that she and her husband had cohabited and that the "Doctor [Hamilton] had behaved to her as a husband ought to a wife."[93] In fact, her boasts to her mother about their love life cause her mother to exclaim, "O Child, there is no such thing in human nature," leaving the reader tantalized by the possibility that the cross-dresser offers sexual pleasures surpassing those offered by a male partner.[94] During Hamilton's trial we learn that the magistrates had seized "something of too vile, wicked and scandalous a nature . . . in the Doctor's trunk"—that is, a dildo.[95] Though Fielding's text purports to castigate women like Hamilton who dupe other young women, especially through the use of such "vile" devices, it is clear from the narrator's tone that Fielding and his readers are enjoying the spectacle—and that they are curious about the female cross-dresser and her fantastic abilities.[96] I discuss the importance of the dildo and its superlative abilities at length in chapter 3, as the missing penis plays a role that, physically and discursively, is similar to that of the missing facial beard. Terry Castle has argued persuasively that Fielding's rendering of Hamilton reveals how the female husband elicits "recoil and fascination, fear and attraction" from an author known for his "awareness of the theatricality and artifice of human sexual roles."[97] In addition, although Fielding's narrator presents Hamilton as dangerous, laughable, and even criminal, there is no doubt that she displays a gender ambiguity that is deeply attractive to several Englishwomen, despite—or, perhaps, because of—her femininity. Hamilton's lack as a woman is precisely what makes her attractive to other women, as it compels her to compensate with seductive letters and gestures, as well as a dildo, an implement that never fails. Again, we see that her beards enjoy her attentions both because of and despite her femaleness.

Even in texts in which a facial beard is not remarked on explicitly, we see the workings of metaphorical bearding and same-sex desires. In yet another famous story of a female soldier, *The Life and Adventures of Mrs. Christian Davies, the British Amazon, Commonly Called Mother Ross*, we see how the cross-dressing Christian Davies is represented as able to appropriate other women's desires as part of her performance of masculinity.[98] Her biography depicts other women as clamoring to claim her male persona as a lover—and even, in one case, as the father of her child. Davies boasts that "a Lady of civil Conversation" attempts to seduce her while pregnant. Davies, dressed as a dragoon in the British Army, rebuffs her, but the lady "swore she would revenge the Slight . . . by swearing me the Father of her Child."[99] She notes that the lady chose her particularly, as "I [Davies] made a better Figure than any private Dragoon in our Regiment."[100] The narrative emphasizes Davies's performance of masculinity as desirable to this woman and appealing to women more generally, presenting the reader with the idea of women who desire other women. In addition to her gender-ambiguous good looks, Davies, like Snell and Leonora, uses her knowledge of "what women want" to attract her beards. In her "Frolicks, to kill Time," Davies admits that she often turned to courting young ladies for fun while passing as a dragoon.[101] She uses her experience as a woman to woo these young ladies, specifically the daughter of a local burgher, employing the "tender Nonsense" conventionally used in such cases: "I squeezed her Hand, whenever I could get an Opportunity; sighed often, when in her Company; looked foolishly, and practised upon her all the ridiculous Airs which I had often laughed at, when they were used as Snares against myself."[102] Surprisingly to Davies, her behavior "had an Effect I did not wish: the poor Girl grew really fond of me, and uneasy when I was absent."[103] Regardless of her intentions, Davies's story emphasizes that her experience as a woman, combined with her good looks, make her the ideal romantic partner for many of her beards. As Dugaw notes, "Encountering such heroes as Christian Davies . . . same-sex desire emerges in the story as a titillating reality."[104] The metaphor of the beard is one of the ways through which we can read this interplay of imagination and reality of same-sex desires and the equality titillating possibility of ambiguous and ever-mutable gender. Further, the narrative detaches masculinity from physical maleness as Davies's masculinity manifests not only materially through her dragoon's uniform but also discursively through her attributed fatherhood.

The memoir of the actress Charlotte Charke, daughter of Colley Cibber and a famous cross-dresser both on and off the stage, likewise represents the relationship between the cross-dresser and her beards. Her autobiography *A Narrative of the Life of Mrs. Charlotte Charke* does not list the lack of facial beard specifically as a problem, yet, like Davies's narrative, Charke's story portrays how her appearance in men's clothing and performance of female masculinity inevitably attract other women.[105] In addition to having a mysterious female partner, or "beard," Mrs. Brown, with whom Charke travels around England as "Mr. Brown," she, like Davies, also complains about ardent female admirers who mistake her for a man.[106] Early on in the text, Charke notes that despite many financial ups and downs, the "want of Cloaths was not amongst the Number. I appeared as Mr. *Brown* . . . in a very genteel Manner; and, not making the least Discovery of my Sex by my Behaviour, ever endeavouring to keep up to the well-bred gentleman, I became . . . the unhappy Object of Love in a young Lady."[107] Like Leonora, who must disappoint her female admirer Laetitia, both Davies and Charke claim to be surprised and saddened when their masquerading leads a female heart astray, and both assert that they refuse to take further advantage of these women. Davies goes so far as to proclaim that, in the case of the Burgher's daughter, "I was fond of the Girl, though mine, you know, could not go beyond a platonick Love."[108] Regardless of the cross-dresser's protestations, however, her appeal to other women is a constant in these works, and the texts emphasize both the physical and emotional appeal of the cross-dresser to her beards. Thus, although some cross-dressers deny romantic or sexual attraction to other women, the desires of her beards remain full of sapphic possibilities for the readers.

The beard, whether facial or metaphorical, functions as a marker of same-sex desire in the stories of cross-dressing women, and the appearance of the beard or smooth face alludes to the problems and possibilities of cross-dressing. It also reveals the desires of the sapphic women who do not cross-dress but instead come to love and desire the cross-dresser and her alluring feminine masculinity. In this way, the female cross-dresser and her beards put same-sex desires at the forefront of these narratives. The appearance and behavior of the cross-dresser attract her beards while marking her as not wholly male or masculine, and the desires of the beards underscore the widespread appeal of the cross-dresser, at least discursively, to other women. Whether these representations are positive or negative, it is evident that the cross-dresser and her beards draw attention to eighteenth-century discourses of gender ambiguity and same-sex desires, both romantic and erotic.

Cross-dressing narratives often focus on how the cross-dresser attracts her beards with her extraordinary skills of mimicking masculinity; at the same time, as these examples reveal, the cross-dresser's masculinity is frequently undercut or informed by female knowledge and the cross-dresser's own rather feminine or ambiguous appearance. Textual references to the missing facial beard and its subsequent replacement illustrate how gender performance and female desires are fraught with ambiguity. This ambiguity not only expands our understanding of gender performativity in the eighteenth century but also suggests a method of reading non-normative bodies and pleasures in texts that initially appear to emphasize heterosexual coupling. If, as Lanser has argued, the eighteenth century saw the rise of the sapphic as a critical lens through which to understand modernity and its entangled relationship to the body and sexuality, then the cross-dresser's beard or beards might function as an embodied marker of this sea change. The beard illustrates, through its relations to bodies, desires, and identities, this notion that "the logic of 'woman + woman' cannot simply be transformed to the logic of 'woman + man.'"[109] The appeal of a feminine-looking man to the women in these texts is a pattern that draws attention to the tenuousness of gender difference, and therefore desire, and the complex nature of these intertwined categories—even as effeminacy in men was reviled and attacked at this time. The women who desire the passing woman's smooth-faced youthfulness reject the obvious marker of masculinity—the facial beard—as a necessary component of maleness; they reject the need for a facial beard to make one male, embracing cross-gendered and nonbinary embodiments. The beards desire a youthful, feminine man (or a woman dressed as a man—the difference is a slippery one). Through the desires of these other women, the cross-dresser is able to perpetuate her adopted gender performance—and attract more women. How we read the cross-dresser and her beards is colored by the fact that the reader is always "in the know": what Braunschneider terms "readerly knowingness" is central to these narratives.[110] The reader is aware of the fact that the cross-dresser is female, for it is her enterprise of cross-dressing as a woman that is often a central point of interest in these narratives. As a result, the act of reading these narratives and, consequently, interpreting these liaisons betrays a secondary knowledge, a moment of seeing beyond what the characters in the text are able to see. For readers, gender and desire are both being questioned, and the queerness of the beard's desires is a result of the transing of the cross-dresser's body. The narratives of cross-dressing women emphasize the reader's privileged position, at times even relishing it and in some cases addressing the reader directly, as the narrator of *The Female Soldier* and *The Female Husband* do.

By drawing our attention to the lack of facial beard, these texts stress the visual dimension of desire and knowledge. Knowledge of the cross-dresser's true identity and lack of this knowledge become central to the possibility of female self-reliance, preservation, and same-sex desires. The problem of beardlessness suggests that knowledge of the cross-dresser's true sex is apparent, yet often unreadable. As Traub argues, discussions of sex and desire in the past must consider how "erotic desires and behaviors . . . are, in crucial ways, inaccessible, resistant to interpretation, even unknowable."[111] Thus, the beard, in its metaphorical register, acknowledges this unknowability, even as it suggests to readers the possibility of erotic same-sex desires, and the breasts, as we shall see, function similarly. In the narratives of the female cross-dresser we can read the same-sex desires evident in the text and the textual knowingness that accompanies these desires. Emma Donoghue reminds us that "every woman who read a crossdresser's signals and related passionately to her took part in that enterprise. I find crossdressing most important not for itself but for the space it gave women to recognize each other."[112] Similarly, the enterprise of cross-dressing, as it is represented textually, gives women, and readers more generally, the ability to recognize the possibility of same-sex desires between women. By focusing on the facial beard, and the consequent "bearding" of the cross-dresser through the desires of other women, these narratives highlight the women in the eighteenth century who passionately identified with and desired an ambiguous gender performance and,

possibly, therefore other women or trans men. The cross-dresser complicates current debates on gender and, especially, masculinity in the eighteenth century, exposing the complex, at times contradictory discourses
on gender and desire in this time period. The beard enters into debates
about masculinity and effeminacy, virility and sexual desire. The female
cross-dresser, like the macaroni, castrati, and molly, functions as a figure
around which discourses of masculinity are momentarily disrupted. The
cross-dresser's appeal to other women because of her feminine delicacy,
rather than in spite of it, alludes to eighteenth-century fears that masculinity was not a clearly defined category but, rather, confirms the modern
notion of ideal masculinity as impossible to achieve. The female breast, by
contrast, emphasizes the ways in which women are represented as bonding in eighteenth-century literature via body parts. The breast, as a feminine feature, and its metaphorical link to the heart further function as
a way to represent sapphic possibilities in eighteenth-century literature,
though one whose meaning is, like that of the beard, also mediated via
imperial and nationalist discourses.

2

>•<

SAPPHIC BREASTS AND
BOSOM FRIENDS

The Female Soldier; or, The Surprizing Life and Adventures of Hannah Snell
(1750) recounts the many adventures of the virtuous, valiant, laboring-class
cross-dressing heroine Hannah Snell. It also reminds its readers of the
difficulties of keeping her gender concealed, such as when she is to be
whipped publicly, an event for which she is obliged to appear shirtless.
The narrator explains, "Her Breasts were then not so big by much as they
are at present, her Arms being extended and fixed to the City Gates, her
breasts were drawn up, and consequently did not appear so large; and be-
sides this, her Breast was to the Wall, and could not be discovered by any
of her Comrades."[1] Immediately following this instance of gender passing,
the narrative explains how Snell manages to hide the groin wound she
sustained at the Battle of Pondicherry, discursively equating the baring of
breasts with the exposure of one's groin area. Clearly, the breast bears the
burden of sexual difference as much as facial hair or even genitalia, signifying, in the case of the breast, undeniable femaleness. The narrator's insistence that no one could read Snell's breasts as feminine due to their small
size and their distortion while she was being whipped discloses anxiety on
the part of the narrator to account for everyone else's lack of recognition,
as well as the believability of Snell's successful passing. In another instance
in the narrative, however, Snell must give a woman "ocular demonstration" of her own femaleness—a moment in which the breast is evoked
through absence and allusion, revealing a potent sapphic possibility.

This chapter examines, first, how narratives of laboring-class cross-

dressers establish the breast of the passing woman as consummately femi-
nine and in need of hiding while, at the same time, suggesting how breasts
can forge sapphic and, at times, explicitly erotic connections between
the cross-dresser and the women who desire her: her beards. The texts
I examine—*The Female Soldier, The Female Husband* (1746), *The Life and
Adventures of Mrs. Christian Davies, the British Amazon, Commonly Called
Mother Ross* (1741), and Captain Charles Johnson's *A General History of the
Robberies and Murders of the Most Notorious Pyrates* (1724), exemplify the
role of the breast as both gender-ambiguous and an enticement toward
sapphic bonding. Together, these texts, all of which were widely available
in the eighteenth century and circulated extensively in reprinted editions,
exemplify the different ways in which the breast functions not only as a
liability for the passing woman's successful performance of masculinity,
but also as a powerful expression of femaleness and female desire. The
end of the chapter examines Maria Edgeworth's novel *Belinda* (1801) and
how its representation of upper-class women's cross-dressing in the domestic novel is informed by the representations of plebeian cross-dressing
in print culture. The novel takes up the notion of female breasts as a site
of sapphic possibility and emblems of female bonds that, by the end of
the novel, take on a much greater importance than the heteronormative
love plot. In *Belinda,* the transgressive cross-dressing Harriet Freke and
the "dying" (and cross-dressing) Lady Delacour together create a narrative
about the cross-dresser's breast and the sentimental breast that further
exposes the breast's ability to index female bonds, both erotic and emotional. Considering these characters together, along with those in *Belinda,*
we see how texts use the breasts of the cross-dressing woman to draw
attention to female-centered relationships and as a motif for the articulation of lesbian desires. Rather than functioning unilaterally to reinforce
patriarchal expectations and normative gender divisions, the breast reinforces female bonding and sapphic possibilities. Like the beard, the
breast functions as a body part crucial to the enterprise of cross-dressing,
but it also functions in a metaphorical or emblematic register through
which cross-dressed and non-cross-dressed women are linked via passionate, female same-sex desires. At the same time, however, as we shall see,

the color and shape of the cross-dresser's breasts are predicated on categories of racial and national superiority, revealing how discourses of gender and desire are inextricably imbricated within discourses of whiteness.

The role of the breast in the narratives of cross-dressing women has special importance at this time, as eighteenth-century discourses surrounding the female breast undergo a significant shift in political and medical texts. Over the course of the eighteenth century, women's physical breasts become firmly established as markers of femaleness, as well as important indicators of femininity and Britishness. Significantly, much of the scholarship on women's breasts and their role in eighteenth-century medical and political discourses focuses on how the breast became de-eroticized through the emphasis on the maternal breast and the increasing insistence over the course of the century on maternal breastfeeding. The work of Valerie Fildes, Londa Schiebinger, Marina Warner, and Marilyn Yalom has traced how the image of the breast changes during the eighteenth century, becoming less associated with eroticism and sexuality and more attached to the maternal role of women in society. Further, Ruth Perry's discussion of the colonized breast links the project of nation building in eighteenth-century Europe to the ways in which the breast and motherhood become vectors for articulating national characteristics and the goals of citizenship.[2] Citizenship and even humanity were being discussed through the lens of the body at this time, and just as some naturalists of the time used facial hair to categorize more or less "civilized" peoples, so others used categories of female breasts to do the same kind of ideological work.[3] Finally, the breast also functioned discursively at the end of the eighteenth century through the visual rhetorics of freedom and revolution, as Yalom and Marcus Rediker have argued.[4]

At the same time, the eighteenth-century breast is not completely emptied of its erotic or embodied connotations.[5] Simon Richter's insistence on the erotic and the maternal together in the same image of the breast, like Yalom's, encourages us to read the breast as a multifaceted locus of meaning in this time period.[6] The moments in which the narratives of cross-dressing women cannot identify exactly how and when the breast is female, even when it is revealed as such, implies that breasts are not undeniable markers of femaleness, as has been argued by Sally

O'Driscoll. She contends that in the narratives of the female pirates Anne Bonny and Mary Read, "The breast takes on a vital role: it becomes the signifier of femaleness that betrays passing women and thus attempts to prove that passing is impossible. The revealed breast upholds the social order by reassuring the reader that the 'truth' of femaleness will always be made evident, and that fraud will eventually be detected."[7] Yet even in the narratives of Bonny and Read, the breast is only ever revealed by Read herself—her desire and ability to reveal her breast are, in fact, not "betrayals" so much as a choice through which to reveal sexual desires, both straight and queer.

In fact, these narratives often play on the erotic quality of the breast in the moments when the cross-dresser's breasts are revealed to others, either purposefully or inadvertently. The exposed breasts of the cross-dresser engender sapphic possibilities as women uncover their breasts to other women and readers are encouraged to consider the spectacle of women exposing their breasts to one another in an erotic context. Thus, while the breast often indexes femininity through its size, shape, color, and relation to nursing and mothering, it is as often incapable of being represented or recognized as female, and it can also function as an invitation or entice-ment to a sapphic bond. To use the example of Read and Bonny, when Read is in men's clothes, she purposefully exposes her breasts to identify her femaleness to a man she wishes to seduce. She also reveals her sex to another man who turns out to be a woman: Anne Bonny. The doubling of this moment in the text—once with a woman, and the next time with a man—suggests the breast's ability to function as a marker of sex, as well as of sexual enticement. Similarly, in *Belinda,* Lady Delacour's breast brings the women of the novel together, thus functioning as a symbol of not only maternity but also intense female friendship and same-sex passions. Discussions of the maternal breast, the sentimental breast, and the erotic breast must be supplemented by the sapphic breast: one that is shared and desired by women.

The narratives of cross-dressing women establish the breast as a sign of femaleness, just as they establish facial hair as a sign of maleness. The physical female breast can expose the cross-dresser as a woman; it is proof of her female-ness; and it must be hidden if she wishes to pass as a man.

The liability the breast represents demonstrates the significance of the female breast to establishing femininity and femaleness. The cross-dresser must hide or camouflage her breasts if she wishes to pass. The narratives of cross-dressing women who do not wish to "pass" must still contend with the breast and its discursive and physical role in defining femaleness. Like the beard, the breast appears initially to belong to one gender and one gender only, yet several texts present the breast as both female and ambiguous or androgynous, a body part whose visibility and legibility rely on not only situation (when and where the breast is revealed), but also intention (why it is revealed, for what purpose). In the example from Snell's narrative, the breast is not always coded as female, and it is not always easy to see: it is both female and not. The breast's invisibility and illegibility underscore how eighteenth-century texts grappled with the concepts of embodied gender, as well as how they enjoyed the titillating possibilities inherent to gender non-normative or transgendered bodies. Thus, as we shall see, the breast functions, to an extent, like the beard: it emblematizes the eighteenth-century fascination with mutable gender and desire, even as it is an embodied marker of lesbian desire. Importantly, though, many of these texts predicate such desires and fluidity on the presumed whiteness of the people involved, calling out strange moments of racialized embodiment that cannot quite be reincorporated into a stable narrative of individual desires.

The Breast in the British Cultural Imaginary

For centuries, the breast has been the locus for a complex and often contradictory set of expectations and representations in Western civilization. From the earliest statues of fertility goddesses whose multiple breasts symbolized abundance and nourishment, to the huge and hideous teats of witches that are the stuff of legend, breasts have been central to positive and negative definitions of femininity. Whether erotic or maternal, the breast, as both literal body part and metaphorical signifier of the motherland, is almost always coded as female. At the same time, however, in English the words "breast" and "bosom" may refer to a woman's breast;

the chest area of a man *or* woman; or the body part that contains a person's deepest emotions, regardless of gender. Eighteenth-century texts often reference all three meanings without attracting much attention to this slippage; what makes this slippage interesting is how it functions textually to make or unmake gender.

The maternal breast and the increasing insistence over the course of the century on breastfeeding are topics that dominate the discussions of eighteenth-century breasts. Works by Fildes, Schiebinger, Warner, and Yalom form the basis for much of the subsequent discussions on how the image of the breast changes during the eighteenth century, becoming less associated with eroticism and sexuality and more attached to the maternal role of women in society.[8] Schiebinger argues, for example, that Linnaeus coined the term "mammal" precisely due to the increasing importance placed on the female breast in the eighteenth century.[9] Yalom explicitly traces this change by arguing that the breast in the Renaissance period was an "erotic breast," while the eighteenth-century breast was connected to political and ideological projects linked to the rise of capitalism, as well as the French Revolution.[10] Perry comes to a similar conclusion.[11] She suggests that it is not just nation building but the act of colonizing that denies women their own breasts and reappropriates them for patriarchal purposes.[12] Like Warner and Yalom, Perry suggests that the emphasis on the maternal aspects of womanhood undermined a sexual identity for women in the second half of the eighteenth century.

The eighteenth-century breast is not completely emptied of its erotic connotations, however. Even within her discussion of breastfeeding mammas of the Napoleonic era and the fashion for loose, uncorseted breasts and gauzy dresses, Yalom admits that, while "the breasts had been separated during the Renaissance into two groups, one for nursing, the other for sexual gratification—[they] were now reunited into one multipurpose bosom. Lactating breasts had become sexy."[13] Alternative views of the eighteenth-century breast have been proposed by other critics, as well. Richter argues that female breasts came to assume a metaphorical congruence with the male penis that perpetuates a version of the one-sex model over the course of the century. He describes the breast as a "contested and unruly signifier, not easily disciplined by biological and medical discourse," and he posits that there is a significant and potentially rich analogy to be found in anti-masturbation and anti-wet-nursing treatises from this time.[14] Richter analyzes this analogy between the breast and the penis to argue that a one-sex model persisted into the nineteenth century, despite the arguments of Thomas Laqueur (and others) that the eighteenth century saw the revolutionary change of a one-sex model to a two-sex model.[15] Richter critiques Perry's view that the sexual breast was colonized completely and turned into a maternal breast, as "certainly eros is involved even in the biological constructions of sexuality, as it undoubtedly is in the construction of motherhood and the maternal breast. How can we possibly keep separate the erotic voyeurism of the male gaze . . . the many fantasies, male and female, private and collective, relating to the breast?"[16] His insistence on the erotic and the maternal together in the same image of the breast encourages us to read the breast as a multifaceted locus of meaning that is constantly shifting.

At times, the eighteenth-century female breast indeed takes on a powerful, threatening aspect. In some texts "there are discursive situations, fantasmatic but real, in which the breast attains phallic—i.e. threatening—proportions," Richter writes. "We may, with due qualification, be justified in speaking of the late eighteenth century as a mammocentric culture in which fantasies of the female breast become dominant."[17] In her discussion of Fielding and Richardson, Nina Prytula argues that "the breast serves as an outward manifestation of intangible qualities of mind."[18] She differentiates between the two writers, however, by arguing that in Richardson's novels, the breast is an instrument of sensibility, while Fielding uses the bosom to assign positive or negative qualities to female characters. Large, loose breasts are equated in Fielding's world with aberrant Amazons, women who manifest masculine characteristics.[19] Thus, the large-breastedness of these women becomes a mark of their supposed Amazonian qualities: physical strength and sexual appetite.[20] Interestingly, though the term "Amazon" is a popular one throughout the eighteenth century for strong, masculine, or self-assured women, it appears without reference to the one-breastedness of the Amazons of legend. In The Culture of Sensibility, J. G. Barker-Benfield remarks that the term "Amazon" was both taken up and disavowed by a variety of female writers throughout the long eighteenth century.[21] Dror Wahrman expands on this, arguing that the Amazon, literal or figurative, "was doing rather well until the last two decades of the eighteenth century, and was routinely seen as an evocation of ancient glory, more a compliment than a complaint."[22] In both cases, as well as in several examples they cite (such as the use of "Amazon" to describe Mrs. Selwyn in Fanny Burney's *Evelina*), the term "Amazon" is used to describe qualities of attitude and mind or even masculine physique (such as Mrs. Freke's "masculine arms") rather than the lack of breast.

The size and shape of the ideal female breast, however, is of great cultural significance at this time. Schiebinger notes that, despite Linnaeus's focus on the female breast and lactation, as well as the growing emphasis on mothers' breastfeeding of their children, the eighteenth-century ideal breast was a "virginal" one. The qualities of the virginal breast—small and rounded—were thought to exemplify a civilized society. Schiebinger points out that the colonial enterprise contributed to this classification: "The ideal breast—for all races—was once again young and virginal. Europeans preferred the compact 'hemispherical type,' found, it was said, only among whites and Asians."[23] While Schiebinger notes that this hierarchy emerged in the late nineteenth century, Kathleen Wilson finds evidence for such emphasis on small-breastedness in the eighteenth century. In *The Island Race,* she argues that British historians and writers on the Cook voyages to the Pacific frequently cite the size and shape of native women's breasts to determine the level of civilization in a society. According to Wilson, the ideal eighteenth-century mother had "round and moderately sized breasts with well-formed nipples."[24] Thus, those societies where the women's breasts were "'round and beautiful' were among those where women were esteemed and well treated, and held to be advancing out of savagery; conversely, in the cultures where women's breasts were 'flaccid and pendulous,' women were wretchedly used as beasts of burden or punching bags by their own offspring."[25]

The female breasts' size and shape were important factors in understanding and asserting British superiority to other races. Their status as a primary determining factor of both beauty and civilization suggests the significance of the breast as a visual marker of femininity and maternity.

Breasts signaled the ability of women to bring up good citizens who, in turn, would treat their mothers (i.e., their country) well. But they also suggest the importance of looking and evaluating; the colonial endeavor contained within it warring desires of recognition and rejection of similarities among other peoples. It is also significant that small-breastedness was a desirable quality in the ideal eighteenth-century woman: a small breast represents the ability to be controlled, confined, and defined by the patriarchal order, while the overly large or pendulous breast is characterized as threatening and even masculine in its aggressiveness. The passing woman implicitly appears to rely on her own small-breastedness to adopt male garb and lifestyle successfully and to pass as a man even as she is frequently described as feminine, attractive, even beautiful. This suggests, perhaps—as does the lack of beard—that a certain amount of androgyny was a desirable characteristic.[26] Further, the small breasts of the female cross-dresser fit well with notions of racial superiority associated with British nationhood, civilization, and, increasingly, whiteness, as we shall see.

Thus, the literal female breast represents femininity, maternity, and nationhood, as well as erotic desire, yet the breast also has a gender-neutral or ambiguous meaning in the eighteenth century. Warner points out that, historically, "for both sexes [the breast] is the place of the heart, held to be the fountainhead of sincere emotion in both classical culture and our own," and "In English, the words 'breast' and 'bosom' were not sex-specific either until possibly very recently."[27] The breast linguistically embraces the possibilities of extreme gender-specificity and gender-neutrality, even in medical texts from the time period. This ambiguity makes it a potent image to explore as it functions on or in the body of the cross-dressed woman. Its presence as a marker of gender is visible in the histories of Hannah Snell and Mary Read, who pass as men and who first must hide their breasts but later use their breasts to vouch for their "true" sex. In Snell's narrative, as well as in that of Christian Davies, the metaphorical breast is also at work, functioning as the locus of sentiment and bravery. Davies's story, however, also incorporates the breast's maternal function, as her narrative suggests some of the issues that will come to the fore in *Belinda*, in which the transgressive cross-dressing Harriet Freke and the "dying" Lady Delacour together create a narrative about the cross-dresser's breast and the sentimental breast that further exposes the breast's ability to function prosthetically and elicit sapphic desires. Considering these characters together, along with those in *Belinda*, we see how the physical breast can function metaphorically to highlight female-centered relationships and rebellion against patriarchal expectations.

The breasts of the female cross-dresser are rarely at the center of discussions of breasts or cross-dressers.[28] Yet the breast is often central to the construction of a coherent gender identity in the stories of female cross-dressers. The breasts of the female cross-dressers not only suggest new ways of looking at the breast, but they also tell us something about the act of looking at the body and understanding embodied desires. By looking at hidden breasts, desiring breasts, breasts that appear only for a short moment, we may understand the breast queerly—as a part of a transgressive, non-normative, and nonmaternal set of discourses that challenge our understanding of the eighteenth-century breast as the locus of patriarchal forces of domesticity and nation building. The cross-dresser's breasts must be examined more closely to understand the construction of gender difference in the eighteenth century, as well as how these constructions fail. The cross-dresser's breasts undo gender, creating a space for trans bodies and queer desires. By looking at different works and different genres, we can construct a narrative of the body that is intimately linked to desire and performances of gender. The breasts are not simply the locus for eighteenth-century cishetpatriarchal expectations of women; they are body parts that articulate a rebellion against these expectations and posit fascinating, fluid identities and embodiments.

Female Cross-Dressers and the Real Soul of a Man in Their Breast

In one of the few studies of eighteenth-century female cross-dressers and their breasts, O'Driscoll makes a compelling argument for the importance of breasts to the story of the female pirates Anne Bonny and Mary Read. She argues, "The pirates' milk-white breasts, flashing from their clothes, are the heart of their enigma. The men's jackets they wear cannot completely contain them, and neither can the narrative—the conundrum of the female figure who exceeds all social bounds is hard to contain in a formally messy narrative that is a crossroads for several literary conventions. . . . The breast becomes the compelling metonymic focus of a swirling debate about appropriate femininity."[29] Similarly, the breast becomes a "compelling metonymic focus" in the eighteenth century regarding sexuality and same-sex desires, not just in Bonny and Read's narrative, but across many of the stories of plebeian female cross-dressers. This section considers four texts of working-class cross-dressing women—two of them laudatory, and two of them condemnatory of the cross-dresser—to look at patterns of representation across texts and genres.

The physical breast often functions in these narratives as a visible marker of sex and gender. We see this clearly in the history of Mary Read, and a similar pattern of representation emerges in *The Female Soldier*, the story of Hannah Snell. Both women pass as men and must hide their breasts to impersonate men successfully, but later these women reveal their breasts to vouch for their "true" sex. In Snell's narrative, as well as in that of another female soldier, Christian Davies, the text establishes the breast as both corporeal and female and as the metaphorical locus of sentiment and bravery. This latter movement in the text suggests how narratives attempted, yet again, to establish the plebeian cross-dresser's superlative performance of masculinity and her (erotic) appeal to her beards. Davies's narrative also incorporates the breast's maternal function, as her narrative foreshadows some of the issues that will come to the fore in Edgeworth's *Belinda*. The narratives of the female pirates Anne Bonny and Mary Read, the female soldier Christian Davies, and the female husband Mary Hamilton also refer to the female breast as an embodied gender marker and an indisputable indicator of femaleness. The narratives of these women emphasize that breasts can "give away" one's gender or make their true sex legible to those around them, often, though not always, for erotic purposes. These texts highlight the visual element of sex identification and erotic desire. When the breast is revealed to another woman (the beard) and recognized as female, the texts allude potently to female same-sex desires and the eros of looking while at the same time reinscribing cisgendered body normativity. The breast, like the beard, functions to identify the perils of cross-dressing for the women who enter into that undertaking, but also its possible pleasures. Unlike the missing beard, the breast serves to anchor sex and gender in the body—but only ever fleetingly.

Snell's whipping in public, for example, offers a moment in the text that the narrator feels he must address explicitly to explain away her breasts, which would reveal her femaleness aboard ship. *The Life and Adventures of Mrs. Christian Davies, the British Amazon, Commonly Called Mother Ross,* published anonymously in 1741, also establishes the female breasts as undeniable markers of gender.[30] Like *The Female Soldier,* Christian Davies follows her husband into the army, commits acts of great bravery, and woos various women along the way.[31] Initially, Davies's breasts appear to pose no obstacle to her ability to pass as a man, even as they are explicitly coded as female. As she prepares her male disguise, Davies recounts, "Having thus ordered my affairs, I cut off my hair, and dressed me in a suit of my husband's, having had the precaution to quilt the waistcoat, to preserve my breasts from hurt, which were not large enough to betray my sex."[32] She quickly and easily accounts for her breasts and how she manages to hide them before entering into the regiments to look for her disappeared husband. This narrative, like that of Hannah Snell and Mary Read, asserts that the breast is female. Davies must protect the vulnerable mark of her femaleness, just as she must cut off her hair, to disguise her femininity. The narrative accounts for and dismisses the female breast, though it asserts the importance of hiding the breasts as the waistcoat is "quilted" to ensure better coverage, thus alluding to practices of both butch lesbians and trans women in the present, such as breast binding.

Despite her precautions, her breasts eventually divulge her sex when she is under the care of a surgeon after being wounded in battle. Davies is carried to a small French town near the battleground. She says, "Though I suffered great torture by this wound, yet the discovery it caused of my sex, in the fixing of my dressing, by which the surgeons saw my breasts, and, by the largeness of my nipples, concluded I had given suck, was a greater grief to me."[33] The breasts are what give Davies away—or, to be more specific, the size and shape of her nipples. It is not necessarily the breast itself that "outs" her but, rather, the bodily signs of breastfeeding—of being a mother—that reveal her secret. Within the ever-growing importance of mother's milk and breastfeeding in nationalist discourses of the eighteenth century, Davies is marked as a good mother, despite her distinctly unfeminine roles as soldier. The allusion to her role as a mother reminds the reader of her femaleness while also marking her as a laudatory female cross-dresser. She fights for her country (i.e., Britain, even though she is Irish), but she is also a mother who gives suck to all her children (and perhaps her country, as she serves as an example of extreme valor on the battlefield). Her breasts take on extra-symbolic meaning that combines the female breast and its links to maternity with the valorous, androgynous bosom of soldier and citizen. Her "grief" at her discovery yet again suggests the importance of her gender fluidity and connects to modern-day stories of transgender people who wish to conceal the physical signs of sex assigned at birth that disturb their gender identity.

The emphasis on Davies's nipples rather than the size of the breasts, however, is reminiscent of when Mary Read's breasts reveal her femaleness aboard ship not through size but through skin color. In both narratives, the gendering of breasts does not rely on any single standard of femaleness; there is no uniformity of type that codes breasts as specifically female.[34] The narratives of Anne Bonny and Mary Read appear in *A General History of the Robberies and Murders of the Most Notorious Pyrates*, published in 1724 under the authorship of Captain Charles Johnson.[35] Both women disguise themselves as men and use their disguises to remain aboard privateer and pirate ships for the purposes of pillaging and plundering along with their fellow pirates.[36] Both also use their disguises to carry on affairs with men aboard ship. In both cases, their cross-dressing begins at a young age.[37] In the story of Mary Read, her cross-dressing begins when her mother passes her off as a boy for financial gain. Even as an adolescent Read remains in men's clothes. At thirteen, she works as a footman for a while until, "growing bold and strong, and having a roving Mind, she enter'd herself on board a Man of War, where she served some Time, then quitted it," only to be a cadet in a regiment in Flanders, where she falls in love with one of the Flemish soldiers.[38] The narrator writes that "as they lay together in the same Tent, and were constantly together, she found a Way of letting him discover her Sex, without appearing that it

"Ann Bonny and Mary Read convicted of piracy Nov. 28th 1720 at a court of vice admiralty held at St. Jago de la Vega in ye island of Jamaica," *A General History of Robberies and Murders of the Most Norotious Pyrates*, 1724, opposite page 117. (© British Library Board, C.121.b.24)

was done with Design."[39] Her method for revealing her sex is unclear until she reveals it again, later in the narrative, to a young man taken captive aboard the pirate ship where she serves. Read uses all her skills to seduce him, first gaining his confidence by disparaging the pirate lifestyle and subsequently revealing her femaleness. "When she found he had a Friendship for her, as a Man," the narrator writes, "she suffered the Discovery to be made, by carelessly shewing her Breasts, which were very white."[40] Thus, it is not the size and shape of the breasts that bear the marker of gender here, but their color.[41] As readers, we may infer that Read's "accidental" revelation of her gender to the Flanders cadet was through a similar means, as the revelation of breasts is the only specific method for the discovery of her sex represented in the text. Thus, in Read's story, breasts *are* gender—or, at least, the white ones are.[42] In addition, Read's story explicitly states how a woman might use her breasts to signal her "true" sex visually. The focus on color rather than size or shape suggests that sex is a constructed category whose parameters are not clearly defined.

The narratives of Bonny and Read in Johnson's *A General History* present both women as accessing sexual independence through their working-class initiative, combined with their cross-dressing and piracy. Their sexual independence, however, is not limited to the pursuit of heterosexual romance. Moments of sapphic possibility arise in their narratives when we learn that the two women met aboard ship, and Bonny attempted to seduce Read. O'Driscoll makes a case for the lesbian overtones of their stories that would have been legible to eighteenth-century readers, arguing that "the possibility of a same-sex affair remains available to the reader, couched in the conventions of cross-dressing theatricality—thus presented as playful misrepresentation. The original edition neatly labels this playful possibility as impossible, yet later editions indicate that readers and publishers found it appealing."[43] Although Read reportedly rebuffs Bonny's sexual overture and reveals her true identity to Bonny instead, the ambiguousness of the exchange and its existence in the narrative at all alludes to the titillating quality of same-sex female desires that were available to contemporary readers, as well as the role of the breast in signifying and mediating sexual encounters between women.[44] The breast becomes one of the bodily sites for representing the vectors of desires between cross-dressers and their beards.

Thus, the attachment of "femaleness" to the breast, via various factors and in certain circumstances, reminds readers of the cross-dresser's status as "woman" and, implicitly, the possibility of women desiring women. Further, the representation of the breast textually establishes female same-sex desire as both a discursive and an embodied phenomenon. The stories of passing women establish the breast as female and a liability to passing, only to then paradoxically suggest that femaleness gives them access to other kinds of pleasurable possibilities: sapphic possibilities. For example, when Bonny attempts to seduce Read, apparently ignorant of Read's own femaleness, she "first discovered her Sex to Mary Read; Mary Read knowing what she would be at, and being very sensible of her own Incapacity in that Way, was forced to come to a right Understanding with her, and so to the great Disappointment of Anne Bonny, she let her know she was a Woman also."[45] By describing Bonny's motivations as "reasons best known to herself," the narrator gestures to the *amor imposibilis* of lesbian desire— the desire that dare not speak its name. Read's decision to reveal her true identity to Bonny is also unclear, as it seems that she took great care, until that point, to keep her identity hidden. Read's decision—or desire—to reveal herself as a woman to Bonny is suggestive of lesbian desire, even more so when we speculate as to how Read and Bonny reveal *their* sex to each other. Given the only specific "revelation" of sex in these two narratives, the reader may imagine that they also showed their breasts to each other as a means of seduction and confession. Although Bonny's "great Disappointment" bespeaks a kind of refusal to acknowledge sapphic possibilities, as well as hetero-disappointment, it also alludes to the possibility of reading trans identifications between two female-bodied people of masculine gender.

Nevertheless, in Read's story breasts are undeniable indicators of sex. Presumably, the whiteness of Read's breast indicates her femininity because a woman's breasts are never exposed to the sun in the way a laboring-class man's might be; however, several problematic points arise here. An aristocratic or middle-class man might also have a very white chest, for example. Second, and more to the point, is the indication of racial preference in a female breast.[46] The sailors and soldiers who see Read's breast, we might surmise, would identify her as female due to the size or shape of her breasts; the text, however, reveals that it is the whiteness of her breasts that makes her recognizable as both female and an appropriate partner for a romantic relationship. If, indeed, the female breast was becoming increasingly "colonized" and recoded as an important part of the imperial project, as Perry has argued, then the whiteness of Read's breast is not merely coincidental. This moment in the text reveals not just Read's breast, but also the growing concerns about who has access to the freedoms of the transatlantic world and who does not.[47] By the logic of romance, these women are self-sufficient, exciting, and desirable, and their ability to transcend gender and sexual expectations is at once extraordinary and acceptable. The romance of Bonny and Read is only possible, though, because they are white and European.[48] Thus, we must consider the sapphic possibilities between these women as made available to the reader through and at the cost of entrenched ideas about race and default whiteness of the heroines.

The possibilities for same-sex desires were and still are part of the allure of these women's stories. The text encourages its readers to imagine the two women baring their breasts to each other: for Bonny, as a sign of a desire, and for Read, as a signifier of her lack of it—or, as the narrator puts it, "her own Incapacity in that Way."[49] Even this phrase, however, implies that Read is unable to return Bonny's desires rather than fulfill them. Significantly, their mutual revelations become fodder for Rackam's jealousy: "This Intimacy so disturb'd Captain Rackam, who was the Lover and Gallant of Anne Bonny, that he grew furiously jealous, so that he told Anne Bonny, he would cut her new Lover's Throat, therefore, to quiet him, she let him into the Secret also."[50] Rackam's jealousy, like Bonny's initial attraction to Read, signifies that Read passes unquestionably as a man to others. Yet the narrator's allusive remark that Bonny's attraction to Read was "unaccountable" calls on the reader to consider the possibility that Bonny was attracted to Read precisely for her female qualities or appearance. As pirate women who transgress norms of femininity and domesticity in addition to transgressing the rule of law, Bonny and Read are perhaps, not surprisingly, coded as sapphic. As O'Driscoll points out, later editions of *The General History* played up the sapphic possibilities in the text: "The togetherness of the two women, their constant presentation as a couple, signals a homoeroticism that some later editions pick up on more strongly: the 1765 edition, for example, adds a slight variation to the story, in which Read refers to Bonny as her 'lover.'"[51] The narratives of Bonny and Read emphasize the importance of the breasts to representations of female desire, symbolically connected as they are to discourses of embodiment, gender, and female bonding, as well as to nation building, empire, and categories of whiteness.

We see a similar movement from breasts as dangerous indicators of vulnerable femininity to breasts as the marker of sapphic desire in *The Female Soldier*, a text that explicitly marks itself as different from that of less virtuous female cross-dressers who use their disguises to have sexual affairs with men (i.e., Bonny and Read), as I discuss in chapter 1. The visual revelation of sex between women via the breast nevertheless functions similarly in Hannah Snell's narrative. Though Snell must hide her female body while aboard ship, she must also prove her "true" sex at the end of her narrative upon her return to England. Snell returns to her brother-in-law's house and "discover[s] herself" to him, after which she is recognized and welcomed into the family home.[52] When it comes time to find her a place to sleep, Snell is introduced to a female lodger. The lodger is asked whether she would take on a sister of Mr. Gray's as a bedfellow, to which she agrees, until she sees Snell, who is still in her regimentals. And although "Mr. Gray and his Wife discovered the Secret [of Snell's true sex], . . . [the lodger] would not Credit [it], until she had occular Demon-stration."[53] The text does not specify the kind of "ocular demonstration" that Snell provides, leaving the reader to imagine how this female soldier proved her femaleness. The narrator tells us only that "this was the first, next to [Snell's] Brother and Sister, that she discovered herself to, and ever since they have been Bedfellows, which made the Neighbours report (imagining her to be a Man) that the young woman was married to a Sol-dier."[54] The reader is left to wonder what Snell could show her as strong enough "ocular demonstration" of her sex for the young woman's peace of mind.

Given the example of Mary Read in *A General History*, the breast comes to mind, though it is possible, given the vagueness of the remark, that Snell bares some other part of her body.[55] However, Snell's "discovery" of herself to the young woman echoes the scene between Bonny and Read, in which the discovery of gender forecloses (hetero)sexual desire (or its threat) by replacing it with a suggestive sapphic possibility. The neighbors interpret the women as a heterosexual married couple because they are unable to recognize Snell's femaleness beneath the regimentals, suggest-ing at least outwardly Snell's transgender identity. Where the neighbors "see" heterosexual coupling and desire, the text explicitly asks the reader to see nothing more than two women sharing a bed, a common enough practice at the time. Yet the emphasis on Snell's femaleness allows the readers a glimpse at yet another close relationship between women. Jux-taposed against the earlier moments in the narrative in which Snell woos her beards, this relationship, too, reads queerly. While Read and Bonny are explicitly unfulfilled by their mutual revelations, there is no explicit lack of fulfillment for Snell and the lodger. Instead, we are confronted with the scene of one woman baring her body—possibly her breast—to another, who subsequently forms a close relationship with her. The moment of exposure is the moment in which the text reveals just how appealing a female cross-dresser may be to another woman.

As with the beard, the breasts function similarly to index not just femaleness and bonds between women, but also the ability of women to adopt certain aspects of masculinity and improve on them. *The Female Soldier* presents us with not only a physical breast but also a metaphorical breast that symbolizes both Snell's masculine courage and her capability for great feeling—feelings that the narrative presents as part of what makes her an ideal partner for other women. In Snell's account, when she realizes that her husband has abandoned her, "She thought herself privileged to roam in quest of the man, who, without Reason, had injured her so much; for there are no Bounds to be set either to Love, Jealousy or Hatred, in the female Mind."[56] Throughout *The Female Soldier,* the narrator ascribes various feminine sentiments to Snell, suggesting she may have felt frightened or fatigued in her journey on account of her "true" sex, her *bodily* sex, which affects the gender of the mind, as well. The narrator suggests that her "mind "—the rational, thinking part of her—is feminine (i.e., not rational). Yet her inner soul is not completely feminized: "That she might execute her Designs with the better Grace, and the more Success, she boldly commenced a Man, at least in her Dress, and no doubt she had a Right to do so, since she had the real Soul of a Man in her Breast."[57] The narrative's rhetoric transforms Snell from an injured woman into a "man"; her mind may be female, but her soul is masculine, and it resides in her "breast." Her breast is, as Warner puts it, "the fountainhead of sincere emotion," and even the seat of the soul.[58] The narrator asserts that Snell's soul is a brave, courageous, and strong one—hence, masculine—that is not driven by petty hatreds, jealousies, or other immaterial sentiments associated with women that, evidently, result from having a woman's *body* or even a woman's *mind* but not a woman's soul. Snell's breast comes to symbolize both masculine and feminine qualities; it is essentially feminine in that it exposes her sex, and it is essentially masculine in that it harbors "the real soul of a man," thus constructing her as a quintessentially transgender subject. The slippage between the metaphorical "breast" that refers to the genesis of human emotions and the literal, female breast, with all its gendered connotations, is evident in Snell's history, allowing for the potent suggestion to arise that true feeling is trans feeling. At the same time, the narrator focuses so much on Snell's actual breasts that it is difficult to ignore his use of the same word to justify her joining the navy in the first place, and this slippage adds to the ambivalence the narrator betrays over Snell's feminine and masculine attributes.[59] Although the breast is feminine and through its exposure can limit the cross-dresser, it can also bring her closer to her fellow women, giving her privileged access. From a trans perspective, these texts foreground the difficulties and fears experienced by trans people in the past (and present) when attempting to transition to a different gender. Thus, cross-dressing narratives themselves reveal not only the transness of gender and the ambiguity of gender definitions, but also the pleasures that can be found in desires predicated on a closeness of minds or bodies rather than strict adherence to gender and sexual binaries.

The breast also reveals the fluidity of gender in Davies's story, even as it ultimately reveals Davies's female sex. The slippage of meanings associated with the breast is evident most clearly when she woos a young woman in the guise of a soldier. She calls it one of her "frolics, to kill time," to woo a burgher's daughter whose spurned lover eventually challenges Davies to a duel.[60] While describing the duel, Davies recounts the various blows exchanged, including a pass that her opponent "aimed at my breast, but hit my right arm."[61] Here the term "breast" refers to the physical, though not necessarily gendered, body part of the chest. Only a few pages later, Christian addresses the burgher's daughter (i.e., one of her beards) with the following gallantries: "No my charmer, though I am no more than a common sentinel, this breast is capable of as much tenderness . . . as that of a general."[62] She addresses the woman in soldier's garb, in the guise of a lover, alluding to her metaphorical breast, the repository for true emotion that is neither male nor female. Thus, her narrative, like Snell's, juxtaposes the embodied breast with the metaphorical breast, in both cases emphasizing the ways in which the female cross-dresser represents the pleasurable and satisfying aspects of having a woman or a trans man for a lover. The female cross-dresser is both bold and tender, and she embodies the physical strength of men in these narratives, as well as the sexualized body of a woman. While the lack of beard reveals the attraction of the beards for an androgynous face, the physical female breasts index an embodied femaleness that functions as an invitation to further bonding.

The role of the breast in the story of the female cross-dresser is likewise evident in Henry Fielding's *The Female Husband,* which exemplifies and develops in its own way the role of the breast as not only a liability for the passing woman, but also the embodied site of romantic and erotic desire between women. *The Female Husband* is by far the most explicitly sexualized account of a working-class, passing woman, even if it is not a laudatory account like that of *The Female Soldier* or the narrative of Christian Davies. Despite the narrator's attempts to condemn Hamilton's behavior, *The Female Husband* presents the possibility of reading the female husband and cross-dresser Mary/George Hamilton as an integral and even positive character in the development of an early lesbian and trans identity, as we see in chapter 1.[63] Fielding rarely desists from his satirical tone of narration, yet his frequent movement between the pronouns "he" and "she" when referring to Hamilton is an unironic confirmation of her/his ambiguous, nonbinary gender. As a narrator, Fielding acknowledges the ways in which Hamilton's character negotiates between these identities, and in doing so he represents a character whose gender is in flux. While Hamilton's greatest problems of proving her masculinity come from her lack of (physical) manhood, as I discuss in chapter 3, her breasts are still at issue. If the men's clothes hide the woman beneath, they never do so perfectly, and for Hamilton, her breasts are at risk of violent revelation whenever they are mentioned. The female breast always presents a hazard for the female cross-dresser wishing to hide her "true identity."[64] *The Female Husband* constructs the breasts as quintessentially feminine and, at the same time, unrecognizable as such, suggesting that the breast is only ever partially visible as a signifier of gender, or that when it is visible, it is difficult to recognize as female at all.

Fielding's short story begins with sapphic seduction. Hamilton's decision to go to Ireland in the guise of a young male Methodist teacher is precipitated by the end of her relationship with Anne Johnson. Anne comes back from six months in Bristol a Methodist and proceeds to seduce Hamilton with the same tricks that were used to seduce her by her "methodistical sisters."[65] Unfortunately for Hamilton, Anne meets one Mr. Rog-ers, whom she decides to marry.[66] When Hamilton hears of the match, Fielding writes, "She became almost frantic, she tore her hair, beat her breasts, and behaved in as outrageous a manner as the fondest husband could, who had unexpectedly discovered the infidelity of a beloved wife."[67] The beating of the breasts holds both symbolic and literal meaning for the female cross-dresser. Like the tearing of hair, the beating of breasts as a sign of despair is a highly symbolic gesture, one that is scripted or done for pure effect, like that of an actor on the stage. Although Mary Hamilton has not yet started cross-dressing, Fielding reveals her passionate feelings for her lover through this gesture, which relies less on the female breast than on the breast as the fountainhead of emotions and, significantly in this scene, masculine emotions. At the same time, with the breasts as a signifier of femininity, is it difficult to forget Hamilton's position as *woman* scorned, *not* husband cuckolded. The beating of the breasts may even be read as an attack by Hamilton on her own breasts—the markers of her unfortunate femaleness. Fielding's use of this symbolic gesture to signify her despair lends some sympathy to the plight of the heartbroken young woman even as he satirizes her extreme outburst of emotions.

The physicality of Hamilton's breasts plays as important a role in the text as the metaphorical bosom, although the female body is not always recognizable as such. In Hamilton's case, the breasts are exposed against her will at a critical moment in her courtship with the innocent young woman in Wells, England: Mary (Molly) Price. At one of the town dances, the Doctor (Hamilton) enters into a dispute with a man. During the scuffle, the man "tore open her wastecoat, and rent her shirt, so that all her breast was discovered, which, tho' beyond expression beautiful in a woman, were of so different a kind from the bosom of a man, that the married women there set up a great titter."[68] We have no indication from the text as to the size, shape, color, or quality of Hamilton's breasts except that they are extremely beautiful. How Hamilton hides her superlatively perfect breasts in the guise of a man is left to the imagination of the reader. According to our narrator, "Tho' it did not bring the Doctor's sex into an absolute sus-picion, yet [it] caused some whispers, which might have spoiled the match with a less innocent and less enamoured virgin."[69] The physical breast is ambiguous—it engenders a suspicion, but not an "absolute" one. As discussed in the introduction, once Hamilton is "outed" beyond a doubt as a woman in front of the magistrate, it is "to the great shock and astonishment of every body."[70] The astonishment of "every body," even those women who saw Hamilton's breasts at the dance, suggests that in this case breasts do not figure as undeniable signs of female sex; the clothes and the identity of male lover and doctor have successfully deceived the people of Wells.[71] Like Hannah Snell, who is flogged shirtless in front of her fellow sailors, Hamilton has her breasts exposed to a crowd of people, yet she retains her assumed identity. Fielding suggests that a discerning eye might have recognized Hamilton for who she was while at the same time emphasizing the sensational discovery, as well as the resourcefulness and ability, of Hamilton in disguise.

Hamilton's breasts emblematize the paradox of her gender performance: they are visible, yet they do not mark her as a woman, while at the same time they *are* visible, and they *do* mark her as female. We know that Mary Price's sex life with Hamilton is fulfilling when Price declares to the judge that Hamilton indeed "had behaved to her as a husband ought to his wife."[72] Simultaneously, the narrator asserts that Price's love and naïveté alone are the reason for her remaining with Hamilton, even after the discovery of her breasts: "And had not her affections been fixed in this strong manner, it is possible that an accident which happened the very next night might have altered her mind."[73] Thus, Price is both innocent and knowledgeable; Hamilton is both man and woman to her; the people of Wells both know and do not know Hamilton's true identity; and the text, as Terry Castle suggests, is both fascinated with and horrified by Hamilton's transgressions. The breast epitomizes the duality of Hamilton's story in its own duality of signifying and not signifying femaleness. The ability to "read" Hamilton's sex at times depends on touch, and at other times it depends on sight. Yet the text uses the breasts at least twice as an index of Hamilton's physical, feminine beauty and appeal, reinforcing to the reader the body parts through which the reader, whether male or female, might enjoy the body of the female cross-dresser.

It is this corporeal quality, the very physicality of the passing woman's body, that makes the breast a meaningful appendage in discussions of both gender and sexuality. It is a place of vulnerability, a chink in the armor; it is a bodily marker signifying inevitable discovery. It implies sex and sexual attraction as a visual and tactile stimulus to desire. At the same time, the stories of passing women also hold out the possibility of reading the breasts more metaphorically and symbolically, not only as markers of ideal femininity, but also as ambiguous parts denoting ideas or concepts—femininity, intense emotion, courage, and strength. Hamilton's story, like that of Snell, Davies, and Read, is full of panache and vigor. We have before us the stories of people who risked their reputations, as well as their bodies, for a variety of reasons, including adventure, love, or revenge—or all three. The reader is always aware that these are female-bodied people, and the text refers to them predominantly as female; however, the texts also blur gender distinctions, though each woman ultimately reveals herself or is discovered by someone else as a woman. Thus, these texts explicitly construct the breast as simultaneously ambiguous and female. We also see here the importance of the female relationships in which the cross-dressed woman engages. Bonny, Snell, Davies, and Hamilton each attempt to engage the desires of other women (i.e., their beards). In the case of Hamilton, her desire for other women is quite clear; in the other texts, the intentions and desires of the cross-dresser are more ambiguous—however, the desires of her beards are evident. As already established in chapter 1, the women who come into contact with the cross-dresser inevitably desire her for her physical beauty and prowess as a lover, as well as for her emotional acuity and tender phrases. The breasts become the signifier of and enticement to desire between women as characters are represented exposing their breasts to other women and narrators ask readers to speculate about the cross-dressers' breasts. Speculation is tied to the specular and spectacle. As meanings congeal around the breast, we can speculate about the many matrices of desire at work in these texts.

Although the breast may be colonized for patriarchal duties, as suggested by Perry and implied through Scarlet Bowen's interpretation of female soldiers, it is difficult to deny the multiple possibilities for female same-sex desires that appear to be taken for granted by the representations of the passing woman's breasts. Not only do the breasts draw our eyes to sapphic possibilities, but at the same time they show us how desire functions: through the body as both a corporeal site of pleasure and a more metaphorical vessel for the heart and soul. The cross-dresser's breasts are not always recognizable as female body parts, and their seemingly gendered breasts are never gendered in quite the same ways through quite the same qualities, allowing the transness of the cross-dresser's body and gender to be read in the text. The reader, as we know already, is informed from the start about the cross-dresser's identity, being in the privileged position of knowing. Simultaneously, the reader can only speculate as to how the cross-dresser hides her female body or why her beards are attracted to her—and the narrators of these stories very often reflect on these elements of the narrative, returning to the moments of impossibility and impossible desires. For the reader, however, the possibility of reading sapphic desires is imbricated in this paradoxical textual logic. Similarly, in *Belinda,* the seductive power of the breast resides even within Lady Delacour's supposedly "diseased" breast, and the novel rewrites the role of the breast as a conduit for sapphic desires within the realm of the domestic novel.

Bosom Friends and the Sapphic Breasts of *Belinda*

Maria Edgeworth's 1801 novel *Belinda* is about relations between women, even as it also a novel about achieving domestic bliss and finding the right mate. One of the central symbols of both female same-sex relations and imperiled domesticity in the novel is the breast of Lady Delacour, and similar anxieties are expressed in the novel through the motif of female cross-dressing. As a domestic novel published toward the end of the long eighteenth century, *Belinda* may be the ideal example of a "middling-class text" in which cross-dressing functions as a whimsical freak of the upper classes, in stark opposition to the laudable, laboring-class cross-dressers of print culture.[74] The "domestic ideal," however, that critics such as Catherine Craft-Fairchild posit as the novel's ultimate representative goal seems untenable when we see in *Belinda* just how complex and ultimately unsatisfying the heterosexual domestic relationships are without the more satisfying female same-sex relationships to bolster them. Instead of reading such novels as a departure from print culture representations of female soldiers and female husbands, this reading proposes that novels take up similar threads of representation and are in conversation with these texts. The novel's themes of deception and masquerade serve as powerful critiques not of female vice but, rather, of social expectations for women and their limitations. Female friendships and intimacies become triangulated through Lady Delacour's breast, whose wound itself is linked to her cross-dressing and, by extension, her chafing under the demands of eighteenth-century high society.

The wound on Lady Dealcour's breast initially appears to be a punishment for her inadequacies as a wife and mother. Earlier critics have read her diseased breast as a mark of rebellion that is subdued once Lady Delacour allows the male physicians and surgeons, rather than her quack doctor, to examine her.[75] Other interpretations have suggested that the injury to Lady Delacour's breast is a result of her attempts "to be like a man, from her attempt to transgress the limitations imposed upon her gender."[76] Conversely, Ruth Perry posits that "Lady Delacour's history could also be read as festering resentment at the colonization of her body, represented synecdochically by the breast that poisons her life."[77] Katherine Montwieler suggests yet another reading: by revealing that Lady Delacour's breast was never diseased in the first place, the novel reveals that Lady Delacour's transgressive behaviors are healthy and positive.[78] In light of her reading and Perry's, we can no longer read the diseased breast as exclusively the symbol of Lady Delacour's punishment for her earlier rebellious behavior. The wounded breast at the center of the novel lends itself to a variety of interpretations, as the breast comes to symbolize not only Lady Delacour's internal battle for happiness, but also her desire for friendship, love, and reciprocal desire; the struggle for female empowerment; and the possibilities for strong, emotional, and possibly even erotic same-sex bonds. The female breast is made visible in the novel, just as it is in the narratives of passing women, thus engendering sapphic possibilities in the relationships of Lady Delacour, Harriet Freke, and Belinda.

The breast takes on a quasi-erotic quality in *Belinda* in one of the novel's earliest moments of intimacy between Lady Delacour and Belinda. The moment of revelation becomes a moment of shared emotions between the two women made possible through physical intimacy—not unlike similar moments in the stories of Mary Read and Hannah Snell. The evening after the masquerade, Lady Delacour shows Belinda the truth—that she, the lively, good-humored society lady, is in fact a farce. Underneath the makeup, Lady Delacour is a wreck: "'You are shocked, Belinda,' said she, 'but as yet you have seen nothing—look here—' and baring one half of her bosom, she revealed a hideous spectacle. Belinda sunk back into a chair—lady Delacour flung herself on her knees before her."[79] The scene initially appears to be about the havoc Lady Delacour's indiscretions have wrought on her body. She bemoans her past errors to Belinda: "'Am I humbled, am I wretched enough?' cried she, her voice trembling with agony. 'Yes, pity me, for what you have seen; and a thousand times more, for that which you cannot see—my mind is eaten away like my body, by incurable disease—inveterate remorse—remorse for a life of folly."[80] In this scene, the intense emotional connection between the women also suggests a suppressed eroticism. We are asked to imagine one woman showing another woman her breast, ostensibly to reveal "the truth." Lady Delacour exposes her complicated truth at the same time that she exposes an intimate, if imperfect, body part—the wounded breast—to Belinda. The wounded breast opens a path to female intimacy just as it is the result of female indiscretion—indiscretions that include female cross-dressing and female dueling.

Lady Delacour risks everything to reveal herself to Belinda. In this way, the breasts become the windows into the soul. Lady Delacour must reveal her breast, which is both erotic and repulsive, to expose her true self to Belinda; the revelation of the breast initiates Belinda into the secrets of her friend, engendering intimacies both emotional and bodily. Significantly, this revelation, which echoes the other revelations of breasts between women, is the prelude to the rest of Lady Delacour's "discoveries" of herself to Belinda. First she bares her breast, then she bares herself, and from this moment on, Belinda is invited to share in Lady Delacour's secrets as well as to enter her mysterious boudoir.[81] The wounded breast lays the foundation for the increased intimacy, physical and emotional, between the two women. Compared with the tableau that ends the novel, this scene is chaotic, emotional, and complex; it focuses on embodied relationships rather than the frozen perfection of the tableau which, by definition, is momentary and fleeting.

The revelation of the imperfect, ruined breast strengthens the friendship between Belinda and Lady Delacour and sets the stage for Lady Delacour's confession of her life and past errors to Belinda. Among her confessions is her failure as a mother. She links her failure in part to her failed attempts at breastfeeding her first child. It is this struggle, in part, that propels Lady Delacour into the arms of female friends—first Harriet Freke, and later Belinda. Lady Delacour explicitly uses the term "bosom friend" in reference to her former friend Mrs. Freke, suggesting both the centrality of the breast to female same-sex relationships as well as the novel's conflation of body part with emotions.[82] Part of the power of Lady Delacour's breast and the bosoms of *Belinda* is the breast's metaphorical resonance, the breast as "the fountainhead of sincere emotion."[83] In *Belinda,* the transgressive cross-dressing Harriet Freke, the "dying" Lady Delacour, and the rational Belinda are affected by the diseased breast as well as the emotional turmoil located in the metaphorical bosom. The erotic breast and the emotional breast mingle in the term "bosom friend."

Belinda and Harriet Freke are linked through the breasts of Lady Delacour: Belinda through the revelation of the wounded breast, and Harriet Freke through the very act of its wounding. Both women also function at one time or another as Lady Delacour's "bosom friends."[84] Lady Delacour tells Belinda that she, Belinda, fills an "aching void" in her heart left vacant by Mrs. Freke, a phrase that illustrates the possibility of a sapphic love triangle.[85] Lady Delacour explains to Belinda the pain Mrs. Freke has caused her, effectively equating Mrs. Freke with a past lover, even going as far as to call her a "rake."[86] She tells Belinda that Mrs. Freke "has cost me my peace of mind—my health—my life. She knows it, and she forsakes, betrays, insults, and leaves me to die. I cannot command my temper sufficiently to be coherent when I speak of her—I cannot express in words what I feel."[87] Lady Delacour asks Belinda to recognize the depth and passion of her former relationship with Mrs. Freke. When Belinda steps in to fill this void, the love triangle emerges. Significantly, Lady Delacour explains the power of female relationships by explaining that "a woman can always hate a woman more than she can hate a man, unless she has been in love with him."[88] Lady Delacour's phrasing implies that her feelings for female friends can be matched only by her feelings for men she has loved. She is even more explicit about her love for Mrs. Freke and her ability to forgive her wily, masculine friend almost anything: "Whilst I thought she really loved me, I pardoned her all her faults—*All*—what a comprehensive word! . . . I always thought that she cared for no one but for me."[89] Lady Delacour speaks of Harriet Freke like a lover who has jilted her; their relationship is revealed as one that was at once deep and intimate, at least on the part of Lady Delacour, and it is intimately linked to the breast.

Mrs. Freke is indisputably linked to Lady Delacour's breast both through the designation of "bosom friend" and through the duel that leads to Lady Delacour's wound. Mrs. Freke is partially responsible for this wound. The rivalry between Mrs. Luttridge and Lady Delacour (which can be read as another sapphic possibility in the novel) climaxes in a duel between the two women that Mrs. Freke orchestrates. Mrs. Luttridge indirectly challenges Lady Delacour to a duel in response to an insulting cartoon.[90] At Mrs. Freke's urging, Lady Delacour challenges Mrs. Luttridge to a duel; when all of the women appear at the dueling site, Mrs. Luttridge and her second, Miss Honor O'Grady, are "both in men's clothes."[91] Later, it is implied that Mrs. Freke and Lady Delacour were also in men's clothes, as Lady Delacour boasts to Belinda that in "Clarence Hervey's opinion . . . I looked better in man's clothes, than my friend Harriet Freke."[92] After some parley, the women all agree to shoot their pistols in the air, leading to Lady Delacour's breast wound: "My pistol was overcharged—when I fired, it recoiled, and I received a blow on my breast, the consequences of which you have seen—or are to see."[93] It is Harriet Freke who encourages Lady Delacour to duel, telling her "that the only way left, nowadays, for a woman to distinguish herself, was by spirit," and Lady Delacour claims that she "had prodigious deference for the masculine superiority . . . of Harriet's understanding."[94] The duel is an initiation ritual for Mrs. Freke, a way to draw her "bosom friend" even closer.[95] According to Lisa L. Moore, "Lady Delacour's wound is, in terms of the novel's sexual economy, a wound to her femininity, the moral consequence of her transgression of gender boundaries in the duel," yet we might also read it as the result of coming face to face with another boundary in the novel: that of sapphic possibility.[96]

The novel alludes to sapphic possibilities through the dissonances in the apparently heteronormative plot, as well as through the congruities between this plot and the plots of other cross-dressing narratives. Cross-dressing serves as an index of sapphic possibility and relations between women that exist beyond the reach of marriage or as parallel to it. Lady Delacour is Mrs. Freke's beard, just as Belinda eventually becomes hers. The novel positions Lady Delacour's breast at the heart of the first half of the narrative: the wounded breast that results from her frolic with Mrs. Freke alienates Lady Delacour from both Mrs. Freke and her husband, yet it paves the way for deeper intimacy with Belinda. On an emotional level, the revelation of the wounded breast and personal history leads Belinda to promise Lady Delacour she will not leave her during her last illness. On the bodily level, Belinda is allowed into the mysterious boudoir containing the laudanum used to alleviate the pain in Lady Delacour's breast.[97] Physically, Belinda is brought closer to Lady Delacour through the wounded breast in tending to it; metaphorically, she becomes the soothing balm for Lady Delacour's aching bosom. When Lady Delacour's carriage overturns on the way home from the king's birthday celebrations, her ankle is hurt, and she is rushed to her boudoir. She immediately asks for Belinda, telling the servants to "lay me on this sofa and leave me to Belinda," rejecting the help of her husband in favor of her bosom friend.[98] Lord Delacour suggests that perhaps a lover of Lady Delacour's is concealed in the boudoir, or perhaps "a lover of miss Portman's."[99] Ironically, in the small space of the boudoir, Belinda and Lady Delacour are as intimate as lovers. Once they are alone, Belinda undresses Lady Delacour, another act of intimacy allowed a "bosom friend." The breast occupies an ambiguous space in the novel as it symbolizes both transgression and repentance, desire and disease. Belinda is in the privileged position as confidante and companion, and the novel alludes to sapphic possibilities through sapphic bosoms and bosom friendships.[100]

Moreover, the novel ascribes to Mrs. Freke all the conventional trappings of the menacing, masculine, "odd" woman—that is, a lesbian. Lady Delacour describes Mrs. Freke as "downright ugly," with a "wild oddity in her countenance" and "more assurance than any man or woman I ever saw."[101] Mrs. Freke brings "*harum scarum* manners into fashion . . . that *took* surprisingly with a set of young men."[102] She is a woman who uses cross-dressing to enter male spaces with hardly less panache than a female pirate or female husband; she boasts to Lady Delacour, who mistakes her initially for "a smart-looking young man," that she had snuck "into the House of Commons" to hear Sheridan's speech.[103] It would seem that Harriet is more interesting, and perhaps even more attractive, in men's clothing than in women's clothing. Lady Delacour tells Belinda that Mrs. Freke "was always quite at ease; and never more so than in male attire, which she had been told became her particularly. She supported the character of a young rake with such spirit and *truth,* that I am sure no common conjurer could have discovered any thing feminine about her."[104] In putting on men's clothes and acting the bold rake, Mrs. Freke "had laid aside the modesty of her own sex," and she encourages Lady Delacour to do the same.[105] While her behavior to Lady Delacour is ultimately reprehensible, as she encourages her friend to take up again with her former flame, Colonel Lawless, and in the end abandons Lady Delacour and decamps to her enemy Mrs. Luttridge, their friendship implicates Lady Delacour in a network of lesbian desires legible in part through Mrs. Freke's butch masculine description.[106]

In fact, however, Mrs. Freke's betrayal of Lady Delacour serves to emphasize a sapphic triangle among Lady Delacour, Belinda, and Mrs. Freke. This love triangle is made explicit after Lady Delacour and Belinda "break up" for part of the novel. Belinda is absolved of her promise to Lady Delacour when Lady Delacour accuses Belinda of making plans to marry Lord Delacour upon her death. Lady Delacour cries out: "'Oh, Belinda! you! whom I have so loved! so trusted!'"[107] Their parting is fraught with accusations, tears, and beseeching, providing one of the most emotionally intense scenes in the novel, rivaled only by the initial revelation of the diseased breast to Belinda. The rift between the bosom friends allows Harriet Freke to court Belinda, ostensibly to strike a blow to Lady Delacour's ego. At the same time, the rivalry for Belinda triangulates desires among all three women. Mrs. Freke approaches Belinda at the Percivals' home and assures her that "Luttridge and I had such compassion upon you, when we heard you were close prisoner here! I swore to set the distressed damsel free, in spite of all the dragons of Christendom."[108] Mrs. Freke uses the language of fairy tales, casting herself in the role of prince to Belinda's "distressed damsel," reminding us of the ways in which Mrs. Freke, as a female cross-dresser, believes she may have something to offer Belinda that another lover cannot. She assumes that, like the damsels in the stories, Belinda wishes to be freed, not realizing that Belinda is still loyal to Lady Delacour and still involved in a sapphic relationship.[109]

Although her attempts to court Belinda are unsuccessful, Mrs. Freke introduces the revolutionary rhetoric of women's emancipation into the novel. Her arguments reflect the novel's conversation about a woman's right to control her body and her desires—logical extensions of Mrs. Freke's cross-dressing adventures, as the endeavor of cross-dressing is often related to the assertion of female independence, mobility, and empowerment (see chapter 4). Although ridiculous in the mouth of a false friend such as Mrs. Freke, these radical sentiments echo the freedoms Belinda shared once with Lady Delacour. Mrs. Freke asserts that feminine delicacy is a trap for women. "This *delicacy* enslaves the pretty delicate dears," she tells Mr. Percival.[110] "'I hate slavery! *Vive la liberté!*' cried Mrs. Freke, 'I'm a champion for the Rights of Women.'"[111] Espousing, perhaps overly simplistically, the sentiments of the French Revolution and those of Mary Wollstonecraft's *Vindication of the Rights of Women*, Harriet Freke is a disturbing force in the quiet, happy Percival household. Deborah Weiss suggests that, "as with most of Freke's declarations, her outbursts here give evidence of the weakness of her ideas and the general impoverishment of her mind."[112] I would argue, however, that while her arguments are unsubstantiated, their existence in the novel is a crucial reminder that other alternatives exist for women, though they may require a revolutionary stance.[113] Mrs. Freke's emphasis on "delicacy," that eighteenth-century ideal, and how it "enslaves" women is potent, given the final result of Clarence Hervey's attempt to cultivate the "perfect" wife and Belinda's own search for the "perfect" husband. Mrs. Freke's rhetoric of female independence and hardiness are evocative of the cross-dressing narratives of working-class women who are represented as tough, resourceful, and strong, though, of course, Mrs. Freke has wealth and social status that can protect her cross-dressing fancies, unlike the much more precarious, if hardy, plebeian passing women. Cross-dressing, in its many iterations, connotes female desire for independence and an assertion of female strength and perseverance, as well as sapphic possibilities in ways that cut across class divisions. Notably, Mrs. Freke's appropriation of plebeian cross-dressers' qualities is a fascinating precursor to twentieth-century butch lesbian gender performances in which working-class masculinities become appropriated by lesbians of disparate social classes. Her form of courtship, however blundering and unsuccessful, establishes her as a suitor to Belinda and a rival for her heart, while her rhetoric advocates for radical female camaraderie and homosociality.

The struggle between Lady Delacour and Mrs. Freke to claim Belinda serves as a reminder of the sapphic desires that are parallel, but not inferior, to heterosexual ones. As with the rare, flowering plant that Lady Delacour steals to upstage Mrs. Luttridge, so Belinda functions: as a prize that the two women both wish to possess—not entirely unlike the beards who function as a kind of prize for the passing female soldier or female husband. Lady Delacour herself explicitly sets up Belinda as Mrs. Freke's replacement and opposite when she half-feverishly cries to Belinda, "For what was Harriet Freke in comparison with Belinda Portman? . . . Oh, Belinda! how entirely have I loved! trusted! admired! adored! respected! revered you!"[114] Moore argues that "the novel opposes Harriot's [sic] freakish courtship of Belinda with Lady Delacour's ladylike attentions, establishing romantic friendship between 'normal' feminine women as an appropriate relationship within which the women can express intense romantic feeling."[115] Lady Delacour, however, is not a "normal" feminine woman, though she is arguably less overtly butch than Mrs. Freke, and even her declarations of love or distrust of Belinda are characterized by a vehemence she does not express for her husband or any other man. In addition, she and Mrs. Freke have much in common: they both cross-dress; they both enjoy masquerades and fooling their friends with disguises; they are both women with imperiled reputations; they both want Belinda; and, ultimately, they are both wounded. Lady Delacour's breast is wounded before the novel begins, and Mrs. Freke's legs are wounded before the novel ends. Lady Delacour and Harriet Freke function as doubles whose attributes and motivations are parallel, making it difficult to argue that Lady Delacour's femininity is the reason she is the better match for Belinda.[116] Belinda has access to Lady Delacour's breast and the feelings therein, and she refuses Mrs. Freke the power to penetrate the innermost feelings of her own bosom. Ultimately, Belinda is the better match for Lady Delacour because she is truly concerned with Lady Delacour's health and well-being. Her bosom friendship with Lady Delacour is reciprocal, and Lady Delacour's sapphic breasts initiate and encourage the intimacy between them.

Notably, Clarence Hervey, who is the declared nominal suitor for Belinda in the novel, also functions as an object of exchange between women. The novel begins with a masquerade ball at which Clarence is set up as interested sexually in both Lady Delacour and Belinda, yet the triangular nature of the relationship among the three of them subverts the traditional triangle of patriarchal power that Eve Kosofsky Sedgwick interrogates in *Between Men*.[117] Although the second half of *Belinda* reprises the "usual" triangular structure through its rivalry of Clarence Hervey and Mr. Vincent, the first half of the novel plays with the notion that Clarence might be a mere triangulation of desire between Lady Delacour and Belinda. The interplay of female same-sex desires and gender play are nowhere more potently revealed than when Lady Delacour convinces Clarence to dress up in women's clothing, ostensibly to prove how well he can wear a lady's hoop. Clarence plays his cross-dressed role as an émigré by the name of Madame de Grignan: "He managed his hoop with such skill and dexterity, that he well deserves the praise of being a universal genius."[118] Clarence's dexterity fails him, however, when he leans down to pick up a comb dropped purposefully by Lady Delacour; his sudden movement "threw down the music stand with his hoop," losing the bet to Lady Delacour that he could wear a hoop as well as any lady.[119] Thus ends Clarence's attempt to get close to Belinda while in women's clothing—a queer kind of courtship if there ever was one, relying as it does on transgender performances. Clarence's failure of femininity, however, is laughable, while Lady Delacour's failures are tragic—an idea foreshadowed by the masquerade costumes of Tragedy and Comedy. We know, however, that these "failures" are not really true ones. Lady Delacour and Belinda remain bosom friends even as Clarence, in the end, wins Belinda's hand in marriage.

Although Lady Delacour is declared healthy once she gives herself up to patriarchal medical authority, and she has given up her cross-dressing and reunited with her husband, yet after her breast has healed she refuses to give up her power completely. She maintains that she has been "won" by kindness, not tamed by it, for a "tame lady Delacour would be a sorry animal, not worth looking at. Were she even to become domesticated, she would fare the worse."[120] Thus, Lady Delacour's breast does not signify patriarchally defined femininity and domesticity; instead, it alludes to her relationships with other women. The breast connects her with Mrs. Freke, Belinda, and even the serving woman Marriot and her rival Mrs. Luttridge, other women who are implicated in the sapphic networks of the novel. It is the medium through which sapphic desire is signified, and it symbolizes Lady Delacour's unwillingness to lose her individuality, even once she is reconciled to her family. The change from her diseased and dying breast to her happy, healthy one is not an about-face, she insists. She is still independent, lively, outspoken, and untamed. It is she who arranges the characters into a tableau at the end of the novel, implying that she is the master puppeteer, and it is she who invites the reader to look into the moral of the story: not rational Belinda, perfect Lady Percival, or innocent Helena. The tableau at the end reminds the readers that the novel is a performance within a performance; perfection is constructed and false while imperfections reveal truth.[121] The imperfections of Lady Delacour's breast represent the truth of sapphic desires among Lady Delacour, Belinda, and Mrs. Freke.

At the end of the novel, Lady Delacour arranges all the heterosexual happy couples into an orderly tableau and finishes with a cryptic moral couplet: "Our *tale* contains a *moral,* and, no doubt, / You all have wit enough to find it out."[122] The moral of *Belinda* is unclear, however, especially given that Lady Delacour speaks it, and she, as we shall see, is a character whose own virtuous transformation is, as yet, incomplete at the end of the novel. Lady Delacour's breast comes to unite the metaphorical feeling organ with her literal female one while remaining intimately tied to the realm of female friendships and sapphic pleasures. If the moral of the story is so easy to "see," then we must return to a consideration of the realm of the visual. In seeing, we must both *look* and *recognize; Belinda* offers us the chance to look and recognize something beyond the heteronormative love story by placing the story of Lady Delacour's breast at the center of the narrative. At the same time, Lady Delacour's breast thematizes the problems of the failure of vision or inadequate vision: only those endowed with the right kind of vision can "find out" the true moral of the story. In this way, the breast's ability to court sapphic feelings through explicit baring of bosoms is the inverse of the beard. The beard is unable to "see" the cross-dresser as a woman, yet she is attracted to the cross-dresser's ambiguous gender performance. Thus, again, we see how eighteenth-century texts predicate same-sex desires on transgender embodiments and performances.

In *Belinda*, the breasts in the novel link the three women together bodily and discursively, just as the breasts link together Anne Bonny and Mary Read and Hannah Snell and her female lodger. Further, the novel's primary network of affections is between the women, even as Lady Delacour is ultimately reconciled to her husband when she reveals her wound to him, and Belinda is engaged to Clarence Hervey once his indiscretions are revealed as benign. The novel intimates that Belinda's engagement to Clarence and Lady Delacour's reconciliation with her husband merely mean that she and Belinda are free to continue their intimate friendship uninterrupted. Rather than reinforcing a heteronormative love story through the tableau, the end of the novel arranges everyone in a way that leaves the reader with the sense that these heterosexual couplings are merely for show. The true emotional bonds are all between the women. The sapphic breasts of *Belinda* unite the wounded breast, the erotic breast, the maternal breast, as well as the feeling bosom. Through the breast the novel portrays a network of female affections constructed through emotional connections, as well as erotic ones—as we saw also with the beards, who admire and are attracted to the cross-dresser for her ability to know what women want. The cross-dressing character of Mrs. Freke, although ultimately rejected as a suitable lover/friend for Lady Delacour *and* Belinda, remains as a foil for them. Her cross-dressing, as well as Lady Delacour's, when read as in conversation with that of working-class female cross-dressers, is a marker of same-sex desires, as well as the expression of independence and empowerment. Although the novel ends with Lady Delacour and Belinda in petticoats, with the cross-dressing "freak" expulsed from the final tableau, the final moments of the novel refuse to be read neatly with one meaning. Like the gender performance of the female cross-dresser, the performance of heterosexual pairing off seems, at best, overly conventional and unsatisfying.

The wounded breast of Lady Delacour is linked discursively to the breasts of the passing woman not just through the act of cross-dressing, but also through the spectacles they create in their moments of exposure. In the same movement, we discern the female desire that is at the center of each of these narratives. These texts use the spectacle of the female cross-dresser to triangulate female desire. The moments of sapphic possibility link the female body to same-sex desires, and the cross-dresser's function as an index of same-sex desires exists in tandem with the heteronormative reading of the text, allowing for a multiplicity of readings in which ambiguity and failures of vision feature as sexual invitation. Similarly, gender codes are not reestablished via the breast; the slippages that arise through the use of the word suggest that, like beards, breasts are only ever partial signifiers of sex, and cisgender bodies are only ever defined contingently. The breasts also function as the reverse or inverse of the beard; it is the *missing* beard that threatens to expose the passing woman, while it is the corporeal, *attached,* already existing breast that marks the passing woman's femininity. The cross-dresser's sex is revealed when her breasts are revealed, though often, as we have seen, not because of their size but, rather, because of their shape or their color, indicating that there is no single way in which the breast is specifically defined as female as opposed to male. Further, the reader already knows that the cross-dresser has breasts; rather, the breasts are revealed to another character, though we rarely see them ourselves. The cross-dresser's body cannot be seen clearly by the reader. Her body is just as vague to us as it is to the other characters, except in the moments when those characters see her breasts. Thus, the breast moves between categories of recognizable and unrecognizable, as well as eroticized and de-eroticized.

The breast comes to embody knowledge (knowledge of that person's sex, sexuality, or desire), as well as sex and desire itself. In these texts the breasts appear as both literal body parts, capable of nursing a child (like those of Christian Davies) or being in pain (like that of Lady Delacour), but they are also the metaphorical "breast" and "bosom" that contain all human emotions and relationships. Karen Harvey also notes this congruence between beards and breasts in the eighteenth century: "Beards and breasts might be important consequences of a person's sex, but they were not the defining aspects of it. . . . Breasts could signal both the construction and the disruption of sex differences, and beards had the same potential."[123] In this chapter, we have seen how breasts, like beards, disrupt notions of sex difference and gendered embodiment. The breast becomes a bodily marker that can, in fact, suggest a non-normative or gender-fluid body full of non-heteronormative desires. Each of the works in this chapter alludes to the possibility of looking *for something else*—for a different kind of desire, possibly a sapphic desire. The very fact that it is the color of Mary Read's breasts or the size of Christian Davies's nipples that reveal these women's gender, rather than the size, shape, or innate female quality of their breasts, emphasizes that there is no single, defining way to read the breast in the eighteenth century.

Importantly, however, the breast draws a clear line connecting bodies with national and racial hierarchies. The whiteness of Mary Read's breasts and the fine beauty of Mary Hamilton's exposed breasts at the dance hall channel eighteenth-century discourses on the perfection and purity of whiteness and virginal breasts as signifiers of advanced civilization. It is no coincidence that *Belinda* contains a discussion on breastfeeding in which Lady Delacour reveals that she sent her daughter Helena away to be wet-nursed because an earlier child had died at her breast. Lady Delacour herself understands her diseased breast as punishment for her bad mothering, even as the novel itself subverts this reading by revealing that her breast was never diseased in the first place. The stories of cross-dressing women thus both rely on received notions of racial and national superiority as expressed through skin color and breast shape while, at times, also questioning those same hierarchies. It is notable and problematic that the sapphic possibilities of these texts are nearly always between white women—as though gender or sexual crossing can be acceptable, titillating, or even possible only where there is no crossing of racial lines, as well. To put it another way, gender ambiguities are tolerated only in places where racial ambiguity does not exist.

Despite the professed ambiguity of the cross-dresser's breasts and the narrative inability to define clearly what constitutes a female breast, the texts are adamant that these breasts are, in fact, recognizable as female and as capable of engendering desire in both men and women. The beards of the cross-dresser become her lovers through desires that are triangulated through the breasts. Thus, it is through the figure of the cross-dresser, her beards, and their body parts that sapphic desires are articulated and made more than discursive: they are embodied, passionate, and brimming with desire. Further, these representations confirm, yet again, that desire is not bounded by heteronormative vectors of desire; indeed, heteronormativity becomes, in *Belinda,* a mere tableau, an ossified and inflexible monument that individual desires often exceed. The penis and its prosthetic replacement, the dildo, draw our attention to these excesses, positing lesbian sexuality as made visible through the dildo while also, paradoxically, rejecting the rhetoric of penetrative sexual contacts as necessary to sexual pleasures. In the next chapter, I consider how normative ideas about genital sex and sexual orientations are challenged by cross-dressing texts in ways that explicitly highlight the instability of heterosexuality as a category and identity.

3

▸◂

PENETRATING DISCOURSE
AND SAPPHIC DILDOS

You would take him at first for no person of note,

Because he appears in a plain leather coat,

But when you his virtuous abilities know,

You'll fall down and worship Signior Dildo

   —John Wilmot, Second Earl of Rochester, "Signior Dildo," 1703

The whole truth having been disclosed before the Justice, and something

of too vile, wicked, and scandalous a nature, which was found in the

Doctor's trunk, having been produced in evidence against her, she was

committed to *Bridewell.*

   —Henry Fielding, *The Female Husband,* 1746

In this chapter, I explore how cross-dressing stories account for the missing penis when passing—and wooing other women—in the guise of a man. The narrative negotiations in texts such as *The Life and Adventures of Mrs. Christian Davies, the British Amazon* (1741) reveal an anxiety on the part of the narrators to explain, for the readers' benefit specifically, how these women passed as men in such extraordinary circumstances without a penis. Christian Davies's purported use of a urination device, in description so like a dildo, then connects to the stories of female husbands—that is, "Women who not only passed as men but who married women."[1] The narratives of Mary Hamilton in *The Female Husband,* by Henry Fielding (1746), and Catherine Vizzani in the biography *An Historical and Physical Dissertation on the Case of Catherine Vizzani* (1751), written by the Italian physician Giovanni Bianchi and translated into English by John Cleland, emphasize how these two women's "detestable impostures" in male attire are imagined as facilitated by dildos. Both texts, while outwardly condemning their behavior, also appropriate a satirical tone that encourages readers to question their moralizing and consider, rather, the erotic possibilities of sex with a woman. Finally, eighteenth-century dildo discourses and cross-dressing adventures merge in the erotic landscape of Cleland's *Fanny Hill; or, The Memoirs of a Woman of Pleasure* (1749). In tracing this arc of sapphic possibility from the stories of laudatory female cross-dressers to vicious or misguided female husbands and the seemingly heteronormative narrative of Cleland's pornotopia, I reconsider these texts as part of a growing discourse on the lesbian in the eighteenth century. Even as these texts capitalize on a voyeuristic quality not unfamiliar to both early modern and contemporary readers, in which lesbian sex is represented by men for male sexual satisfaction, they cannot fully recuperate the sapphic for the male gaze. Rather, female same-sex desires are, as in the case of the beard and the breast, represented so as to appear available and pleasurable to many women, not only the ones who overtly transgress social norms through the donning of men's clothing.

At the same time, though, the female husbands and passing women represent the clearest possibilities for reading trans identities in the past. In writing and presenting about Catherine Vizzani, some scholars have discussed Vizzani as trans, using the masculine pronoun, and taking seriously the possibility that Vizzani's story is one about a person born female-bodied but who identified as a man, regardless of the beliefs of the author and translator of the text, who focus nearly obsessively on Vizzani's female-bodiedness. The story of Mary/George Hamilton, as related by Henry Fielding, while winkingly ironic, gestures strongly to the gender fluidity or transness of Hamilton. Fielding, as narrator, often goes back and forth between masculine and feminine pronouns, presenting a character who is in transition, caught between what she is born as and what he wants to be. Notably, both Fielding and Cleland, the English translator of Vizzani's story, understand these people to be women and motivated by lesbian desires, implicitly or explicitly. But their characterizations leave room for reading both lesbian and trans identities, as we see in this chapter. Importantly, Gayle Rubin has claimed that the discontinuity between butch lesbian and transgender need not be read as such, arguing that "drag, cross-dressing, passing, transvestism, and transsexualism are all common in lesbian populations."[2] Further, Rubin argues that "categories like 'woman,' 'butch,' 'lesbian,' or 'transsexual' are all imperfect, historical, temporary, and arbitrary. We use them, and they use us. We use them to construct meaningful lives, and they mold us into historically specific forms of personhood."[3] As newer generations come into their own in our world today, terms such as "lesbian" and "woman" are being replaced or supplemented by "queer" and "gender-fluid" or "gender-nonbinary," while others identify as gender-nonbinary lesbians, and so on. As this chapter explores the lives of people who could fall into many of these categories, it will become evident that these stories foreground the fluidity of gender and desires in ways that play with body parts, gender norms, and sexual orientations to the point that even heterosexual sex appears queer, and cisgendered bodies are transed. Curiously, these possibilities arise even when (especially when?) texts try to base gender on genitalia and, specifically, the penis.

In this chapter I analyze how the stories of female cross-dressers account for this problematic absence by taking up a prosthetic replacement that becomes a material object through which same-sex desires are imagined by male authors. *The Female Husband* and *An Historical and Physical Dissertation on the Case of Catherine Vizzani* feature women-loving women who use dildos to pleasure their conquests.[4] The dildo in these texts functions as unmentionable and unacceptable yet also as titillating and impressive, revealing both an anxiety about and an interest in the woman-loving woman. In addition, these texts reveal that a dildo may provide women with certain pleasures that a real penis cannot, as they echo ideas from dildo poems in the earlier part of the century. Finally, a close look at the language of Cleland's *Fanny Hill* shows that it is not just the dildo that is prosthetic; the erect penis becomes a prosthesis itself, further challenging the implied heteronormativity of a text such as Cleland's.[5] Once we understand the penis itself to be prosthetic and even unnecessary to maleness, and prosthetic devices such as the dildo become superior to the penis, we establish yet another facet of eighteenth-century embodiment: the possibility that no body and no appendage can be represented clearly in terms of gender.

Second, the possibility of reading the penis itself as prosthetic allows us to find sapphic pleasures throughout novels of the eighteenth century that are often predicated on transgendered categories of embodiment.

Cultural Understanding of the Penis and
Dildo in the Eighteenth Century

As it is today, the penis and its penetrative capabilities were associated closely with maleness and masculinity in the eighteenth century and earlier time periods, though the penis's relationship to sexuality was, at times, markedly different. Thomas Laqueur notes that during the Renaissance, the penis was "a status symbol rather than a sign of some other deeply rooted ontological essence: *real* sex. It could be construed as a certificate of sorts, like the diploma of a doctor or a lawyer today, which entitled the bearer to certain rights and privileges."[6] Such a concept reveals the extent to which female cross-dressing was associated with a usurpation of male prerogative. Further, anatomy was often regarded as controlling or defining desire—a notion that exists long into the eighteenth century, even as it becomes gradually replaced with a more psychologically rooted notion of sexual identity. Early modern texts frequently discuss female same-sex acts and desires as a result of unnatural anatomy, portraying women who exhibit such desires are actually possessors of enlarged, penis-like clitorises that mark them as male and only temporarily or mistakenly female. Large or monstrous clitorises were often thought to give rise to "unnatural" desires, and in some cases these women were eventually branded "hermaphrodites" and therefore women who were not women at all. It is important to note here that the term "hermaphrodite" was used in the eighteenth century, but this term is now considered offensive, the preferred term being "intersex."[7] The enlarged clitoris-*cum*-penis of the intersex person could be explained "in the Galenic medical tradition, as a vagina which prolapsed or popped out because of increased body heat or sudden motion."[8] A variety of stories proliferated in the early modern period about cases of young women who desired other women, only to suddenly have their penis "pop out," legitimizing their same-sex desires by turning them into heterosexual ones in making one of the women a man. One of the most popular of these stories is that of a young French woman named Marie, whose story is documented by Michel Montaigne. While leaping over a fence and engaging in boisterous physical activity, Marie suddenly developed testicles and a penis and was henceforward known as Germaine. In the Galenic medical model of the humors, a "bit more heat or acting the part of another gender can suddenly bestow a penis, which entitles its bearer to the mark of the phallus, to be designated a man."[9]

Thus, the "inverted male" theory of the body and sexual difference points to two distinct yet linked possibilities: that desire must relate to biological sex and can even change one's biological sex, and that the presence of male genitals is the discerning marker of male power, privilege, and desire for women.[10] The fear of the "monstrous clitoris" persisted into the eighteenth century, with pamphlets by pseudo-medical writers such as Nicholas Venette and Louis Lignac betraying alarm at the idea of a monstrously large clitoris and its power to become erect, "like the part which distinguishes the man."[11] Both compare the clitoris to the penis, revealing and perhaps even reveling in anxieties/fantasies of an overly large clitoris that will cause women to penetrate other women.[12] For seventeenth- and early eighteenth-century anatomists, the ability to penetrate another woman during sex was equivalent to being male. In this case, the penis is male in that it is the organ that allows for penetration, but it is also not male, as every woman contains the possibility of her penis "popping out" under the right circumstances. Further, while the accounts of female "hermaphrodites," whom we would call intersex people today, establish the power of the penis to define male qualities as well as desire for women, this apparent power becomes destabilized in eighteenth-century narratives of female cross-dressers, especially female husbands, who are described as—and reviled as—women who seduce and desire women. Thus, rather than being immediately replaced with a two-sex model in the eighteenth century, the Galenic model of sex persists in parallel with new ideas about sex and gender, with the narratives of female husbands functioning in part as a space in which to negotiate these ideas and their relation to desire and sexuality. These discussions can and should be seen as crucial to the understanding the evolution of both queer desires and trans or gender nonbinary identities in the eighteenth-century imaginary. The medial, scientific, erotic, and pseudo-medical discourses that proliferated in the time period were often concerned with categorizing and labeling, a discursive movement that should remind readers of similar discussions in our world today. And yet the fascination with characters and person-ages whose desires, orientations, and bodies cross categories suggests an underlying challenge to such categorization in the past and now.

The eighteenth-century female cross-dresser is rarely, if ever, portrayed as a woman who turns into a biological male, as in these earlier narratives of serendipitous transformation. Narrators instead emphasize that the passing woman is biologically female, as many of the plot points revolve around keeping her body hidden or disguised for fear of being raped or otherwise debauched, as in the case of Hannah Snell and Sarah Scott's cross-dressing Leonora in chapter 1. The fear of discovery in those texts echoes similar fears among twentieth- and twenty-first-century passing transgender people, such as Brandon Teena, but also illustrates Jack Hal-berstam's "bathroom problem" that both transgender people and butch/gender non-normative women face when they enter a highly policed single-gender space such as a women's public toilet.[13] The crossing of gender boundaries can result in violence, a point of which eighteenth-century texts often remind their readers. The clothing and behavior that beard the female cross-dresser are enough to let her pass, initially, though they are never quite enough—at least according to the narrators of these texts. Still, the cross-dresser is able to access the eighteenth-century codes of masculinity and convincingly show that one can be a man without a penis and appeal to other women. The stories of female husbands who use dil-dos complement and complicate this code of masculinity while adding fuel to the fears of female appropriation of male power. These stories, as men-tioned earlier, also provide the clearest possibility for reading transgender identities in the past, as people such as Hamilton and Vizzani evidently wished to live as men, regardless of motivation.

Although the female husband who made use of a dildo was often the most reviled of cross-dressing women, eighteenth-century popular liter-ature in England was full of examples of dildo usage, including examples of women using dildos for their own pleasure. This kind of phallic woman,

The dildo shop. Frontispiece to *Elegantiæ Latini sermonis*, by Joannis Meursii, 1690. (© British Library Board, P.C.30.i.10)

who has the ability to penetrate herself or another woman without the aid of a man, was the subject of bawdy humor as well as tales of warning. Emma Donoghue has noted that "dildos were always good for a laugh in erotic literature, but they had a certain aura of danger as well."[14] Some of the more conspicuous appearances of dildos in eighteenth-century British texts are in the Earl of Rochester's play *Sodom; or, The Quintessence of Debauchery* (published in England in 1707), as well as his poem "Signior Dildo"; the 1706 pamphlet *Dildoides, a Burlesque Poem,* by Samuel Baker; the anonymously published poem *Monsieur Thing's Origin; or, Seignior D—'s Adventures in Britain* (1722); and the story of Theodora and Amaryllis in *A Treatise of Hermaphrodites,* from 1718, attributed to Giles Jacob.[15] James Caulfield's *Blackguardiana* (1795) defines a dildo as "an implement resembling the virile member . . . made of wax, horn, leather, and diverse other substances, and if fame does not lie more than usually, are to be had at many of our great toy shops and nick nackatories"; his definition implies that they were not difficult to come by.[16] It is reasonable to believe that references to dildos in the stories of female husbands, for example, were legible and recognizable to a contemporary public. Similarly, the texts I discuss almost always portray the dildo as being used by women, together, and the ever-increasing anxiety about this pleasure without men suggests that these textual representations posit lesbian desires as not fully consumable by the male gaze.[17]

The representations of dildos in the eighteenth century often attempt to make light of this prosthetic replacement to minimize its sapphic possibilities. Satirical poems portray the dildo as an anthropomorphized entity of foreign extraction.[18] The Earl of Rochester's poem evokes the figure of Signior Dildo to satirize various ladies at court. The women are so pleased with Signior Dildo's performance that "real" penises do not stand a chance, and eventually they try to quash their prosthetic rival:

> A Rabble of Pricks, who were welcome before,
> Now finding the Porter deny'd 'em the Door,
> Maliciously waited his coming below,
> And inhumanely fell on Signior Dildo.[19]

The poem constructs the dildo as better than a "real" penis, though it will always also be lacking because it is inauthentic. The dildo is superior and false, while the penis is inferior but true or real. Thus, the female husband is, in some ways, also constructed as superior to a "real" husband but also false (i.e., fraudulent).[20] Further, Signior Dildo is simultaneously constructed as a dildo (false, prosthetic, mechanical), as well as human and male, though a foreigner and therefore not English. In the poem *Monsieur Thing's Origin; or, Seignior D—o's Adventures in Britain*, printed 1722 in London, the trope of dildo as man is also apparent.[21] Women of all kinds come to love him—in particular, two milliners who are the first ones to take Seignior into their own hands, literally:

> One of the Girls ty'd *Monsieur* to her Middle,
> To try if she the Secret could unriddle:
> She acted Man, being in a merry Mood,
> Striving to please her Partner as she cou'd.[22]

Monsieur, however, is displeased with this usurpation of his power. He is almost "suffocate[d]" during the indulgence of their "Lustful Inclinations" and "with that, of all things, that at last he hated." He finally leaves the two milliners "to run the Frisk together by themselves."[23] The poem constructs female masturbation with a dildo as sex between a man (the anthropo-morphized dildo/penis replacement) and a woman. When a woman ties the dildo to her own body and uses it to have sex with another woman, the man/dildo is smothered. When he leaves them to "frisk" themselves, the poem implies that the dildo is not really needed; the women can take care of themselves, and he wants nothing to do with it.[24] Instead of Rochester's humorous allusions to insatiable female desire and male homoerotic nu-ances, *Monsieur Thing's Origin* betrays overt anxiety at the use of the dildo by two women together rather than just one alone.[25] Texts about female husbands often follow this line of representation. In *The Female Husband*, Mary Hamilton's use of the dildo is ridiculous and dangerous, while Cle-land's framing of the story of Catherine Vizzani is full of allusions to the moral perils inherent in such behavior.

Both poems cited here construct the dildo as male, thus ensuring that when women are described as using the dildo, the sexuality described is still a heterosexual one, diffusing the possible threatening qualities of the dildo as penis replacement.[26] In fact, the dildo's use by the women in the poems only serves to remind the readers just how much women desire the penis, to the point that they lust for any replacement when they cannot get at it.[27] The texts construct the dildo as a foreigner to exoticize the threat of penis replacement, just in case anyone "misreads" the poems as being an endorsement of non-normative sexuality. Although the dildo poems ridicule or condemn the phallic woman and the ease with which she appropriates phallic power, they, like the stories of female husbands, ultimately suggest the sexual pleasure available to women without men. Regardless of the authorial intent, the dildo comes to signify an improved masculinity that deconstructs the naturalness of the penis and challenges its ability to define maleness. The dildo suggests a multiplicity of mean-ings, and these meanings in turn blur the line between authentic male-ness and the performance of it, thus offering a transgender reading of the penis. The very inauthenticity of the dildo, yet its ability to usurp both masculine prerogatives and maleness, destabilizes notions of both.[28] The female cross-dresser is able to "pass" because she acquires prostheses to her masculinity, yet she is always defined by the absence of a penis. The physical deficiency, characterized in the eighteenth-century slang term for vaginas, "flats," is never far from the text.[29]

Many stories of passing women are ambiguous or even silent on the topic of the "penis problem." Guyonne LeDuc emphasizes that "most women warriors' narratives remain vague on the subject of stratagems used to avoid betraying themselves, for example while urinating."[30] While "standards of hygiene were low" in the eighteenth century, "to avoid being discovered, the women had to be continually on the alert, especially when washing, dressing and urinating."[31] Further, men's fashions up until the 1770s disguised this lack through an emphasis on baggy breeches and long waistcoats that obscured the groin region, making it unnecessary to account for the cross-dressing woman's ability to pass without a penis.[32] Generally, clothing was a powerful determinant of gender, and the appropriation of masculine apparel itself lent authority to the gender performance of these women. The cross-dresser had the advantage that by donning men's clothing, she instantly acquired the appearance of maleness. Rudolf Dekker and Lotte van de Pol note that many passing women were aided by the time period's "strictness of the differentiation between the genders. . . . A sailor, in trousers, smoking a pipe, with short and loose hair, would not easily be thought of as anything but a man."[33] Interestingly, however, cross-dressing narratives focus on how clothes are not enough to ensure credible gender performance. Although these narratives portray a woman who can pass as soon as she puts on the clothes of a man, they inevitably allude to the cross-dresser's problematic missing male appendage.

And yet, although the passing woman is often aware of her insufficiency, most tales of passing women do not include the use of a dildo or other penis replacement as part of the masquerade. Texts that did not circulate as medical or erotic (including quasi-medical texts that doubled as erotic texts, such as the *Onania*) infrequently mention male or female genitalia.[34] *The Life and Adventures of Mrs. Christian Davies,* therefore, is remarkable because its second printing included a note by the publisher that attempts to address readers' curious questions not regarding sexual activity but, rather, regarding how Davies could relieve herself as a

female-bodied soldier in disguise. The narrative represents Christian compensating for her missing mark of maleness by embodying a masculine
persona that swears, fights, flirts, and allegedly fathers a child. Despite
the ease with which she appears to adopt this persona, the second edition
of the anonymous text, published in 1741, makes a specific reference to
a "urinary instrument" that supposedly helps Davies pass while in the
military. Other editions of *The Life and Adventures of Mrs. Christian Davies* contain no mention of this "instrument"; it appears only in "From
the Bookseller to the Reader," the publisher's note in the 1741 edition. In
the note, the author acknowledges the earlier publication of *The Life and
Adventures* and some issues that caught readers' attention pertaining to
Davies's ability to pass as a man despite her female body. The writer of the
note wishes "to gratify the Curiosity of many, who, as we understand, have
been greatly puzzled to conceive how a Woman could so long perform a
certain natural Operation, without being discovered; since Soldiers are
obliged to perform it, not only standing, but often publickly, and even at
the Head of the Regiment."[35] Like the anonymous narrator of *The Female
Soldier*, the bookseller emphasizes the veracity of Davies's account, though
he does so in a rather unbelievable manner: by ascribing to her a "urinary
instrument" that is not mentioned in the body of the text. The narrator
acknowledges that "this indeed seems a difficult task; and yet it was very
easy to her by Means of a Silver Tube painted over, and fastened about
her with leather Straps."[36] The urinary instrument sounds very much like
a strap-on dildo, with its "leather Straps" that "fastened about her." The
leather straps conjure an image of Davies wearing this tube at all times
while she is passing, like an accessory to one's outfit, but also in mimicry
of a dildo. In addition, Davies's prosthesis, her "tube painted over," is not
only the means by which she can pass, but also part of the incitement
to pass in the first place: "This Urinary Instrument belong'd to the brave
female Captain, who, hurry'd with the Alarm, mentioned p.6. of her Life,
forgot it, and left it behind him [*sic*] in the Bed, where she and the Maid
found it; And this it was which determined her, in Imitation of that Heroine, to put on Man's Apparel: For without such an Implement she could
never have hoped to pass long concealed"[37] The tube's genealogy "suggests
a kind of secret tradition of cross-dressers."[38] While the bookseller's note

attempts to cast this tube as a normative part of women's passing, its prosthetic attachment to Davies's narrative opens up a space for considering the rather tenuous connection between gender and the body. Further, the narrator's use of the masculine pronoun in reference to the "brave female Captain," whose urinary instrument is Davies's gender-bending inheritance, encourages reader to consider the fluidity of gender and the transgendering of both characters.

The urinary instrument also alludes to the possibility of same-sex female desires through its similarity in form to a dildo. The bookseller's note implies that Davies easily performed the call of nature using the tube, and she was discovered to be a woman (purportedly) when surgeons saw the size of her nipples rather than her genitalia, as discussed in chapter 2. Donoghue argues that "fictions about 'female husbands' and erotic stories of dildo-users . . . must have spread the knowledge that a dildo could give women as much pleasure as a penis could. If Christian Davies could strap on a urinary instrument she could strap on a dildo too."[39] Thus, "Readers could only find her flirtations with women totally 'harmless' if they shut their ears to all the stories about dildos that were circulating" in the mid-eighteenth century and earlier.[40] Davies engages in many flirtations with women over the course of The Life and Adventures and at one point is accused of being the father of another woman's child; in another situation, which I discuss in chapter 2, a burgher's daughter falls in love with cross-dressed Davies and wishes to marry her. Sapphic overtones saturate Davies's narrative, and, as Donoghue suggests, in conjunction with eighteenth-century popular knowledge about dildos it becomes difficult to ignore the sexual possibilities inherent in the urinary instrument. Like many stories of passing women and female husbands, Davies's story offers the possibility of reading trans bodies and same-sex desires simultaneously, refusing just one reading and allowing for the multiplicities of transness and queerness to occupy the same body.

The bookseller's tacked-on note, its own strapped-on textual appendage, creates a queer space in the text—one whose very presence is added to rectify an absence in the previous edition. The note also anticipates Hannah Snell's narrator in the last third of The Female Soldier, where he returns to certain moments in the text in which Snell's passing seems improbable. The narrators of both works position the strategies of passing as additions or addenda to the text—just as for female husbands, dildos become important addenda to the cross-dresser's gendered or sexual passing. Thus, the situation of the female soldier is a complex one, especially in the case of Snell and Davies, both of whom resist using their disguises to facilitate sexual relationships with men (as opposed to the female pirates Bonny and Read, for example), but whose stories are fodder for sapphic sexual imaginings, as we see in chapter 1.[41] The narrators of these texts insist that the absence of a penis is inherently a female condition, but it is not necessarily an impediment to passing as a man—and yet narratives such as that of Christian Davies allude to the more titillating ways that these female-bodied people compensated for their missing male appendage. Davies's urinary instrument thematizes the way that these narratives were concerned with the cross-dresser's gender performance and its relation to the body while also betraying anxiety over gender fluidity or indeterminacy. A material body needs material prostheses to one's gender to pass. Within the context of female husband narratives, the overt use of a dildo brings sapphic possibilities to the forefront of the cross-dresser's representation in the eighteenth century, even as they also powerfully allude to the lives of transmen and gender-fluid people in the past, marking out an important element of eighteenth-century transgender history. Further, the texts that represent female husbands—passing women who use dildos to marry and have sex with other women—indicate how the overt prosthesis, the dildo, could function as a superior male appendage to the penis within the eighteenth-century literary imaginary. The representations of female husbands destabilize the penis as a necessary appendage to maleness, overtly connecting the female cross-dresser to sapphic possibilities, but also questioning the parameters of heterosexuality and cisgenderedness.

"No Such Thing in Nature": Dildos and Female Husband Narratives

Despite its obvious emphasis on sex as penetrative, the dildo functions as a destabilizing and transgressive object. Carellin Brooks discusses the possibilities of the dildo for female empowerment by focusing on the ability of the dildo to question dominant patriarchal discourses. She argues that "the dildo, far from being a penile imitator, erases the idea of a stable body, the kind in which a penis would either exist or not exist," in part because "the dildo's real role is as a destabilizer of sexual difference, a threat and a desire."[42] This destabilizing power comes from the fact that "[the dildo] is modelled upon both penis and Phallus, yet when worn by a woman, forcefully contradicts the very concept of the natural body. The dildo-wielding woman is self-consciously fictional, the mythic phallic possessor."[43] For the female cross-dresser who also engages in sex with other women using a dildo, the dildo becomes yet another prosthetic device that supplements the other prostheses of masculine behavior and apparel. In *The Female Husband* and *An Historical and Physical Dissertation on the Case of Catherine Vizzani,* the dildo functions as a superior appendage, capable of bringing pleasure to other women in excess of what they can get from a "real" penis. Its prosthetic and "fraudulent" nature cannot negate the pleasures that it bestows. Because it is not a real penis, the dildo functions as a queer appendage that opens up a space in the text for the articulation of sapphic desires that are not subordinate to heteronormative ones. The narratives of these two female husbands explicitly address the sexual, embodied possibilities between the cross-dresser and her beards, revealing explicitly to readers the mechanics of sexual penetration between female-bodied persons.

In these narratives, the dildo represents the quintessential moment of the usurping of male privilege by women in the eighteenth century. According to Lillian Faderman, "The claim of male prerogative combined with the presumed commission . . . of certain sexual acts, especially if a dildo was used, seem to have been necessary to arouse extreme societal anger."[44] In some cases of exposed female husbands on the European Continent, such an accusation could warrant the death penalty, as it did in the case of Catharine Margaretha Linck, among others.[45] At the same time, these executions were few and far between; even on the Continent, there are almost no reports of executions of female cross-dressers after the first half of the eighteenth century. In the case of the English female husband Mary Hamilton, the real-life Hamilton was caught, tried, and whipped publicly for her crimes. This punishment was meted out for the crime of defrauding the women she married and for marrying them as a woman and not telling them that she was not a man (i.e. lying). In Fielding's fictionalized account, *The Female Husband,* the narrator notes that Hamilton is tried under "a clause in the vagrant act, *for having by false and deceitful practices endeavoured to impose on some of his Majesty's subjects.*"[46] Hamilton is tried for fraud rather than sodomy or some other explicitly sex-related crime, as was often the case in England, yet Fielding's narrative emphasizes how the fraud was enacted: via a dildo.[47] In Fielding's text, the dildo is unmentionable and indescribable, like the "unspeakable" crime of sodomy in the eighteenth century, which emphasizes the titillating aspects of the story, while the emphasis on Hamilton's cupidity reads as a possible indictment of the economic imperatives inherent to all marriages.[48] In Bianchi's *An Historical and Physical Dissertation on the Case of Catherine Vizzani,* the dildo is the instrument of her "detestable imposture," even as the locals find it nothing more than a piece of leather stuffed with rags.[49] The dildo enables lesbian sex, providing titillating narrative thrills even as the narrator works to disavow Vizzani's seductions and minimize the importance of the dildo. Both texts ultimately reveal the vicarious pleasures inherent in the representation of the female cross-dresser's appropriation of male sexual power even as they acknowledge that such these women appealed to other, non-cross-dressed women, or "beards," as well.

As discussed in chapter 1, the stories of female husbands were not unknown to the eighteenth-century public, even before these particular narratives appeared at midcentury. Rictor Norton has documented several instances in popular publications detailing the adventures of cross-dressing women who seduced other women. For example, a story in the *Female Tatler* in 1709 describes two women who dress in men's clothes and who, purportedly, "have seduc'd Miss Lack-it from the boarding-school," while a satirical poem from 1728, "Two Kissing Girls of Spitalfields," describes a butch-femme couple.[50] Other instances of women living as men and pursuing relationships with women were documented in newspapers of the time. Fraser Easton's study of major publications such as the *Daily Advertiser* (1731–96) and the *Gentleman's Magazine* (1731–1830) reveals that such notices were not uncommon.[51] An example from the *Daily*

Advertiser details a long-term relationship between two servants, a man and woman, who were married for eighteen years: "Some Difference happening between them, the House-keeper declar'd the cook was no Man, but a Woman, and had Reasons to believe that her said pretended Husband was with Child; which we hear upon Examination prov'd so."[52] Thus, by the time Fielding's and Bianchi's texts were published in England, the female husband was a culturally recognizable character. Decidedly, such notices point to both butch lesbian and transgender histories that were available and legible to eighteenth-century readers, and they would have provided a background of cultural knowledge against which readers encountered texts such as Fielding's or Bianchi's.

Published anonymously in 1746 but generally attributed to the novelist Henry Fielding, *The Female Husband: or, The Surprising History of Mrs. Mary, alias Mr. George Hamilton* is the highly fictionalized story of the real-life female cross-dresser Mary Hamilton.[53] The pamphlet was immediately

Mary Hamilton whipped for vagrancy and lying. Frontispiece to *The Surprising Adventures of a Female Husband!* by George Cruikshank, ca. 1810. (Carl H. Pforzheimer Collection of Shelley and His Circle, New York Public Library Digital Collections)

a sensation and sold more than a thousand copies.[54] While the overall tone of *The Female Husband* is what Theresa Braunschneider calls "censuring" of the female cross-dresser, many critics argue convincingly that Fielding, either purposefully as a satirist or subconsciously as a writer and actor, is not completely condemnatory of Hamilton.[55] Terry Castle is one of the earliest critics to draw attention to the contradictory impulses displayed by the text's narrator, focusing on how he displays both disgust and admiration for Hamilton's exploits. Although "Fielding attacks sartorial ambiguity because sexual hierarchy (and the maintenance of masculine domination) depend on the sexes being distinguishable," Castle notes that "Hamilton's theatricality, as Fielding seems half to realize, may allude ultimately to deeper human aspirations toward transcendence."[56] In Castle's analysis, it is impossible to read Fielding as unilaterally condemnatory of Hamilton. Despite the challenge Hamilton poses to the readability of gender, Fielding still appears to enjoy writing about her.[57] This complex attitude toward the female husband rejects a simplistic reading of the text as unilaterally disapproving of sapphic practices or gender fluidity. Instead, Fielding draws attention to the constructed nature of both gender and bodies and how our ability to see and identify what we see is often incomplete or faulty.[58] *The Female Husband* solicits a queer vision of the female cross-dresser by asking us to look at her as both a fraud and a symbol of sapphic possibility—a possibility that Fielding's narrator alludes to through Hamilton's initiation into lesbian sex acts by her friend Anne Johnson, a debauched Methodist.[59]

Throughout *The Female Husband*, Hamilton appropriates male power for herself, even as the reader is constantly reminded that Hamilton is not, in fact, a man. She is defined by contradiction: she is masculine and often referred to by a masculine pronoun, yet as a woman she is always lacking and thus in need of a dildo to supplement her performance of biological maleness in the bedroom. Thus, the act of "passing" in the bedroom is a negotiation between opposing ideals; in this case, it is between possession and deficiency of the male appendage. Hamilton's inability to perform might be read as a performance of masculinity, albeit failed masculinity. One night in bed with her first wife, the Widow Rushford, Hamilton does not have "at that time *the wherewithal* about her" to please her amorous partner.[60] Donoghue notes that "Hamilton's more-than-phallic sexual power comes and goes, however, since she does not always have her dildo in place. . . . Fielding casually compares this to male impotence—which begs the question, if all men are liable to drops in potency, is maleness itself a matter of flux, of luck?"[61] Hamilton is simultaneously an ideal man, an impotent man, and a biological female. The dildo and the "lacking" female genitals vie for significance in Hamilton's case. Perhaps for this reason, "for Mary Hamilton at least, a masculine identity is never secure."[62] Though her masculine identity is subject to being discovered as lacking, the comment on Hamilton's "wherewithal" is both a humorous double-entendre and a serious comment on the tenuousness of embodied sex.

And yet, to a certain extent, *The Female Husband* depicts Mary Hamilton as portraying an idealized version of masculinity. In addition to her powers of seduction, Hamilton is able to offer greensick girls "sexual pleasure without reproduction."[63] When Mr. Ivythorn's daughter discovers that Hamilton has not what she "ought to have" beneath her breeches, Hamilton tells her they should stay together for "she would have all the pleasures of marriage without the inconveniences."[64] Catherine Craft-Fairchild suggests that this phrase "encapsulates all of Fielding's fears" of unbridled female sexuality.[65] Part of this fear is that a woman might "out-do" a man at his own skills, although Fielding is also satirizing such fears. Further, as Donoghue points out, "The sexual satisfaction [Hamilton] offers is not illusory. Hamilton's lovemaking pleases the widow far more than her previous heterosexual experiences."[66] When Hamilton is discovered, it is, in part, because she performs her role of lover with her final wife, Mary Price, *too* well. When Mary Price finally tells her mother what goes on between the sheets every night with her "husband," her mother exclaims. "O child, there is no such thing in human nature."[67] Hamilton and her dildo exceed expectations, using the dildo to fulfill desires that do not even exist "in human nature," reinforcing the paradoxical nature of the female husband, who, like a dildo, is simultaneously too perfect and not real enough.

The passing woman, therefore, is herself like the dildo in Rochester's poem: she is better than the "real" thing, but she can never fully replace the "real" version—she is always fake or fraudulent. The female husband uses the dildo, this superlative-yet-fraudulent instrument of pleasure, and she becomes a superlative-yet-fraudulent husband. *The Female Husband* depicts Hamilton as offering an alternative but very attractive rendering of masculinity that is still always fake or fraudulent, not the "real thing." Although the initial opposition appears to be that of penis or no penis, Fielding's text complicates this dyad with these other possibilities, emphasizing the prosthetic quality of the penis and its ability to be completely removed from constructions of masculinity. Thus, as Misty G. Anderson notes, "Fielding has himself undermined the notion that gender is grounded in 'propense inclinations' for the opposite sex and inadvertently argued that it is an unstable construct, fueled by more amorphous desires."[68] Even as Fielding pokes fun at the women, the "beards," who fall for the dildo's inauthenticity, his narration allows readers to explore and imagine the possibility of such "amorphous desires" and how they might be facilitated by the dildo.

The construction of masculinity in the text results from the narrator's interest in that other perfect-yet-fraudulent thing, the dildo. *The Female Husband* not only presupposes the dildo as the ideal and necessary implement for sexually seducing other women, but it delights in its presence. The dildo, like sex between women, is described in terms of unmentionability. Fielding uses terms such as "unnatural lusts," "the most abominable and unnatural pollutions," and "transactions not fit to be mention'd" to describe sex between women.[69] When referring to the dildo—the means by which these unmentionable lusts are enacted—Fielding describes it as a "means which decency forbids me even to mention" and as "something of too vile, wicked and scandalous a nature."[70] At the very end of the narrative, the author asserts that "not a single word occurs through the whole [of this narrative], which might shock the most delicate ear, or give offence to the purest chastity."[71] The euphemistic nature of these descriptions belies Fielding's own interest in saying what cannot be said. The mode of euphemism "is a way of mediating the unspeakable, of presenting that which is in every way unrepresentable. Euphemism suggests psychic tension, between impulses of denial and acknowledgment. Fielding tries at once to take note of Hamilton's doings, and pretend that he doesn't know what she has done."[72] These euphemistic phrases point out not only that Fielding is, of course, "in the know," despite his protestations to modesty and propriety, but that readers are also constructed as "in the know."[73] The dildo is not secret, and the gesturing toward the "decency" and "purest chastity" of the readers is itself an ironic admission of the very opposite tendencies. The titillation of the text relies on euphemism that allows Hamilton and her "wherewithal" to be read in multiple ways.

The dildo often functions as an object that cannot be spoken of in the narrative or referred to directly, suggesting the kind of "slanted" desire couched in "oblique" language that Sarah Ahmed has identified as common to lesbian representation.[74] The use of euphemism in the story is noteworthy, as it points to the ambiguity of the cross-dresser and her prosthesis, and yet Fielding's narrator seems ironically invested in the issue of perception and orientation. *The Female Husband* investigates the "queer slants" that make Mary/George Hamilton so very fascinating, demarcating a "queer space" within the text.[75] In many ways, Fielding's text only "works" under the explicit assumption that readers would immediately recognize "something of too vile, wicked, and scandalous a nature."[76] His use of metaphors and euphemisms for Hamilton's dildo "constitutes readers as an in-group: to get the joke, we must share secret knowledge (which, of course, is therefore not so secret)."[77] Thus, Fielding's "language of hyper-propriety" in reference to lesbian sexual acts or Hamilton's dildo highlights the common knowledge available to the readers about such sexualities and dildos, as well as transgender identities.[78] These euphemisms, while serving to codify Fielding's text as "appropriate" for all readers, ultimately serve same-sex ends by emphasizing the female cross-dresser's sexual power. Bonnie Blackwell suggests that "Fielding's narrator protects virgins by encoding meaning through the text's many puns and double entendres. Yet the narrator also teaches them the pleasures and conveniences of having a female husband,"[79] while Donoghue writes that "these indirect descriptions may be intended to titillate male readers, but they actually serve to inflate the unmentionable dildo to the point where it far outdoes the penis it is meant to imitate."[80] The euphemistic quality of Fielding's narrative may inadvertently or even purposefully posit an alternative, sapphic sexuality that is both recognizable and pleasurable to the reader.

This tension in the text between the successful, pleasing abilities of the dildo that exceed cisgender categories of masculinity and the vile, monstrous, unnatural usurpation of male sexuality echoes the tension between reading Hamilton as a man and as a woman. The text insists on both, revealing boundaries between the genders that are rooted in neither biology nor desires. Braunschneider notes that "passing women are sympathetic in some circumstances because they are men, in others because they are women."[81] In the case of Hamilton, to read her as a woman is, according to the narrator, to read her as having "unnatural" desires; to read her as a man is to read him as having an "unnatural" body. The text consistently reminds readers that Hamilton is only ever a woman masquerading as a man, despite Fielding's frequent use of the pronoun "he" to refer to Hamilton when she courts women. The dildo functions as a prosthetic piece of masculinity that endows Hamilton with male powers, ultimately functioning to expose him/her as female, first through the bragging of wife Mary Price, and later through the discovery of the instrument in the trunk. Blackwell argues that, "when the case is tried before a justice . . . , [s]urprisingly, he turns his gaze not on the offending female husband, whose body presumably reveals the truth of her birth sex, but upon the bride and the dildo."[82] Price is asked whether "she imagined the Doctor ha[d] behaved to her as a husband ought to his wife," and "she at last answered she did imagine so."[83] Hamilton's conviction rests on proving that she used a dildo to impose on Mary Price and the other people of the town—that is, to hide her true sex with a disguise. However, Fielding's narrative is ambivalent as to the true nature of sex and sexual desire precisely through its satirical use of euphemism that constructs the dildo as an illicit but still widely recognizable implement of sexual pleasure between women.

Thus, the dildo and the female cross-dresser become the emblems of the problem of defining maleness through genital sex and ascribing masculinity to male-bodied persons. Valerie Traub has argued that early modern depictions of dildo-wielding women often function as a "discourse of containment, a way of enjoining insignificance and immateriality onto per-formances of (for lack of a better term) female masculinity. We can resist this containment by noting the ways in which the tribade displaces and supplements masculine privilege, exposing it as nothing more (or worse) than a simulacrum."[84] But we do not need to actively "resist" this reading, as texts such as Fielding's, and Cleland's, are already playing with the no-tion of masculinity as a simulacrum. The female husband, like the tribade, displaces masculine privilege, and even masculine anatomy, by exposing both of them as illusory. Further, rather than functioning as a "discourse of containment," Fielding's text makes Hamilton's impotence seem potent, even as it is punished and imprisoned. Hamilton's "most monstrous and unnatural desires" survive this imprisonment and her public whippings; nothing can deter her desires. While her insatiable appetites are coded as feminine, as they hark back to dildo poems that satirize insatiable female sexual appetites, Hamilton's strength and determination are often coded as masculine. Fielding further conflates genders when he admonishes his readers to recognize that "unnatural affections are equally vicious and equally detestable in both sexes."[85] Unnatural affections between women, however, are "most shocking and odious" because "modesty be the pe-culiar characteristic of the fair sex."[86] Hamilton is modest only when she must hide her genital lack from her female partners, whose own sexual ap-petites are, at times, those of a "tigress."[87] The desires of the other women are complicit in Hamilton's deception and the sexual satisfaction it can facilitate as they beard her lack of masculinity. *The Female Husband* con-structs sexual desire as being particularly female, despite the "modesty" that is supposed to characterize "the fair sex." The "problem" of female sexuality appears to be the central issue in the narrative, one that must be policed, controlled, and critiqued while, at the same time, furnishing the writer with a humorous tale of missing, or excessive, masculinity. In addition, Hamilton's gender-fluidity casts important doubts on what, ex-actly, women like Mary Price and the Widow Rushford desire. While some women reject Hamilton for appearing too feminine, these others em-brace Hamilton's androgynous appearance or possibly see him as actually masculine. The text questions the common idea that lesbian desire is the desire for sameness and that Hamilton's female masculinity re-encodes heterosexuality within homosexual relations. Already in Fielding's text, the parameters for heterosexuality and cisgenderedness are being both challenged and defined, ironically exploded even as same-sex desires and transgender embodiments provide fodder for both sexual excitement and moral outrage.

The combination of satire and sexual titillation in *The Female Husband* finds a parallel in Cleland's translation of the Italian pamphlet on Catherine Vizzani, the notorious female husband in Italy. *An Historical and Physical Dissertation on the Case of Catherine Vizzani,* published in England in 1751, was originally written in Italian by the physician Giovanni Bianchi, who also dissected Vizzani's body after her death to prove she was a virgin and, ostensibly, to check whether there was any physical evidence that she was a man.[88] The English text, attributed to Cleland, contains the translation along with "certain needful Remarks by the English Editor."[89] Vizzani's story bears a passing similarity to Hamilton's in its basic components: Vizzani woos young ladies while in men's clothing until she is discovered; she runs away and lives in disguise; finally, she meets a young woman with whom she falls in love and successfully enters into a relationship with her.[90] Rather than being imprisoned and whipped like Hamilton, Vizzani's story ends when she dies as a result of a bullet wound to the leg. As she is dying, she is found to have a dildo in her possession that she had kept tied around her waist. After she dies of her wound, Bianchi, who was an acquaintance of Vizzani's when she was in disguise, takes the opportunity to perform an autopsy. At the end of her tale he proclaims that the other doctors, like himself, "not only discovered her to be a Woman, but also a Virgin, the Hymen being entire without the least Laceration."[91] His own results confirm that "the *Clitoris* of this young Woman was not pendulous, nor of any extraordinary Size, as the Account from *Rome* made it, and as is said, to be that of all those Females, who, among the *Greeks,* were called *Tribades,* or who followed the Practices of *Sappho;* on the contrary, her's [Vizzani's] was so far from any unusual Magnitude, that it was not to be ranked among the middle-sized, but the smaller."[92] Vizzani has no corporeal markers that explain her turn toward wearing men's clothes and loving women.[93] Like Mary Hamilton's story, Vizzani's story represents the dildo as, despite its inauthenticity, a superior appendage

Frontispiece to *The True History and Adventures of Catharine Vizzani,* by Giovanni Paolo Simone Bianchi, 1755. (© British Library Board 1490.c.68)

that confuses rather than defines the borders of gender while also serving as an attractive additive to the appeal of the cross-dresser to her "beards." Similarly, Vizzani's story, perhaps even more than Hamilton's, suggests the possibility of both lesbian butch gender performance and transgender representation.

Vizzani and her dildo are, like Hamilton, extremely successful at seducing other women. Again, the female cross-dresser/female husband, while a false man, is the perfect lover. Vizzani cross-dresses as a means to an end: to facilitate amours with other women. Her first serious romance with a young woman in Rome, Margaret, "whose Company she used to court, under Pretence of learning Embroidery," begins with Vizzani's self-presentation as a woman. However, "not satisfied with these Interviews by Day, scarce a Night passed, but she appeared in Man's Cloaths, under her Charmer's Window. . . . This whimsical Amour went on very quietly for above two Years."[94] Vizzani's first love affair with a woman is clearly one in which the courted lady, Margaret, knows very well that Vizzani is a woman, marking their passions as explicitly sapphic on both sides—even as Vizzani's later life in men's clothing suggests other kinds of desires and gender performances. Once Vizzani runs away from home and dresses as a man full time, she passes completely, to the point that she convinces a surgeon and a local laundress that she is a young man who has contracted a venereal disease because "the Girls teased him [Vizzani] out of his very Life."[95] Vizzani is represented as a shrewd manipulator of identity. She/he complains to the laundress, only then "adding (as she knew that Prohibition is with most People an Incentive) a strict Charge to the Laundress, that she should not betray his Confidence by dropping the least Hint, in any Place, either of his Abilities or Distemper."[96] Vizzani's plan is a success, and very soon "it was whispered about that *Giovanni* [Vizzani] was the best Woman's Man, and the most addicted to that alluring Sex of all the Men in that Part of the Country."[97] Vizzani's ability to seduce women is something she/he is shown to be well aware of: "This Character, the Acquirement of which had cost her so many Artifices," was for her a source of "Pride and Delight."[98] Her/his undoing at the end is, in part, due to successes with the ladies, just as it is for Mary Hamilton, and the overwhelming appeal of the cross-dresser to other women correlates to idea of beards and bearding, as we saw in chapter 1. Notably, though, as in Hamilton's story, the narrator cannot quite decide which pronoun to use, he or she, and at times switches back and forth. The feminine pronoun, however, appears the most often, and the translator's final comments, like those of Fielding's ironic narrator, betray the men's discomfort, not necessarily with women dressing as men, but with women's seducing other women.

Even as her decision to run away with a female lover may have brought about Vizzani's untimely death, in some ways her death vindicates her while also revealing the prosthetic device that was hidden in the text all along. When Vizzani decides to elope with a gentlewoman, the gentle-woman's sister, Maria, insists on going with them. The burden of an ex-tra person in their escape party slows them down, and eventually they are caught, and Vizzani is shot. As in the case of female soldiers such as Christian Davies, Vizzani's wound exposes her true sex. She is taken to a nearby hospital, where it is revealed that her wound has become infected, eventually causing her death. Once the end is near, Bianchi notes that, "in this Extremity, a leathern Contrivance, of a cylindrical Figure, which was fastened below the Abdomen, and had been the chief Instrument of her detestable Imposture, became so troublesome, that she loosened it, and laid it under her Pillow."[99] With the removal of the dildo from her body, Vizzani immediately becomes female again, and the text focuses on prov-ing not only her biological femaleness, but also her virginity, which func-tions somewhat ironically, given Vizzani's status as "ladies' man." In fact, lesbianism becomes implicated in the preservation of feminine virtue. As Donoghue notes, "On one level [she is] a virile stud, [and] on another Catherine Vizzani is presented as the epitome of purity," and yet the fron-tispiece to the text proclaims that Vizzani, "being found, on Dissection, a true Virgin, narrowly escaped being treated as a Saint by the Populace."[100] She is, in other words, the perfect woman and the perfect man in one.

Further, both Vizzani's body and her dildo are "dissected" after her death: "The leathern Machine, which was hid under the Pillow, fell into the Hands of the Surgeon's Mates in the Hospital, who immediately were for ripping it up, concluding that it contained Money, or something else of Value, but they found it stuffed only with old Rags."[101] These dissections identify Vizzani as a woman, and perhaps a saint, while the instrument of pleasure that she uses to supplement her performance of masculinity is nothing more than rags. The value of the dildo lies in its attachment to Vizzani's body and the pleasures that the dildo and Vizzani together bring to other women; once it is detached from a female body and in the hands of men, it is useless. Cleland's translation ultimately casts the dildo as a material marker of lesbian sexual pleasure—and more to the point, perhaps, the dissection of the dildo and its fate as a pile of rags conveys the notion that pleasure between women is less about the instrument than about the women who use them.[102] Vizzani, accompanied by her dildo, is, like Hamilton, extremely successful at seducing other women, and in some ways both she and Hamilton play the role of the male rake. Like Hamilton, Vizzani is described as consummately male and female; her desires, however, tend only toward other women, and just like Hamilton, Vizzani is insatiable in her seductions. She is accused of being "the most abandoned Whoremaster that ever seduced Woman," and in the case of one "lovely young gentlewoman," Vizzani "prosecuted [her addresses] with such ardor and success, that they both grew passionately in Love with each other."[103] Although the text gives little clue as to the feelings and desires of Vizzani's conquests, her successes in this arena seem to point to the pleasures she provides for them.

Cleland, as translator, denounces Bianchi's sympathetic view of Vizzani, as well as her supposed virtue, attributing Bianchi's suspect sympathies to his Italianness.[104] He rejects the authority of the medical gaze to the extent that it does not adequately explain the sources of Vizzani's inclinations. He suggests a variety of theories, including the idea that she might have heard lewd stories being told that, coupled with "Incitements from her Constitution, might prompt her to those vile Practices."[105] Cleland disavows any kind of sympathy for Vizzani, presenting her as the perpetrator of "odious" and "unnatural" vices, and he criticizes Bianchi for not assigning a mental reason for her behavior. He writes that that "this irregular and violent Inclination, by which this Woman render'd herself infamous, must either proceed from some Error in Nature, or from some Disorder or Perversion in the Imagination."[106] Because her body contains no irregularities, so to speak, he concludes that "we ought, therefore, to acquit Nature of any Fault in this strange Creature, and to look for the Source of so odious and so unnatural a Vice, only in her Mind."[107] Cleland seems to have forgotten, however, that these "vile practices" are predicated on a prosthetic enhancement not unlike the penises he describes in *Fanny Hill,* as I discuss later.[108] Further, Cleland's own narratorial voice is marked by ambivalence and satirical inflection that cast doubt on the sincerity of the "needful remarks" from the editor. Roger Lonsdale surmises that Cleland's editorial comments condemning Vizzani's behavior had one main function: "to give some air of respectability to the publication."[109] The language of condemnation here echoes Fielding's narrator in *The Female*

Husband, suggesting yet again that such condemnation is pro forma, while the titillating aspects of her narrative—her status as "Whoremaster," her dissection, the discussion of her clitoris, and the description of the dildo's materiality—are not at all "veiled" for reasons of morality. Further, as Hal Gladfelder notes, for Cleland "stories inciting desire," which he suggests may have encouraged Vizzani's own inclinations, are responsible for making individuals aware of "what we want ourselves. Certainly the reader's imagination is full, by the end of the text."[110] Like Fielding's editorializing, Cleland's "needful Remarks" may have stemmed from a desire to "moc[k] the moralism of antimasquerade and other reformers of manners."[111] Thus, both texts, rather than demonizing the dildo as a horrifying object of the women's "detestable imposture," emphasize instead the pleasurable possibilities of lesbian sex with a dildo. Similarly, Cleland's censorious comments also suggest possibilities for understanding gender as not grounded in embodied sex, thus marking a moment in which transgender and gender fluid categories of the self can be distinguished.

By comparing the stories of Mary Hamilton and Catherine Vizzani, we can begin to trace a pattern in which the female husband is constructed as the perfect man *and* the perfect woman, which also means being an imperfect woman and an imperfect man. Although female husbands are generally thought to have been represented negatively in the eighteenth century, especially compared with the laudatory narratives of brave female soldiers, it is evident that these representations contain many similarities. Both kinds of passing women embody an ideal of virile masculinity with the ability to please women. They are able to access the codes of eighteenth-century masculinity to appear male and perform the male role in a variety of capacities. The stories of female husbands, specifically, when compared with *Fanny Hill,* subvert notions of what constitutes embodied maleness even further, making dildos into penises and penises into dildos. If what appears innately male can become prosthetic, and the prosthetic enhancement can equal the male member in its performance, then genital gender loses all of its claims to a biologically based definition. Within this ambiguous space of gender and sex definitions, the sapphic possibilities proliferate and expand to encompass even that which is often coded as explicitly phallic or heterosexual. Thus, female same-sex desires can penetrate even heterosexual exchanges.

The Penis as Dildo: The "Sapphic Supplement" to *Fanny Hill*

In the stories of female husbands, as well as in early eighteenth-century pamphlet culture, the dildo functions as an object that enables intercourse between women. Textually, the dildo is an imaginary appendage of excess proportions whose powers to pleasure are only ever undercut when the dildo goes missing or is destroyed. The dildo is both more than man and, conversely, an indicator of being less than man; the dildo reveals the embodied pleasures a dildo-wielding woman or a trans man can provide another woman, while also implicating itself in the discourses of masculinity and impotence. Cleland's erotic novel *Fanny Hill; or, The Memoirs of a Woman of Pleasure* initially poses lesbian sex as inadequate for the satisfaction of female sexual desires, suborning them to the primacy of heterosexual intercourse between beautiful young men and women. And yet even in this purported "pornotopia,"[112] we can detect aspects of what Susan Lanser calls a "sapphic supplement that turns sex between a man and a woman into sex 'between women' at the level of discourse."[113] The perfect penises of *Fanny Hill*, those "instruments" or "machines" that Fanny both delights in and is horrified by, take on a dildo-like quality in the text, undergoing a narrative process that "resists the trajectory of cross-sex desire that has already been filtered through same-sex affiliation."[114] In the following section, I consider how the "sapphic supplements" to *Fanny Hill* put into question the novel's heterosexual investments through a "dildoization" of the male penis.

In *Fanny Hill*, the titular character, Fanny, writes about her sexual exploits to an unnamed female friend. She recounts in detail the sensations of both pain and pleasure she experiences in a variety of sexual encounters between herself and both men and women, in addition to regaling her audience with descriptions of assignations between others. Cleland consistently emphasizes the naturalness and correctness of sexual encounters between men and women and, more specifically, between ideal masculine men and young, nubile girls. The novel abounds in examples of inferior masculinity and aged femininity that are described in no uncertain terms as unworthy of Fanny's attention, except as opportunities for expressing ridicule or contempt. Notably, the greatest derision and even censure comes from Fanny when she is confronted with same-sex desires and acts. The woman who initiates Fanny into the secrets of sexual pleasure, Phoebe Ayres, is described as having "one of those arbitrary tastes, for which there is no accounting."[115] Fanny subsequently declares that sex with a woman is not enough for her: "For my own part, I now pin'd for more solid food, and promis'd tacitly to myself that I would not be put off much longer with this foolery from woman to woman."[116] And while the act of sex between women does not resurface in the text, anal sex and male homosexuality do, and Fanny is morally opposed to both. When confronted with the sight of two men engaged in anal sex, she is on the verge of turning them in to the authorities, except that she falls from her position of watching and is knocked out before she can communicate "so criminal a scene" to anyone else.[117] Throughout the rest of the novel, Fanny has few qualms about the sexual acts in which she engages. The only requirements for her satisfaction are that her lover be strong, healthy, and in possession of a "machine" capable of sating her sexual appetites. The machine-like erect penises, however, take on a prosthetic quality in the text; their ever-present hardness equates them metaphorically with a dildo, complicating Cleland's emphasis on clearly defined heterosexual couplings and normative bodies. After all, Vizzani's penile prosthesis is referred to as a "machine" and an "instrument," as well.

The novel's insistence on heteronormative sexuality as ideal sex is contradictory. Fanny's outright condemnation of nonheterosexual sex is a reinscription "of masculine dominance and authority."[118] However, her loving descriptions of the male anatomy suggest that "Cleland creates a female voice that thinly disguises a masquerading homoerotic male voice" through which "he . . . critiques both conventional novel plots and the sociosexual ideologies they embrace."[119] Fanny's participation in orgy scenes offers both male and female homoerotic possibilities.[120] When Fanny watches the other women having sex with their male partners, the gazes the women exchange take on the quality of the homosexual gaze. Lisa Moore also argues that Phoebe's role in "breaking in" the young women at the brothel for Mrs. Brown becomes another layer of female same-sex desires, "rendering Phoebe's seduction of Fanny not just a homosexual act but a complex construction of a homosexual voyeurism unmediated by heterosexual economics."[121] The novel's emphasis on voyeurism as the primary means of seduction is saturated with same-sex possibilities, both male and female—though these possibilities are never acknowledged by Fanny herself.[122] Much scholarship on the novel, like Gladfelder's, has already focused on the important role that sapphic desires play in the novel.[123] Thus, it is possible to read the homosexual and heterosexual sex acts of the novel as along a spectrum of sexual possibilities that are each made visible to the reader in turn. The sapphic possibilities of the novel are often found in the way Fanny's gaze functions, in how she describes bodies and sex acts, and in the way that the novel intersects with by then common stories of female husbands and dildo narratives.

The bodies of the novel are ambiguous and fluid, and they change depending on who is gazing on what. The penises in the novel appear under a variety of names. Cleland refers to the penis in mechanical terms, the term "machine" being used the most consistently.[124] Other terms include "weapon of pleasure," "the engine of love-assaults," a "truncheon," "a maypole," an "engine," a "pick-lock," a "delicious stretcher," a "superb piece of furniture," a "pleasure-pivot," "a splitter," and "instrument."[125] The penis itself is never referred to as a penis.[126] It is occasionally referred to as a "member," but more often it is described in terms of the sexual pleasures it provides and its hardness, a pattern that identifies penises discursively with dildos. While such metaphors and euphemisms may be accepted descriptors for pornographic or erotic texts, they take on an added importance when we consider them in light of the descriptions of dildos in the tales of female cross-dressers. Cleland upholds and perhaps even creates some of the stock generic requirements for erotica, emphasizing the beauty and youth of the appropriate participants in sexual acts that he sanctions as pleasurable, as well as the size, girth, and destructive power of the penis. At the same time, he undermines the "naturalness" of these arrangements by emphasizing the male member's mechanical, unbending characteristics. In the novel, the ideal penis is always erect and always ready to perform, metaphorically taking on the qualities of a dildo.

The penises of *Fanny Hill* are rarely flaccid; instead, the novel is predicated on the dildo-like quality of the many penises Fanny and her friends encounter. Susan Bordo explores the prosthetic nature of the penis in *The Male Body* when she discusses the emphasis on the erect penis and the terminology used to describe it in Western culture. The male bio-fantasy of the penis is one defined by "mechanical penile metaphors. Big rig. Blowtorch. Bolt."[127] These metaphors offer "protection" to the penis fantasy against becoming soft. Bordo continues, "Interestingly, such names are often given to dildos too," thus turning the penis "into some species of dildo: stiff torpedoes, wands, and rods that never get soft, always perform."[128] In this sense, the slang terminology of the sex shop, pornography, and certain kinds of erotica not only lends a mechanical quality to the flesh-and-blood body part, but it also encompasses the discrepancy between the fantasy (hardness that is always ready to perform) and the reality (the penis can be soft or vulnerable or refuse to perform). Unlike a dildo, the penis can feel; the metaphors for the penis, however, deny this quality. Cleland's penises can thus be read as dildos, putting into question the naturalness of the body and even heterosexuality, suggesting a queer vision of the glorified male member that identifies the penis as completely prosthetic rather than a normative element of cisgendered masculinity.[129]

In light of this discursive reorienting of the penis as prosthetic, it is worth revisiting the history of Emily in *Fanny Hill*, the young woman in the brothel who cross-dresses and is unwittingly picked up by a man who mistakes her for a young boy. When he discovers her femaleness at the bagnio, the gentleman expresses "a mixture of pique, confusion, and disappointment" and exclaims, "By heavens a woman!"[130] For whatever reason, the gentleman decides to have sex with Emily anyway, laying her face down on the bed, "so, that the double-way between the double rising behind, presented the choice fair to him, and he was so fiercely set on a mis-direction, as to give the girl no small alarms."[131] This scene of attempted anal sex between man and woman—or, at least, its possibility— has already been proposed in the text. Earlier, Fanny has sex with a young man who enters her from behind. She describes the act in terms that might be a prelude to anal sex as much as vaginal: "[He] open'd himself the prospect of the back avenue to the genial seat of pleasure."[132] Not too many pages later, in a spontaneous liaison with a sailor, Fanny recounts that she could feel "pretty sensibly that it [the penis] was going by the right door, and knocking desperately at the wrong one."[133] Fanny corrects him, and they have vaginal intercourse, though only after the sailor rather nonchalantly replies, "Any port in a storm," to Fanny's "correction."[134] Thus, cross-dressing Emily's escapade is not without precedent. While she is also able to "correct" the gentleman who initially mistakes her for a boy, this incident becomes a moment in which the female cross-dresser's body suggests the possibility of non-heteronormative desires.

While Fanny declares that this gentleman's tastes are "universally odi-ous, [and] absurd" and perhaps even "impossible to gratify," her descrip-tion of Emily's encounter is not wholly condemnatory. For example, the text offers two explanations for why the gentleman decides to have sex with Emily even after her femaleness is revealed: "For now, whether the impressions of so great a beauty had even made him forgive her, her sex, or whether her appearances or figure in that dress still humour'd his first illusion, he recover'd by degrees a good part of his first warmth."[135] Like Mary Hamilton, Emily in drag is extremely attractive.[136] Once Emily's true sex is discovered by the gentleman who thought she was a boy, Fanny surmises that Emily's beauty as a woman might keep his attraction. At the same time, Emily's body may still be attractive to the man if he chooses to ignore her femaleness; Fanny is unsure about this point, and the multiple interpretations leave open the possibility to the reader that Emily's own gender is fluid. The novel proposes that clothes can make gender as much as bodies can, and Cleland "shows that imaginative compromises are not only possible but can even be pleasurable."[137] The imaginative compromise in this scene is that of the man who pretends to himself that Emily is still a boy, despite the genital proof—the "extremities which instantly discover the sex"—which reveal quite clearly that she is not a boy.[138] This imaginative compromise, however, relies on the clothing Emily wears and the "figure" she cuts in them. Her attractiveness, like Mary Hamilton's, is simultaneously feminine and masculine. This scene also demonstrates how lack of a penis does not foreclose the possibility of being seen as male; Emily's missing male appendage does not affect her ability to have anal sex with the stranger, even if Cleland disavows this possibility. Female cross-dressing, whether it attracts the attentions of men or women, not only puts gender and sex categories into question but also suggests queer desires and possibilities. Even when Emily convinces her partner to have heterosexual sex, the possibility of male homosexual desires is still present. The conflation of homosexual and heterosexual desires continues into the next passage, where Fanny witnesses the scene of sodomy between two men—and where she initially believes that one of the men must be "a girl in disguise."[139]

Given Phoebe's own earlier exclamation that she wished she could "be a man for [Fanny's] sake," and the novel's further examples of cross-dressing, the novel makes a strong case for cross-gender identification, even within its heterosexual pornotopia.[140] Felicity Nussbaum argues that "Cleland also radically implies that Fanny Hill's body is both male and female."[141] Donald Mengay posits that "Fanny is representative of a third-sex . . . [who] affirms both homosexual and feminist roles: she is at once both male (implied narrator) and female (narrator proper) behaving on the whole as an egalitarian actor in relationships with other men."[142] Dildos do not make an appearance in this text, which seems to imply that the novel is committed to exploring only the pleasures, economies, and exchanges of fleshly bodies. We know, though, that this is not true; the unbending, ever-tumescent quality of Cleland's penises belies the novel's apparent obsession with the flesh. If women's bodies can be read as male—as in the case of Emily—then by the same logic we are able to read male bodies as female. If the men of the text are discursively in possession of dildos rather than penises, then the text offers the reader the possibility of reading these "men" as women in possession of dildos. Nussbaum has noted that in the final sex scene between Fanny and Charles, there is a reversal between the penis and the breast: "In this bizarre description of Fanny's last recorded intercourse, ejaculating during orgasm makes her vagina literally milk Charles's penis dry. . . . The penis becomes the breast to which hungry infants (her vagina) attach themselves. . . . The passage loosens the penis from the male body, and the breast from the female."[143] The penis and the breast, dissociated from their respective bodies, recirculate as prosthetic qualities that might attach themselves to other bodies, creating new gendered configurations and putting even heterosexuality into confusion and disarray. As Gladfelder points out, Charles, Fanny's first and also final, apparently heterosexual partner, is consistently feminized and made androgynous through the novel's narration: "Charles and Fanny can thus be read by turns as sodomites, as tribades, as man and wife."[144] The changing gender roles that Charles and Fanny inhabit, as well as the novel's insistence that the penis function as an impeccable dildo, reveals that the penis no longer has a monopoly on pleasure or power or even on the male body. If the penis is a dildo, then anyone might have it and use it.

Although Fanny characterizes lesbianism as an unaccountable taste (like flagellation) while male sodomy is a criminal act, the specter of both is apparent in the novel's scene of cross-dressing.[145] Emily, even without a penis, can be a boy; her partner, who has a penis, can be a woman with a dildo.[146] The novel's penises, which play such a central role, are described in a way that constructs them as prosthetic, even as they fulfill the novel's notion of the idealized masculine form. The machines and instruments that do the penetrating in *Fanny Hill* bear a remarkable similarity to the actual dildos in stories of female husbands, and Cleland's rhetoric of the amazing male penis gives way to a discourse of dildos and female prosthetic pleasures. As an erotic novel, *Fanny Hill* constructs pleasure through the visual, as well as the tactile. The novel introduces Fanny to sex through pleasurable yet inadequate lesbian sex; the rest of the novel, however, does not foreclose sapphic possibilities. The construction of maleness and heterosexual pleasures through the unbending dildo-like penis suggest the ambiguous quality of gender that is predicated on an erection. While Emily's cross-dressing scene is only one of many adventures related in the novel, it, like the stories of female soldiers and female husbands, suggests the gender-destabilizing possibilities made legible through the cross-dresser, as well as the men and women who desire her.

In the narratives of female cross-dressers, we can see that, like breasts and beards, penises are not exclusively the domain of one gender. In fact, their very existence and necessity are questioned in these texts, even as their authors focus obsessively on how the cross-dresser can "make up for" her missing penis or otherwise hide her female inadequacy. The dildo, the ultimate sexual prosthesis, takes on a reality and a corporeality often denied the penis. Like the beard, the lacking penis might be made up for by the female cross-dresser through other means. The skill at wooing women exhibited by the female soldiers and female husbands, and even by "masculine" women such as Mrs. Freke, becomes a way of accessing male privileges—of bearding themselves. The penis and the dildo are, to an extent, ambiguous and interchangeable in these texts. The female cross-dresser brings this interchangeability to light and urges us to re-examine how the biological bases for sex are put into question by the very body parts that purportedly define it. Gender is increasingly difficult to read as the penis is unnecessary to successful impersonation of maleness, the dildo outperforms the penis, and the penis is described in dildo-like terms. Further, these texts potently suggest the possibility not only of lesbian butch performance and sapphic desires, but also the ways in which transmen could access prosthetic supplements to their gender.

While these texts allude to the problem of not having a penis, they do not supply these women a replacement by portraying them as having excessive appendages of their own. The missing penis becomes foremost a problem of prosthetics. As a detachable/reattachable prosthetic device, the dildo can indeed be circulated among women, although it is not always necessary to the fulfillment of female desires. It can also be an appendage passed down among butches or transgender men. While the penis-like qualities of the dildo seem to emphasize the importance of heteronormative sex acts, a closer look at these descriptions demonstrates that it is the penis that is dildo-like. While the use of a dildo earned the female cross-dresser time in prison or even execution for an apparent usurpation of male privilege, the stories of cross-dressers represent the dildo as the means through which not only to access and fulfill female same-sex desires, but also to destabilize heterosexuality more generally.[147] Although the dildo is often denounced or even satirized as being less authentic than a penis, even the early dildo poems admit its superior performance. This ambivalent view of the penis and the dildo not only question the way in which gender is constructed in eighteenth-century narrative. It also opens up the possibility of reading sapphic possibilities in texts that initially appear to reinforce heterosexual norms.

The prosthetic quality of the penis and the penis's various prosthetic replacements—dildos and "urinary devices," as well as masculine behavior, swords and guns, and female "beards"—trans the body and gender, revealing how the sexed body can be illegible, desirable, and both male and female at the same time. The penis and the dildo do not shut down the possibilities for sapphic pleasures; instead, their mutability and prosthetic nature make room for a variety of queer desires, including sapphic ones. In challenging the "necessity" of a penis to a satisfactory sexual encounter, the stories of female cross-dressers propose to readers the possibility of female-centric desires fulfilled by women (or transmen), for women. The various tales of female husbands and female soldiers often allude to the possibility that the women they court know them to be not male, like Vizzani's lover Margaret, and perhaps this knowledge is the wellspring of their desire. In this case, like the women who "frisk themselves" in "Seignor Dildo," readers can imagine sexual encounters both with and without a dildo that privilege female eroticism and reciprocal same-sex desires. Thus, the beards, the breasts, and the penis become body parts around which cross-dressing texts organize and question sex, gender, and sexual desires. Heterosexuality itself becomes a vexed category that other eighteenth-century texts will seek to reimagine and stabilize as time goes on; the cross-dressed narratives, however, consistently ask readers to question just how stable a category heterosexuality truly is. The legs, by contrast, do not function as explicitly gendered. Yet, as I show in chapter 4, they come to epitomize analogous debates about the representation of women's bodies and desires while also putting into question issues of masculinity and heterosexuality and reframing them in terms of mobility and able-bodiedness.

4

▶◀

PUTTING ON GENDER,
ONE LEG AT A TIME

Legs, and especially women's legs, occupied a contentious space within the eighteenth-century British imaginary. Stage reviewers, documentarians, and nameless poets extolled the beauties of cross-dressing actresses' legs, as well as their ability to appeal to both sexes, openly acknowledging the titillating sapphic possibilities inherent in such performances. By contrast, actress memoirs and novels often ignore the sexual aspects of legs, just as some admirers of female legs onstage often ignored the gender-bending possibilities of cross-dressed actresses, even when they portrayed rakes and fops who court other women. Lisa Freeman notes, "In an age that both featured and censored cross-dressers like Charlotte Charke, transvestism came to constitute a particularly provocative site for the expression of cultural anxieties over the stability of gender hierarchies."[1] The legs of the cross-dresser in many ways epitomize these anxieties, encompassing concerns about gender production, performance, sexuality, and female independence. As Helen Brooks explains, "In claiming this new level of physical and social freedom simply by dressing and behaving as male, actresses also drew attention to masculinity's status as something achievable—displayed, worn, and ultimately performed through gesture, clothing, posture, and vocal presentation—rather than innate."[2] In this way, actresses' legs overtly suggest the performativity of gender, and specifically masculinity, but also its materiality. The legs of the cross-dressing actress have been analyzed by a number of previous studies, but they have rarely been discussed in relation to sapphism in the eighteenth century; instead, they have often been discussed in terms of their viability as sex symbols onstage for the consumption of the male gaze. Here, however, I examine how legs function similarly to beards, breasts, and genitalia in their ability to solicit and signal female same-sex desires to other women, as well as to readers or audience members, while also revealing cultural investments in keeping transgendered performances onstage. In putting legs into conversation with other body parts, we see how authors and audiences acknowledged and enjoyed the possibility of same-sex desires or transgender or gender-fluid embodiments, even as these body parts also reveal intimate and authentic emotional relationships between women. Further, in considering the legs of actresses and their prominence in stage culture in relation to female cross-dressing writ large, we begin to see how legs function in other genres, as well.

This chapter explores how the exposed legs of the female cross-dresser often have the power to seduce other women, further establishing the legs as a sight/site of lesbian desires, while also carrying non-heteronormative, transgender, and antipatriarchal qualities arising from the combination of mobility, power, and sex. The representations of the legs of eighteenth-century female cross-dressers further merge these concepts by explicitly connecting greater freedom and independence to the pursuit of sapphic relationships. Although in some cases female cross-dressing and exposed legs could elicit socially acceptable admiration and desire from both men and women, various texts also suggest the sapphic possibilities inherent in greater female mobility, as achieved through the transing of gender norms.

I begin by situating legs within eighteenth-century discourses of sexuality, gender fluidity, and mobility before moving on to the phenomenon of the breeches role and travesty parts. I draw on the representations of actresses who specialized in these parts—in particular, Charlotte Charke in *A Narrative of the Life of Mrs. Charlotte Charke Written by Herself* (1755) and Margaret (Peg) Woffington in James Quin's *The Life of Mr. James Quin, Comedian* (1766) and Robert Hitchcock's *An Historical View of the Irish Stage* (1788). Last, I look at how legs function as both embodied markers of femaleness and metaphorical sites of female desire and independence in two novels from the end of the century: Elizabeth Inchbald's *A Simple Story* (1791) and Maria Edgeworth's *Belinda* (1801). Together these

texts demonstrate how legs appear as indeterminate and therefore ambivalent markers of gender, a confusion that leads to same-sex outcomes
even as the texts struggle to construct domestic narratives of cisgender
heteronormativity—an element of which we already saw in chapter 2
with regard to the breasts in *Belinda*. The appeal of these legs to women,
and the connections that the cross-dresser makes to other women—her
beards, as discussed in chapter 1—through the social mobility offered her
by breeches, render sapphic desires legible to readers and audiences while
also revealing how sapphism becomes aligned with female freedom of
movement and an explicit challenge to patriarchal expectations of female
domesticity and comportment. Thus, yet again, sapphic possibilities arise
through the apparatus of transgender performance.

While the penis and breast and even the beard represent body parts that
appear in one way or another obviously gendered, both men and women
have legs. Historically, however, women's legs have nearly always been
covered by long skirts, while men's legs have been displayed in trousers
or tights, a contrast that constructs gender difference through clothing
and legs, in part by denying that women's legs exist. Most women's legs
were out of sight in the eighteenth century, and breeches and tights were
primarily the means for displaying men's legs, along with men's heeled
shoes that clearly defined the calf muscles.[3] In *The Fable of the Bees* (1714),
Bernard Mandeville sums up his thoughts on the exposing of female legs
in the early eighteenth century: "If a woman at a merrymaking dresses
in Man's clothes, it is reckon'd a Frolick amongst Friends. . . . Upon the
Stage it is done without Reproach, and the most Virtuous Ladies will dis-
pense with it in an Actress, tho' every Body has a full view of her Legs and
Thighs, but if the same Woman, as soon as she has Petticoats on again,
should show her Leg to a Man as high as her Knee, it would be a very im-
modest Action, and every body will call her impudent for it."[4] Mandeville's
commentary clearly delineates acceptable versus unacceptable women's
legs through a dichotomy of playacting versus reality. In day-to-day life,
he suggests, women's legs should be out of sight. His comments reflect the
standards of the time period: while the outline of male legs were discern-
ible in the breeches of this time period, women's gowns were large, cumbersome, and heavy and nearly always incorporated a skirt, thus keeping

her legs, and often even her feet, completely hidden.[5] Petticoats were the dominant female garment of the eighteenth century and were synonymous with femaleness, just as breeches were synonymous with maleness.[6] While men's clothing tended to emphasize the body and "demonstrate the existence of a trunk, neck and head with hair, of movable legs, feet and arms, and sometimes genitals," women's clothes, and particularly the skirt, according to the fashion historian Anne Hollander, "hid women from the waist down and thus permitted endless scope for the mythology of the feminine." The skirt "had become a sacred female fate and privilege, especially after it became firmly established as a separate garment."[7] Along with its ability to hide women's legs, the skirt is directly synonymous with the female genitalia. Legs have a sex, and dividing women's legs with fabric was a "sexual sacrilege" or even "profound blasphemy"—as implied by Mandeville's commentary.[8] Thus, the separation of the legs alludes, all too clearly, to the genitalia between them, making women in breeches and their exposed legs an overtly sexual spectacle.

Women's legs were exposed most notably and spectacularly on the stage in this era; the women who first walked the stage in the Restoration undertook "breeches roles" and eventually even the parts of male characters (so-called travesty parts), titillating audiences with the novel sight of women's legs on display. According to Jones DeRitter, "the 'breeches part' on the Restoration stage seems to have come into vogue largely in order to put the bodies of the leading female performers on display."[9] Certainly, the appearance of women's legs must have been part of their attraction onstage.[10] Felicity Nussbaum notes that breeches roles were responsible for "increasing nightly receipts because of the audience's wish to admire women's curves in pants."[11] From the actress's point of view, however, Nussbaum also argues, breeches parts, and the breeches themselves, "allow[ed] [actresses] to exercise greater mobility than most women."[12] Similarly, working-class women often wore trousers when doing heavy, dirty, or physical work for reasons of practicality. At the same time, though, these social associations did nothing to remove the moral stigma associated with women's wearing of trousers. Hollander explains that certain working-class women wore trousers before the twentieth century: "Trousers had certainly been worn by female mine-workers, fisherfolk, and agricultural laborers, and naturally by dancers and acrobats, and actresses or singers in 'breeches' parts; but the low status of all these female occupations kept women's pants firmly associated with lowness in general."[13] Masquerades, a prevailing eighteenth-century entertainment, also featured both men and women with exposed legs and even some men in skirts, as cross-dressing was an accepted element of masquerade balls, which themselves occupied a contentious space in eighteenth-century discourse. Further, even actresses had to contend with the condemnation of eighteenth-century moralists on the topic of breeches parts and travesty,[14] and most women were aware that the showing of legs was an immoral act often associated with prostitution.[15] Further, seventeenth-century texts such as *Hic Mulier* and *Haec Vir* (both 1620) very clearly raged against the crossing of gender norms and gender fluidity, anticipating more modern social prohibitions regarding transgender and gender-fluid identities.[16]

In this way, both women's legs and transgender identities are co-opted for the pleasure of the male gaze even as their exposure in public is coded as immoral. Importantly, however, the sex appeal of legs is not restricted for the male gaze; exposed female legs attract female same-sex or other non-normative desires. And just like the lack of beard, the ambiguity or even the femininity of the cross-dresser's legs may in fact be what appeals to other women. In "The Story of Leonora and Louisa," Leonora cross-dresses without exposing her legs: she chooses the garb of a clergyman precisely because it "left her Petticoats tho' it took from her her Sex, and obliged People of any Degree of Politeness to behave with much the same kind of Decorum in her Presence as if she had appeared a Woman."[17] For Leonora, the clergyman's habit (which she must abandon later) is the ideal male costume, as it allows the sexualized appendages to remain hidden and, so she thinks, guarantees a certain level of decorum from those she meets. Leonora's body logic is rooted in the idea that to expose the legs would be to court unseemly overtures from those she might meet on her travels, indicating that the parting of the legs has moral as well as sexual implications. Yet the male clothes are what provide her and Louisa the freedom to move about the countryside, just as they do for many other female cross-dressers and "passing" women, including Hannah Snell, Christian Davies, Mary Hamilton, and Edgeworth's Harriet Freke.

The antipatriarchal quality of female mobility, coupled with the sexualized nature of exposed legs, indicate that legs are gendered appendages capable of signifying both power and desire.[18] The cross-dressing woman who "puts on her legs" when she appropriates male garb creates sapphic possibilities around her, even as the cross-dressing narratives (at times) attempt to dispel these desires by normalizing them or ignoring them. The women who see the cross-dresser's legs and admire them demonstrate the sexual power of the legs, while, again, the reader, knowing that the cross-dresser is in fact a woman, is also endowed with the ability to identify the sapphic possibilities in the narrative. Thus, the mobility and independence that come with the exposed legs of the cross-dresser consequently lead to sapphic pleasures and desires. Rather than thinking of the cross-dressing actress or novel heroine as a temporary aberration, an appealing spectacle for the male gaze, or a difficult woman who is ultimately punished, this chapter argues that the legs of the cross-dresser refocus our understanding of women's and transgender men's self-fashioning through clothing and narrative. Further, both cross-dressing actresses and cross-dressing novel characters teach their readers that legs equal independence, not only of movement, but also in matters of love and desire, potently suggesting the allure and opportunities in transgender performances alongside their risks.

The concepts of independence and mobility are vexed ones in the eighteenth century, however, and a growing body of scholarship on disability studies and the history of sexuality points to how the equating of masculinity with mobility were both crucial to the making of the modern self and modern gender dichotomies, even as they were highly problematic correlations. As Jason Farr has noted, dominant social discourses of the time privileged "heterosexuality and able-bodiedness," yet many works of literature "use the intersections of disability and queerness to stage an array of eighteenth-century debates" that included feminism, among many others.[19] The debates about legs and the sexualization of legs clearly intersect with models of able-bodied masculinity in the narratives of female cross-dressing, revealing how such intersections questioned gender binaries and, at moments, dismantled them. Cross-dressing narratives often defined female masculinity through access to normative ideals of able-bodied masculinity, and yet the embodiedness of these women and their relationships is often framed in terms of fatigue, illness, and even injury or maiming. Actresses' legs are exploited by theater managers and sexualized for audiences while the cross-dresser's legs off stage function metaphorically as sites of women's bonding at the moment when partners are most tired, exhausted, or in harm's way. Thus, these narratives expose how masculinity becomes synonymous with able-bodiedness while femininity is often considered a type of disability in eighteenth-century discourses of embodiment.

Legs as Sexual Accessories

In general, eighteenth-century fashions, as in earlier time periods, emphasized exposed legs as masculine and a lack of visible legs as feminine. As many historians of dress have already noted, however, the tightening of breeches and the change in menswear that began in the Restoration and continued to evolve over the course of the eighteenth century altered the masculine silhouette to emphasize the male leg in new and sexually suggestive ways. Karen Harvey traces these changes, arguing that "cultural representations reveal yet other meanings attached to the male leg: those of beauty, power, and sensuality."[20] Certainly these ideas existed prior to the eighteenth century, as the case of Henry VIII attests; the notorious king was exceedingly proud of his bulging calves, and his athletic legs were a vaunted feature of his for much of his life. Ample scholarship by historians of sexuality in the early modern time period attests to the sexualized nature of men's legs and male fashions. Mario DiGangi notes, for example, that "strong legs" were "a major criterion of male beauty in the Renaissance," an idea that Susan Vincent explains in terms of male fashion and power: "Fundamental to this matter of appearance were legs . . . the corporeal shorthand for elite manliness."[21] Men's legs of the early seventeenth century required a certain amount of "daintiness about these limbs, a neatness: the sort of legs on which the phrase *well-turned* would sit nicely."[22] Interestingly, Vincent notes that in the eighteenth century, women's legs were often considered thicker and less well-proportioned than those of men, suggesting the importance of the dainty, graceful, aristocratic *male* leg.[23] Such distinctions take on added significance when we consider the gender-bending performances of female masculinity on the eighteenth-century stage and how actresses displayed their own "well-turned" legs.

Over the course of the eighteenth century, men's fashions increasingly emphasized elongated, elegant, yet slightly muscular legs in tight breeches and stockings.[24] The shortening of the waistcoat and jacket meant that more male leg was exposed during the eighteenth century, and "an elegant leg in a white silk stocking was an important part of fashionable appearance."[25] The male costume of coat, waistcoat, and breeches—essentially the beginnings of the three-piece suit—became the general fashion by about the 1670s and lasted with only minor modifications throughout the century.[26] While the tightness or colorfulness of some men's breeches comes under attack by moralists of the time, the breeches themselves are a standard piece of clothing for nearly all men.[27] Hollander writes that "close-fitting silk knee-breeches and skin-tight doeskin pantaloons of the late eighteenth century . . . had shown off the male legs and crotch without much room for compromise."[28] While moralists and satirists frequently reviled the fops and macaronis for their ostentatious clothes—the types and colors of fabrics they wore, the perfumes they used, the size and shapes of their enormous wigs—men had to make do with breeches of some sort.[29]

By contrast, as noted earlier, women's gowns were cumbersome and kept legs, and often feet, hidden. The skirt and its ability to hide women's legs is directly synonymous with the female genitalia. In fact, for many admirers of the female form, this hidden division between the legs was a powerful erotic enticement to imagining what lies between them. Will Fisher begins his discussion of the homoerotic qualities of male legs with their origins in typical heterosexually themed blazon poems focused on praising women's thighs and the practice of intercrural sex—that is, "thigh sex." Fisher explains, "It was quite conventional for poets to praise the beauty of their beloved's thighs," and such praise was often linked to fantasies of what lies between said thighs.[30] In fact, Fisher identifies the middle of the seventeenth century, right around the time of the Restoration and the return of women to the stage, one might add, as the starting point for the rising popularity of women's thighs as erotic body parts in poetry. Thus, the eroticization of women's legs and the focus on legs and thighs as explicitly erogenous zones dovetailed with homoerotic (male) discourses, while the dainty, well-turned, appropriately muscular male leg of courtiers and dandies became a way of playing with gender performances by cross-dressing actresses.

The sexualized nature of female legs is evident in print culture, as well, especially in caricatures of the late eighteenth century. Several caricatures by James Gillray—most notably, *A March to the Bank* (1787)—depict legs splayed or awry as a way to juxtapose sexual and political satire. In *A March to the Bank,* Gillray satirizes the heightened security at the Bank of England in the wake of the Gordon Riots. A crowd of pedestrians lie sprawled on the street as guards march over them, including a thin, mincing soldier who flourishes his dainty leg even as his other foot tramples the ample stomach of a woman whose legs—and very nearly her entire crotch—lie exposed to the viewer. Another woman, a well-dressed and coifed lady, lies on the ground nearby, with her shapely leg in the air, while a barber takes advantage of the situation to slide his hands between her legs. Like Thomas Rowlandson's *Exhibition "Stare" Case* (ca. 1800), Gillray's caricature is an excuse to depict many pairs of exposed and sexualized legs. Rowlandson and Gillray satirize eighteenth-century modes of looking and desiring by providing the viewer an up-skirt perspective. The use of legs to signify social standing as well as sexual availability, political pressures as well as class membership can be seen in many of Gillray's prints. In his *Fashionable Contrasts; or, The Duchess's Little Shoe Yielding to the Magnitude of the Duke's Foot* (1792), tiny female slippers are interpenetrated by large buckled men's shoes. The rumored delicacy of the feet of Duchess Frederica, eldest daughter of the King of Prussia, becomes the means through which not only to satirize public interest in her upcoming wedding with Frederick, Duke of York (second son of George III), but also to depict clearly and satirically the mixing of political and sexual elements via the feet. Despite the prints' focus on political commentary, they rely on the sexual element of legs to make their meaning clear.[31]

By showing legs in men's trousers rather than through upturned skirts, the cross-dressing woman offers an alternative sexual possibility: she is sexualized, but she is not vulnerable. The female cross-dresser's legs are exposed even as her genitals are not—though they are suggestively alluded to merely by the lack of petticoat—making her a seductive presence on the Restoration and eighteenth-century stage. Further, the cross-dressing actress becomes yet another type of cross-dressing woman: one whose explicit raison d'être is often to seduce men *and* women in the audience. Certainly performances by Charlotte Charke, Margaret Woffington, Dorothea Jordan, and Elizabeth Inchbald, among others, over the course of the century helped saturate the British imaginary with the spectacle of seductive androgyny and female masculinity. As Brooks notes, "Just as the popular 'women warrior' ballads and the stories of women like Hannah Snell and Christian Davies all relied on their readers' knowledge of their subjects' multiple identities, theatrical travesty thrived on the juxtaposition, rather than the effacement, of the female actress with the male character."[32] Building on the ephemeral performances that we know of but that we cannot access, the personal narratives and theater histories add to our understanding of how eighteenth-century audiences and readers would have understood, enjoyed, and thought about women dressing in men's clothing, performing masculinity through the juxtaposition of masculine and feminine. In many of these texts, the legs take center stage as appendages through which to read sexual desire and ambiguous gender.

Staging Legs: Theatrical Cross-Dressing On and Off the Stage

In England, women gained the stage in the second half of the seventeenth century. Male cross-dressing onstage had been a matter of course in the early modern period, as young men and boys played the parts of all female characters. Many popular plays from that earlier time period, such as Shakespeare's *Twelfth Night, As You Like It,* and *The Merchant of Venice,* also contain female characters who pass themselves off as men, parts that in the eighteenth century came to be known as breeches roles. Rudolf Dekker and Lotte van de Pol note that, "of more than three hundred plays first performed in London between 1660 and 1700, eighty-nine contained roles in which actresses donned male clothes."[33] The fashion for women in men's clothes persisted throughout the eighteenth century and continued into the nineteenth.[34] While detractors condemned the practice as immoral, its popularity indicates that it was enjoyed and embraced by spectators, actresses, playwrights, and theater owners and managers. The proliferation of women onstage in breeches and tights meant that the sight of a cross-dressed woman was not unusual, and yet, although the sight of women's legs was acceptable onstage, it was still taboo offstage.

While actresses such as Margaret "Peg" Woffington were praised for their ability to play male roles and admired for their shapely legs, they were also, at times, at the center of controversy. Even from the earliest decades of the eighteenth century there were detractors of the theater and theatrical cross-dressing. While such cross-dressing obviously afforded the audiences much specular pleasure, and many, as Mandeville's earlier quote articulates, accepted onstage cross-dressing as a matter of course, there is a strong sense that cross-dressing transgressed certain accepted social boundaries.[35] There were many outspoken critics of female cross-dressing on the stage, including the Yorkshire theater manager Tate Wilkinson, as well as the actors Charles Dibdin and Charles Lee Lewes.[36] The criticism of female cross-dressing onstage appeared to intensify toward the end of the eighteenth century, when commentators of the 1770s and 1780s found such performances laughable and unrealistic.[37] Moralists throughout the century labeled female cross-dressers dangerous and immoral to society, threatening to the state of British masculinity, or improbably silly and pathetic. These critiques existed in parallel with the continued appearance of cross-dressed women onstage and audiences' positive reactions to them. Susan Lanser argues that "London public culture . . . depends on events such as opera and theatre, where castrati, and actresses playing 'breeches parts,' help to create the very conditions for heterosociability,"[38] drawing attention to how heteronormative British culture of the eighteenth century rested on queer constructions of gender and sexuality—to which we might also add transgendered embodiments. Thus, cross-dressed actresses channeled same-sex desires through their appeal to other women and their superlative performances in male roles, even as they were also desired by men. The exposed legs of these actresses function as embodied markers of mobility and sapphic desires. Thus, the fashion in men's clothing that allowed a gentleman to "show off a well-turned leg to advantage" became, in theatrical drag performances, the vehicle through which to put the female leg on display while also playing with notions of gender fluidity that had long been a part of stage culture in the past.[39] Although this aspect of female cross-dressing has been examined by critics of gender studies, as well as performance studies, not enough attention has been paid to how such performances functioned as opportunities for expressing and engendering same-sex desires. Further, the cross-dressed actress of the eighteenth-century English stage becomes an early symbol for women's, and especially lesbian, social and sexual freedom via transgendered embodiments.

In this section I focus on two actresses particularly known for their performances in breeches on (and at times off) the stage: Charlotte Charke, a daughter of the actor-manager Colley Cibber, and the Irish actress Margaret Woffington. I argue that textual evidence of their cross-dressing reveals to readers how actresses' legs function as markers of independence and sapphic possibilities, while Charke's story in particular also invites us to read her cross-dressing life off stage as an early trans autobiography. Charke rose to fame through family connections, only to be cast out of the family and forced to make her own way in life, a journey she documents in her autobiography, *A Narrative of the Life of Mrs. Charlotte Charke*. She made a career of breeches and travesty roles, though she eventually took her cross-dressing off the stage, as well, an element of her life that may have contributed to the break with her family.[40] In Charke's memoir, breeches signify not only increased mobility and economic opportunity, but also sexual ambiguity. Charke authors herself by offering an authorized story of her life by her own "Female pen," and her autobiography becomes a specific performance of her gender, as well as her life. As Jade Higa notes, "Charke makes clear to her audience that she is aware of her own gender performance and introduces herself by provoking her audience to question her gender."[41] By contrast, Woffington, whose beauty and sexual charms were often an object of praise by her admirers, appears in various midcentury texts, but never in her own words. A range of stories circulated about her and her ability to seduce both male and female members of the audience during and after her lifetime. Some of these anecdotes appear in *The Life of Mr. James Quin, Comedian* and *An Historical View of the Irish Stage*.[42] Importantly, Woffington's celebrity was based in part on her appeal to the sexual desires of both men and women through her highly praised breeches roles. Woffington's appearances in breeches, often as a female soldier in epilogues, as well as her popularity *en cavalier*, reveals, according to Felicity Nussbaum, that, like Charke, "Woffington . . . created an ambiguously gendered persona . . . that promoted national loyalty but also implied a critique of that identity by exposing through sexual impersonation its constructed nature."[43] Thus, Charke and Woffington serve as case studies for understanding how cross-dressed actresses functioned as both popular commodities with salable bodies and figures that disturbed gender and sexual hierarchies on and off the stage.

Charlotte Charke, Gender Outlaw

Charlotte Charke, the youngest daughter of the well-known eighteenth-century actor-manager-playwright and poet laureate Colley Cibber, published her autobiography in 1755, in the wake of a rather public split between herself and her father.[44] *A Narrative of the Life of Mrs. Charlotte Charke* is both a memoir and a picaresque novel, and it has attracted much critical attention.[45] Charke's work poses many questions about her life and how to interpret it, as the memoir frequently jumps in chronology, rarely describes any other characters at length, and resists extended self-examination.[46] Even more ambiguous are Charke's bouts of cross-dressing, most of which we are only aware of after the fact, when she mentions that she was *en cavalier* during an episode in the text.[47] She is at times quite mysterious as to her motives for dressing in men's clothes, while at other times she states clearly that the clothes functioned as a disguise from her creditors. Men's clothing facilitates Charke's easy movement along London's streets and as a strolling player; the word "strolling" is particularly appropriate to Charke's story, as she very frequently traversed long distances on foot. *A Narrative of the Life of Mrs. Charlotte Charke* infrequently describes bodies and body parts; thus, the appearance of legs in the text

Portrait of Charlotte Charke (née Cibber), engraving after unknown artist. (© National Portrait Gallery, London)

is notable. In *A Narrative,* Charke's legs contribute to her attractiveness to other women while also serving as her primary mode of locomotion. She accesses male privilege by cross-dressing, even as she disavows this privilege by portraying herself as a struggling single mother and rejecting the power her appearance has on other women. The narrative of her life and adventures is additionally queer in its lack of continuity and lack of clarity, leaving open a space for the articulation of sapphic possibilities, while her life in men's clothes offstage and her donning the name "Mr. Brown" opens up the possibility of a trans reading of Charke. Crucial to each of these hermeneutics are her legs, vaunted appendages that channel masculinity and independence at once.

Charke begins her memoirs with an entertaining account of herself at four years old, attempting to ape her father. The various tales of her financial and health problems and the stories of her youthful frolics are in many ways an appeal to her father's sense of decency and his fonder memories of Charke as a child.[48] At the same time, the story of youthful cross-dressing is a popular trope in the narratives of female cross-dressers, positing cross-dressing as destiny, as in the narratives of the female pirates Mary Read and Anne Bonny, which I discuss in chapter 2. For Charke, this anecdote is explicitly a precursor to all her later "oddities," and she focuses on the clothes she needed to complete the outfit. Notably, "odd," "oddness," and "oddity" are words frequently associated with lesbians.[49]

An exact Representation of Mrs Charke Walking in the Ditch at Four Years of Age,
F. Garden, 1755. (© Trustees of the British Museum)

Charke's own characterization of her behavior as an "oddity" or a "freak" anticipates the characterization of Mrs. Freke in *Belinda*. Charke describes how she "paddled down Stairs, taking with me my Shoes, Stockings, and little Dimity Coat; which I artfully contrived to pin up, as well as I could, to supply the Want of a Pair of Breeches."[50] She also takes her father's wig and her brother's waistcoat and a large silver-hilted sword, foregrounding her desire to cross-dress as a desire to be like her father. She points out that "'twould be impossible for me to pass for Mr. *Cibber* in Girl's Shoes," and so she decides to march in a ditch, ostensibly to disguise her improper footwear.[51] Once discovered, she writes, "the Drollery of my Figure render'd it impossible . . . to be angry with me," and she is put on one of the footman's shoulders and taken indoors to be "forc'd into my proper Habiliments."[52] Charke's antics, portrayed for the reader as an explanation for her cross-dressing as an adult, cement the link between female cross-dressing and seduction; although she appears foolish, she is able to seduce others in men's clothes even as a child. By extension, she also seduces the reader: no one can resist her cross-dressed figure. Her freedom to act, stroll, and don men's clothes are emblematized by legs, which are explicitly the means for mobility and implicitly the means of seduction, whether playful or passionate. Charke's anecdote also underscores the gendered nature of legs and footwear.

When Charke is an adult, her legs figure in her relationships with various women in *A Narrative,* including her admiring audience at the theater. As an actress known for breeches parts and travesty roles, Charke shows her legs onstage, where her performance in drag elicits same-sex desires. In *A Narrative,* Charke gestures toward only a few of her many performances, including her travesty role as Captain Plume in *The Recruiting Officer.* At this time, Charke was performing sporadically in London while dodging her creditors. She notes, however, that "notwithstanding my Distresses, the want of Cloaths was not amongst the Number. I appeared as Mr. *Brown* . . . in a very genteel Manner; and, not making the least Discovery of my Sex by my Behaviour, ever endeavouring to keep up to the well-bred gentleman, I became . . . the unhappy Object of Love in a young Lady."[53] Charke appears to enjoy wearing men's clothes, as when she describes at length how at a young age she developed "a passionate fondness for a Perriwig."[54] Conversely, Charke refuses to use her disguise to swindle the women who fall for her. Her attractiveness in drag to other women is a theme that comes up several times in the memoir, reinforcing the notion that such occurrences were part of the genre of cross-dressing memoirs while also referring back to the possibility of sapphic desires and androgynous, gender-fluid, or transgender embodiment. Like other female cross-dressers discussed in chapter 1, Charke has her share of beards who desire her *en cavalier*. Charke's asseverations in the memoirs that she never took advantage of another woman's passion for her aligns her with the valorous cross-dressing soldiers Hannah Snell and Christian Davies, as discussed in chapters 1 and 2, and yet allows the readers of her autobiography to consider the attractions of a woman in men's clothing, as well as the performative nature of gender. Thus, the cross-dresser's legs become, like her face, markers of sexual and gender ambiguity, and yet legs thematize most clearly the many possibilities for freedom of move-ment that cross-dressing provided women of the past. In this way, texts that posit lack of beard, presence of breasts, or missing penis as hazards for cross-dressing women might be understood as conservative warnings to women against seeking such freedom. Legs, however, remind readers that such dire warnings can never truly hide the truth that cross-dressing allowed women certain freedoms, whose textual representations then, served as potent reminders of alternative possibilities for women, includ-ing sapphic and trans possibilities.

Despite Charke's protestations that she refused to use her cross-dressing specifically to facilitate same-sex desires, her *Narrative* depicts how cross-dressing elicits these desires, thus performing sapphic possibility textually. Charke represents herself in the narrative as a handsome young gentleman in men's clothes who is convincing enough to seduce a young lady, even if she also represents herself as uninterested in taking advantage of this seduction.[55] A young lady in particular who falls in love with Charke's male stage persona refuses to believe her when she learns from Charke herself that Charke is "not the Person she conceived me!"; the young lady "en-treated [Charke] not to urge a Falshood of that Nature, which she looked upon only as an Evasion, occasioned, she supposed, through a Dislike of her Person."[56] Significantly, Charke provides no other proof to the young lady of her own femaleness other than asserting she is the daughter of Colley Cibber. This explanation is apparently unconvincing: "Notwithstanding all my Arguments, she was hard to be brought into a Belief of what I told her; and conceived that I had taken a Dislike to her."[57] The young woman's persistence in refusing to believe Charke suggests the extent to which gender and desire are linked through heteronormative expectations of the time, yet it is also reminiscent of the other "beards" who fall in love so ardently and passionately with the female cross-dresser in story after story. As Kristina Straub notes, "While this process of denial and negation is surely self-protective, it also situates her [Charke's] encounters with other women somewhere between the commodifiable and recuperable ambiguity of the cross-dressing actress and the dangerous and marginalized transgressiveness of the female husband."[58] Charke, having written the autobiography in part as apologia and in part as a self-justification, cannot acknowledge openly the sapphic qualities of her appeal to women. At the same time, Charke's boasting of her ability to seduce young women impresses on the reader the skill with which she passes as a man but also the ease with which one might fall in love with another woman or, at least, with Charke herself. According to Brian Glover, "Despite her claims to have passed for 'Mr. Charles Brown,' it seems almost certain that people generally recognized her as in some sense a woman playing a man's role, rather than a man as such, if only because her face and body had become quite recognizable in London through her profession."[59] This argument reinforces the notion that Charke's appeal to other women is predicated on her ambiguous gendering in men's clothing. For Charke, men's clothing allows her greater movement but also engenders same-sex attraction. Her exposed legs, the most prominent feature of the cross-dressed actress, become part of her performance of male freedom as well as physical attractiveness, and increased mobility likewise provides greater opportunities for eliciting same-sex desires. Importantly, the admiration of her fan and her insistence that Charke is in fact a man makes her autobiography crucial to studies of butch masculinity, proto-lesbianism, and gender-fluid or nonbinary identities, as well as transgender identity.

These tensions are visible also in Charke's relationship with the woman she calls "Mrs. Brown." Aside from her theater admirers, Charke had a very close relationship with a fellow actress, a woman who figures in important moments in Charke's life in the autobiography and whose close relationship with Charke is instigated through an incident involving legs. It is unclear as to whether Charke had what we would today call a "lesbian" relationship with another woman; as discussed already, her representation of female same-sex desires and relationships in the autobiography is enigmatic.[60] Charke's relationship with "Mrs. Brown" is perhaps one of the most elusive relationships among the eighteenth-century tales of cross-dressing women as it functions only intermittently in the text, with Mrs. Brown herself residing primarily in the background of the story, a barely visible yet persistent shadow in the narrative. It is also, though, the most significant relationship Charke has in the autobiography, the descriptions of her relationships with men being very brief. For Emma Donoghue, the long-lasting relationship between Charke and her female companion, only ever referred to as Mrs. Brown, is "one of the fullest accounts of a long-term partnership between working women."[61] She points out that many previous analyses of Charke's life have glossed over this relationship, in part because Charke's references to it are "marked by so little gushy sentiment, so few elaborate declarations of fidelity, that it is possible for the heterocentric reader to miss the quiet documentation of love between women."[62] Catherine Craft-Fairchild corroborates this point of view when she writes that "complicating Charke's self-portrayal is the fact that, while she refers to Mrs. Brown using theatrical stereotypes, she also writes with the tenderness of a genuine spouse."[63] The close relationship of the women mirrors those tender relationships of other cross-dressing women and their beards, as Charke and Mrs. Brown are always of one mind. Although Charke's story does not detail sexual intimacies, physical intimacy between herself and Mrs. Brown are important elements of Charke's survival of the financial and emotional disasters in her life.

Significantly, Charke's first mention of Mrs. Brown involves baring of legs. The connection between the two women is often characterized in terms of the body, and their first meeting is mediated through legs. As Donoghue explains, "The *Narrative* mentions how a 'gentlewoman' and fellow actress whom Charlotte has known for years shows her kindly character one evening by lending her stockings to the lead actor, performing herself with a severe stoop in order to make sure her dress covers her bare legs; Charke is both amused and impressed."[64] Charke attributes this lady's lending her stockings to "an unprecedented Instance of even a Superfluity of good Nature."[65] She watches the lady in question stooping and bending over onstage, and she asks her how this came to be: "Presently the Royal Dame was obliged to descend from the Stage into the Dressing-Room, and made a Discovery, by the tossing up of her Hoop, of a Pair of naked Legs."[66] Charke is "angry and pleased" at the lady's show of good nature which also exposes her, literally, to "the Hazard she run of catching Cold."[67] For actresses and strolling players, health is wealth; Charke herself suffers bouts of illness and hoarseness that render her incapable of performing, throwing her again and again into poverty. Her concern for her friend's legs and her admiration of the lady's "humanity" converge in the moment at which legs are both real appendages and the tools of performance and profit. Thus, while Charke's well-turned legs are the means of channeling masculinity and masculine beauty, legs also function as markers of precarity for women—and actresses, in particular—the specter of illness and ill-health always dogging Charke and her fellow performers. By contrast, the moment when the skirts are lifted and the "naked Legs" are exposed to Charke in the dressing room echoes the functioning of the breast in chapter 2. In the stories of cross-dressing women such as Mary Read, Hannah Snell, and even Lady Delacour in *Belinda*, the baring of the breast functions to thematize "bosom friendship," but also to elicit sapphic desires. Similarly, Mrs. Brown's naked legs, which she must hide onstage even more stringently than stockinged legs, is the first allusion to the bodily closeness of Charke and Mrs. Brown. Mrs. Brown exposes her legs for Charke, and the reader is invited to look at these legs and to see the admiration of a fellow player, yet she is also privy to the tenderness of Charke's gaze, reinforcing the notion that cross-dressing actresses' bodies were consumed and desired by the female gaze. Thus, the moment of baring legs functions to link the women through their work onstage and the ethics of care among fellow female performers while suggestively inviting the sapphic gaze.

Charke, going by the name of Mr. Brown, and her friend, who adopts the name Mrs. Brown,[68] portrays their friendship in many adverse situations throughout the autobiography. Throughout the text, legs function as important appendages that cement the women's relationship.[69] The lengths to which the women will go for each other are literalized through the journeys they undertake across the countryside, often on foot. Mrs. Brown puts up with all of Charke's admitted faults and stays with her even in the direst of circumstances. When the two of them move to the harbor town of Pill, which Charke in retrospect deems akin to "the Anti-Chamber of that Abode we are admonish'd to avoid in the next Life," they run into serious financial trouble.[70] The ladies are forced to leave the town in disguise to pick up Mrs. Brown's inheritance, as the landlord believes they wish to escape paying the rent. As they are without "a single Groat," Charke and her "Fellow-Sufferer . . . set out, without either Hat or Money, fourscore Miles on Foot."[71] Charke's lack of hat and the necessity of walking are meant to indicate the direness of their circumstances. Later in the narrative, when Charke decides to visit her grown daughter, she and Mrs. Brown are forced again to travel as cheaply as possible: they travel in part on foot until they decide to "par[t] from our last Three Half-pence to ride five Miles in a Waggon, to the great Relief of our o'er-tired Legs."[72] She and her companion are linked by their travels and travails, which often take the form of moving on foot. Their shared journeys and distresses make them partners, and the corporeal aspect of their poverty is emblematized by their legs. The closeness of the relationship between these two women, which begins with a show of legs, continues in the text via legs, as well. Their tired legs emphasize their mobility as well as their close relationship, which remains strong despite Charke's ruinous financial decisions, indicating just one of the places in which sapphic possibilities are legible in the text. Importantly, though, this mobility and independence are rendered discursively different from that of female soldiers: Charke's autobiography reveals the brutal necessity of good health and a strong body for those of lesser means, exposing heteropatriarchal expectations of good health as necessarily classist and drawing attention to her own, dire circumstances as gender outlaw, disowned daughter, and actress.

For Charke, legs are clearly appendages of power, even as, at times, they function as the signifiers of her poverty. The mobility they provide and the passions they allude to become part of Charke's narrative performance that combines celebrity lineage, her stage persona, and performance of different family roles: daughter, mother, and partner to another woman. Her legs are one of the only body parts she discusses overtly in the narrative, and they are theatrical and performative, even as the appendages themselves function as body parts propelling Charke across the countryside, through the streets and theaters of London, and into the hearts of her audience. The legs are one of the main appendages linking Charke and Mrs. Brown; they are connected through exposed legs and tired legs, through sexual innuendo, and through the bonds of companionship and shared trials. Charke's decision to pose as Mr. Brown to her companion's Mrs. Brown emphasizes their partnership, however ambiguous, while their legs function metonymically as appendages of female desire, freedom, and companionship. Charke's appropriation of male accoutrements, such as breeches and stockings, in addition to the hats and periwigs she enjoys, signal her ability to channel male modes of bodily expression even as she uses them for seduction, female bonding, monetary gain, and increased mobility—not unlike other female cross-dressers, such as the female soldiers Hannah Snell and Christian Davies, the female husband Mary Hamilton, or the female pirates Anne Bonny and Mary Read. At the same time, Charke's autobiography potently alludes to the expectations for health and able-bodiedness to make one a success on the eighteenth-century stage.

Margaret "Peg" Woffington, Alluring Actress

While Charke's performance is self-consciously written by herself, Woffington's is described through the pens of others. Interestingly, Charke actually refers to Woffington in her memoir, writing, "Mrs. *Woffington* stands equally in the Rank of those, whose Merits must be sounded in the Song of grateful Praise, and many more of the generous Natives of *Ireland*."[73] Woffington was one of the most popular actresses in her time. She began acting at a young age in Dublin and was from the start considered a beauty. Like Charke, she became associated with breeches parts from the beginning of her career, making the roles of Sylvia in George

Farquhar's *The Recruiting Officer*, as well as the travesty role of Sir Harry Wildair in *The Constant Couple*, her own. It is for these roles, and that of Lady Townley in Colley Cibber's *The Provok'd Husband*, that she was best known. Offstage she was known for a lively love life that included a long-term relationship with the actor and theater manager David Garrick.[74] The unauthorized memoir of her life that surfaced soon after her death, a pamphlet entitled *Memoirs of the Celebrated Mrs. Woffington* (1760), focuses mainly on her various liaisons with other men, including several scenes of lovemaking.[75] Nussbaum characterizes *Memoirs* as "racy, anonymous, and largely apocryphal . . . which positioned her [Woffington] as an appealing and celebrated personage, but a whore nonetheless."[76] Woffington was also the subject of various poems and songs printed in newspapers after her performances, many of which indicate that, although she was

Mrs Margaret Woffington in the Character of Mrs Ford in the Merry Wives of Windsor, Edward Haytley, after John Faber Jr. (© National Portrait Gallery, London)

never linked with another woman romantically in her private life, many considered it plausible that women in the audience were swooning for Woffington's version of Wildair. In fact, Woffington's exposed legs are the appendages most associated with her powers of seduction. The ability of the cross-dressed actress's legs to seduce both male and female spectators marks the erotic power of legs and their potential for encouraging sapphic possibilities.

While many songs merely sung the praises of the beautiful "Peg," several focused on Woffington's ability to seduce both sexes via her cross-dressing, and one in particular, reprinted in Hitchcock's *An Historical View of the Irish Stage,* focuses on the beauty of her exposed legs. Hitchcock reports that in April 1740, Woffington appeared for the first time as Harry Wildair to great success in Dublin. The poem that appeared following the performance was titled, "On Miss Woffington's Playing Sir Harry Wildair":

> Peggy, the darling of the men,
> In Polly won each heart;[77]
> But now she captivates again,
> And all must feel the smart.
>
> Her charms resistless conquer all,
> *Both sexes* vanquished lie;
> And who to *Polly* scorn'd to fall,
> By *Wildair* ravish'd die.
>
> Wou'd lavish nature, who her gave
> This *double power* to please;
> In pity give, *both* to save,
> A *double* power to ease.[78]

The poem, like many that followed it, indicates the erotic quality of Woffington's appearance in breeches.[79] The sexual element of the poem is clear: the author relies on the language of seduction and battle to describe Woffington's powers of pleasing. Her "charms resistless conquer all," and both men and women "vanquished lie" as they are "ravish'd" and "die" by the power of her performance in breeches. The plea at the end that Nature provide a "double power to ease" suggests Woffington's own ability to

"The Female Volunteer; or, An Attempt to Make Our Men Stand," 1746. (University of Illinois Theatrical Print Collection, Rare Book and Manuscript Library University of Illinois, Urbana-Champaign, ID no. W844–29)

"please" both sexes and "ease" their desires in the bedroom. The poem implicates both men and women in Woffington's seductions onstage. Similarly, eighteenth-century stage commentators could not decide whether Woffington performed masculinity perfectly or her appeal stemmed from her ability to combine elements of both genders: "To stage a convincing man whether in breeches or travesty meant, for many viewers, that Woffington separated herself completely from the gestures associated with female form and persuasively affected the style and manners of a gentleman; for others it involved combining the sexes in a harmonious fashion."[80] She was so popular in breeches that she frequently performed epilogues in men's clothes, including one as "The Female Volunteer," the text of which explicitly shames men to volunteer as recruits for the British military, thus harnessing the desirable image of the female cross-dresser for imperial projects, as Scarlet Bowen has previously discussed.[81]

Woffington's appeal to women in men's clothes is evident in a popu-

lar anecdote from *The Life of Mr. James Quin, Comedian* in which Woffington, coming off the stage after a successful performance as Wildair,
purportedly says to Quin, "With no little triumph, 'Lord, I believe the
whole house think I am a man'—'By G-d, Madam,' says he, 'half the
house knows the contrary.'"[82] While the anecdote is likely apocryphal, its
popularity as a much-repeated story about Woffington argues for the attraction her performances had for both men and women, and the appeal
she had to both—while also perhaps making a dig at Woffington's well-
publicized sex life. Nussbaum states that this was "a much-repeated and
almost certainly apocryphal anecdote" about Woffington, and she notes
that "this teasing exchange clearly compromises Woffington's transvestite
achievement by denigrating her dramatic victory as a sexual come-on. The
anecdote erases her extraordinary acting talent to align the travesty role
with prostitution."[83] At the same time, it is unclear as to which half of
the house "knows" she is a woman; her popularity was well established,
and most people would have known she was female because her named
appeared on playbills and advertisements. This knowledge of Woffington's
femaleness suggests the pleasure that audiences gained from desiring the
cross-dressed actress without necessary subsuming the sapphic desires of
the women in the audience for Woffington, much in the way that Charke
represents herself and her appeal to her audiences in *A Narrative*. Further,
the anecdote and the song lyrics suggest the attraction of the *men* for
Woffington in men's clothes, and homoerotic tensions and female same-
sex desires overlay the heteronormative ones. Like Sarah Scott's Leonora
and Henry Fielding's Mary Hamilton, Woffington makes an excellent
"man" precisely because she is a woman: she combines the seductive powers of both to present an image of ambiguous gender that is attractive to
men *and* women. Further, her cross-audience appeal marks just one of
many moments in British theater history in which transgender embodiments and performances are cannibalized for mass-market appeal and
monetary gain.

The link between Woffington's cross-dressing and her appeal to both
men and women is therefore well established in the eighteenth-century
theater world, and her bared legs, whose gender is likewise ambiguous,

are constructed as part of this appeal. Another popular poem explicitly praises her exposed legs in a verse that also appeared after her first performance as Wildair:

> That excellent Peg
> Who showed such a leg
> When lately she dressed in men's clothes—
> A creature uncommon
> Who's both man and woman
> And the chief of the belles and the beaux.[84]

Woffington's bared legs seduce "the belles and the beaux," even as she herself is "chief" of them—both, that is, the best example of each. Other comments about her legs indicate some of the qualities that may have contributed to her popularity on the stage. In his description of Woffington onstage in breeches, Quin mentions that "she was so happily made, and there was such symmetry and proportion in her frame, that she would have borne the most critical examination of the nicest sculptor."[85] He goes on to compare her to Ned Kynaston and his successful impersonation of women on the Restoration stage, concluding that, with regard to Woffington, "It was a most nice point to decide between the gentleman and ladies, whether she was the finest woman, or the prettiest fellow."[86] The Victorian author and biographer Charles Reade echoes these sentiments in his nineteenth-century biography of the actress: "From her high instep to her polished forehead, all was symmetry. Her leg would have been a sculptor's glory; and the curve from her waist to her knee, was Hogarth's line itself."[87] Reade is likely rephrasing the praise of earlier biographers but ignoring the same-sex appeal and focusing instead on the appeal of women's legs to the male gaze and the representations of women's bodies in art. Importantly, however, these perfect legs are allowed to be exposed only through her performance as a man onstage; her legs, with their admirable symmetry and the "curve" of her thigh are sexualized female features that otherwise would be hidden and also highly reminiscent of seventeenth-century blazons. As noted earlier, the cross-dressing actress combines the sexual taboo of exposed women's legs with the expectation for "well-turned" aristocratic male legs in breeches that functioned as so

crucial to ideals of masculinity at the time. In this melding of expectations, the cross-dressing actress's body potently alludes to trans embodiment and the idea of "transitioning" that the trans scholar Jay Prosser
argues is so critical to transgender identity.[88] Woffington's transgender,
cross-gender appeal stems from a body that, while onstage, is perpetually
in transition, enticing the audience with the juxtapositioning of masculine and feminine qualities.

Cross-dressing onstage is one of the central sites through which women's
legs are exposed in this era, reminding us of the queerness inherent in
even the heterosexual male gaze that consumes the actress's legs onstage.
Pat Rogers comments that "the display of leg enhances the sexual display
of womanhood even as it pretends to mimic manhood."[89] Onstage, the
well-turned leg of the eighteenth-century gentleman becomes the sexualized female leg that is capable of seducing both "the belles and the beaux,"
as she is now "both man and woman." The leg seduces both genders even
as it belongs to either or both, and the cross-dressed actress's legs double
and triple the sexual possibilities in their appeal to both men and women.
The actress's legs elicit the sexual attraction of both, making them the in-
stigators to desire while also becoming the appendage onto which desires
are projected. The power of the sexualized leg is evident even in the texts
that celebrate Woffington's abilities to perform masculinity or androgyny.

Breeches parts and travesty roles complicate the actress's role on the
eighteenth-century stage, both literally and figuratively, as her body becomes exposed and fetishized as female, while it is evident that eighteenth-
century audiences also enjoyed the cross-gendered aspect of these performances. For Charke, cross-dressing onstage is only one aspect of her
cross-gender persona, which she uses to make money and to pose as a man,
work men's jobs, and take on a "wife." Even if Charke's sexuality is unclear,
her body, like Woffington's, elicits female same-sex desires for the readers
of her work while also building on female husband narratives that portray
women dressed as men as superior partners for other women. The ability
of the cross-dressed actress to seduce other women relies on her gender
ambiguity, which is emblematized by her legs, but also in part on the audience's knowledge that this is a woman in men's clothes. The actress's
body is both hidden and on display onstage, an object of scrutiny and

observation that illustrates sapphic possibilities as well as transgender embodiments, both functioning as consumable performances and therefore lucrative moneymakers.

Similarly, in novels from the end of the century, the body becomes a central object of observation, and the female cross-dresser's body in particular comes under heightened scrutiny. The increasing pressure on women to perform moral character through their bodies makes the exposure of the cross-dressed body not merely titillating, but dangerous to society, as the undisciplined body of one woman may influence that of another. The exposed legs of the cross-dresser, so often revered as seductive and clearly marked as necessary to accurately imitating maleness onstage, become one of the central appendages through which female same-sex desires are made visible in novels. The depiction of legs in Elizabeth Inchbald's *A Simple Story* and Maria Edgeworth's *Belinda* likewise illustrates the transgressive possibilities of these exposed body parts, as Miss Milner and Harriet Freke, respectively, come under censure for their exposed legs. The novels emphasize the sexual aspect of the legs and their ability to elicit and signify female same-sex desires, thus putting into question their admonition against female cross-dressing and female freedom.

Novel Legs in *A Simple Story* and *Belinda*

In a cursory reading, the novels *A Simple Story,* by Elizabeth Inchbald, and *Belinda,* by Maria Edgeworth, both appear to condemn gender ambiguity and female cross-dressing, deeming them inappropriate and unfeminine. Craft-Fairchild notes that novels across the eighteenth century frequently "punished" female characters who attempted to cross-dress: "If, by the turn of the century, theatre reviewers and biographers were somewhat hostile to the practice of cross-dressing both on and off the stage, novelists anticipated their hostility by several decades. . . . Socially ostracized or killed, these fictional characters met with a harsher fate than the living women they partially resembled."[90] However, a closer reading of the novels reveals a potent counternarrative to the obvious one of domestic hardship replaced by domestic harmony. The cross-dressing and gender ambiguities present in the novels disrupt the heterosexual couplings and posit sapphic possibilities—as we saw in my discussion of sapphic breasts in *Belinda* in chapter 2. The overwhelming critical attention that has focused exclusively on the relationships between Miss Milner and Lord Elmwood and Matilda and Lord Elmwood has obscured the importance of the female same-sex relationship that forms one of the central bonds of *A Simple Story*. The relationship of Miss Woodley and Miss Milner contains sapphic possibilities, as Miss Woodley loves and supports her friend, even bringing up her daughter Matilda and taking care of her after Miss Milner's death. The sapphic possibilities are most clearly articulated in one of the most dramatic moments of the novel, when the servants cannot determine the gender of Miss Milner's revealing masquerade costume. This event leads to an emotional break between Miss Milner and Lord Elmwood (one of several), but it also makes legible the ability of legs to serve as conduits for female same-sex desires. At the center of the controversy is the exposing and clothing of Miss Milner's legs: the length of Miss Milner's petticoat and the height of her boots. Her legs bear the brunt of her gender performance in this scene while also exposing female desires. Legs function similarly in *Belinda*, in which Mrs. Freke's transgressive, exposed legs are maimed at the end of the novel, in contrast with the breast that starts out maimed but is ultimately pronounced healthy (see chapter 2). Both novels construct female legs as signifiers of female freedom that lead to female desires.

Inchbald's *A Simple Story* is distinctive in its plot and characterization. It tells essentially two stories, separated from each other by fifteen years. The main character from the first section, the outspoken and worldly Miss Milner, dies half way through; in the plot she is replaced by her much tamer daughter, Matilda.[91] Several of the main characters—Sandford, Lord Elmwood, and Miss Woodley—are Catholics, like Inchbald herself, and their representation is sympathetic, especially in light of how Miss Milner's incomplete Protestant education compares to the other characters' Catholic values.[92] The novel also contains several elements that are common to other eighteenth-century novels: the theme of improper female education, a strong female friendship, and many representations of sentimental masculinity.[93] The first half of the novel recounts the tumultuous courtship of Miss Milner and her guardian Dorriforth, a priest, subsequently released from his vows and known as Lord Elmwood. Miss Milner is brought up in the Protestant faith of her mother, and the novel emphatically denounces her education at a Protestant boarding school as made up of "merely such sentiments of religion, as young ladies of fashion mostly imbibe. Her little heart employed in all the endless pursuits of personal accomplishments, had left her mind without one ornament."[94] *A Simple Story* returns to this theme of female education at the very end, when we learn that we have "beheld the pernicious effects of an improper education in the destiny which attended the unthinking Miss Milner."[95] Matilda, who is brought up "in the school of prudence—though of adversity," is a much better model of "a proper education."[96] But whether this "proper education" would be more to the benefit of society and men or the benefit of women themselves for their own happiness is left unclear, just as the moral at the end of *Belinda* is also ambiguous.[97] Miss Milner's cross-dressing masquerade costume functions as one of the critical moments in which her lack of proper education leads her to commit an impropriety in the eyes of her guardian. The bodily ambiguities of that scene complicate the novel's representation of gender roles and heterosexual desires while also highlighting the limited means that women such as Miss Milner had for asserting their independence.

Like *Belinda*, *A Simple Story* makes a complex argument against the restriction of female independence while criticizing the social pressures that enforce and police these restrictions.[98] In *Masquerade and Civilization*, Terry Castle argues forcefully for a proto-feminist standpoint in the novel, pointing out that in almost every instance "the heroine's desires repeatedly triumph over masculine prerogative; familial, religious, and psychic patterns of male domination collapse in the face of her persistent will to liberty."[99] Although Patricia Meyers Spacks and Catherine Craft-Fairchild have challenged this triumphant reading of the novel, they acknowledge that its representations of women at the mercy of patriarchal values implies a critique of those values.[100] In fact, Craft-Fairchild argues that *A Simple Story* has subversive power in its ability to portray thwarted female desires and "intense female suffering."[101] The text speaks through "silences and gaps" to critique "destructive male authority and pathological female submission."[102] Despite struggling against his various dictates, the incorrigible Miss Milner marries Lord Elmwood, only to eventually betray him and die prematurely, leaving her daughter to fulfill the role of passive female sufferer and heal the wound between herself and her father. The first half of the novel explores the willful female rebellion of Miss Milner, yet even as the novel appears to cast Miss Milner's stubbornness negatively, the masquerade scene situates this stubbornness as an outgrowth of the limitations of women in the late eighteenth century. More interestingly, the scene offers a possibility for Miss Milner beyond the dyad of rebellion and punishment: sapphic possibility.

Miss Milner's attendance at a masquerade—and her exposed legs in the masquerade costume—offers a critical moment in the text for examining the struggle between masculine and feminine prerogatives, specifically through the transgendering of Miss Milner's masquerade costume. Her desire to attend the masquerade provokes an argument with Lord Elmwood, to whom she is, at this point, informally engaged. Elmwood sees the masquerade as an improper place for any person of virtue, while Miss Milner views it as a pleasant entertainment, in addition to providing an opportunity for testing Lord Elmwood's affection. When Miss Milner insists on attending the masquerade, her companion Miss Woodley reminds her of Lord Elmwood's disapproval. Miss Milner responds to her friend, "As my guardian, I certainly did obey him; and I could obey him as a husband; but as a lover, I will not."[103] Unknown to her—despite Lord Elmwood's initial forbearance—Lord Elmwood, with Sandford's advice, also decides to put Miss Milner to the test. He tells Sandford, "My own judgment shall be the judge, and in a few months, marry, or—*banish me from her for ever*."[104] The situation illustrates the limited power Miss Milner has over her intended while underscoring the patriarchal power that Lord Elmwood wields and the very real repercussions this power has for the women of the household. Amy Pawl reads this moment as crucial to the development of the *bildungsroman* narrative of the novel, arguing that this scene "demonstrates both the sexual license associated with masquerades and Miss Milner's willingness to invoke her own sexuality now that she is an adult woman and not a ward."[105] The masquerade ball becomes the defining moment in the power struggle between Lord Elmwood and Miss

Milner as she calls on the transgressive power of dress to articulate her desires for freedom and independence, to challenge the notion of femaleness as a congenital disability—and yet this moment of gender fluidity also opens up the possibility of reading same-sex desire between women, thus exposing another layer of sexual and emotional independence.[106]

In the eyes of the household, in addition to her poor choice of attending the masquerade in the first place, Miss Milner commits a further indiscretion through her choice of masquerade costume. Although she jokes to Sandford and Lord Elmwood that she will go in the habit of a nun, in the end she chooses to go in the guise of Diana, the goddess of chastity.[107] The amount of leg showing in the costume, as well as Miss Milner's buskins (half-boots) is enough to make the gender of the costume confusing, in effect transing Miss Milner's gender, however momentarily. For Miss Woodley, the buskins and shortened petticoat imply indiscretion and a lack of virtue. For the footman who helps Miss Milner into her chair for the evening's entertainment, they define a male costume. When questioned by Sandford and Lord Elmwood, the footman replies, "She was in men's cloaths."[108] By contrast, Miss Milner's maid replies that Miss Milner "went in her own dress," and, when questioned about the gender to which the clothes belong, she begins to laugh and says, "A woman's dress to be sure, my lord."[109] Exasperated by the lack of coherence in these two accounts, Sandford has the footman and serving woman confront each other. When they disagree, Sandford starts to ask more pointed questions:

> "Had she on, or had she not on, a coat?" asked Sandford.
>
> "Yes, sir, a petticoat," replied the woman.
>
> "Do *you* say she had on a petticoat?" said Sandford to the man.
>
> "I can't answer exactly for that," replied he, "But I know she had boots on."
>
> "They were not boots," replied the maid, with vehemence, "indeed, sir . . .
> they were only half boots."
>
> "My girl," said Sandford, kindly to her, "your own evidence convicts
> her.—What has a woman to do with *any* boots?"[110]

For Sandford, it is evident that any kind of boots are inappropriate for women. In *Dress in Eighteenth-Century Europe, 1715–1789*, Aileen Ribeiro notes that around the midcentury, boots were a common article of clothing for peasant women.[111] By the 1780s, however, half-boots had become fashionable among upper-class women in London: "Boots were the fashionable walking footwear and the *Ipswich Journal* (1786) noticed that 'The ladies begin to wear morocco half-boots and Hussar riding habits.'"[112] However, Ribeiro emphasizes that not everyone approved of the move toward masculine looks in women's fashions: "To many people. . . . the new liberty given to women by their adoption of masculine clothes caused a freedom of gait that the more conservative . . . found at best unappealing and at worst potentially immoral."[113] Thus, while she does not cross-dress explicitly as a man, like the female soldier Hannah Snell or Edgeworth's Harriet Freke, Miss Milner wears an ambiguous costume that is well within the realm of cross-gender representation. The expanse of legs open to view—legs whose upper parts lead directly to the female genitals—is sexually suggestive for a woman, even as the costume itself appears masculine. The exposure of the legs and the half-boots simultaneously channel an image of the eighteenth-century male figure and of female indiscretion and desires. Further, the presence of coat versus petticoat is significant to defining the gender of one's clothes and, by extension, one's gender performance. The petticoat is ambiguous in Miss Milner's costume, thus rendering her without a clear gender.

Beyond this, Miss Milner's donning of her costume is the scene of one of the clearest moments of sexual desire between women in the novel. The only person whose reaction is laudatory is Miss Woodley's. Miss Woodley is a woman of "thirty, and in person exceedingly plain, yet she possessed such an extreme cheerfulness of temper . . . that she escaped not only ridicule, but even the appellation of an old maid."[114] Significantly, Dorriforth (Lord Elmwood) is also "about thirty" when Mr. Milner dies and leaves him in charge of his daughter.[115] Like Miss Woodley, he is not obviously handsome; he is described as having "not one feature to excite admiration," but "he possessed notwithstanding such a gleam of sensibility diffused over each, that many people mistook his face for handsome, and all were more or less attracted by it."[116] While his physical features appear more pleasing than Miss Woodley's, the two characters mirror each other, despite their obvious differences. The same age, inhabitants of the same home, they are both tied to Miss Milner by emotional bonds. Even their names—Woodley and Elmwood—contain the same word, "wood," while Miss Milner's name alludes to the mill where wood is processed. Neither Elmwood nor Woodley can escape the power Miss Milner exerts on them, as destructive as it is. While Lord Elmwood embodies the strict father-figure, Miss Woodley channels the trope of the indulgent mother. By the same token, both appear as convincing lovers to Miss Milner. Miss Woodley's admiration of Miss Milner in the masquerade scene illustrates the sapphic possibility between them. To my knowledge, there have been no previous studies done of the sapphic possibilities in *A Simple Story,* and very little criticism discusses the relationship of Miss Milner and Miss Woodley at any length. If Miss Woodley is discussed, it is with regard to her prohibition against Miss Milner's loving Dorriforth while he is still bound to his priestly duties. Mary Anne Schofield notes, "It is Miss Woodley (another woman) who is able to unmask her [Miss Milner] and who discovers an extraordinarily mature and sophisticated woman underneath the ingénue."[117] However, Schofield goes on to say that "both Woodley and Dorriforth force Miss Milner to mask; like the controlling feminine ideologies, they must keep the woman in her place and that means she must be disguised."[118] Here I propose a new way of reading Miss Woodley and her important role in the novel.

Miss Woodley is Miss Milner's constant companion, a woman who tries to see only the good in Lord Elmwood's ward. In this way, she embodies the elements of both a mother and a lover to Miss Milner. As the theme of incestuous passions resurfaces in the novel several times, it is not surprising that Miss Milner's relationship to Miss Woodley carries similar resonance—however, the maternal role is only one facet of her relationship with the younger Miss Milner.[119] Miss Woodley admires and loves Miss Milner, she attempts to protect her, but in the masquerade scene, she abandons logic in favor of desire. Miss Milner's decision to go to the masquerade as Diana emphasizes her desire for freedom and the pursuit of pleasure. Castle points out that "Diana also symbolizes autonomous female sexuality—a sexuality without reference to men or male authority. More than Aphrodite, whose charm across the epochs depends upon a world of masculine desire, the 'Goddess of Chastity' personifies utopian femininity."[120] Importantly, Diana refuses the companionship of men, making this costume suggestively sapphic. Further, Miss Woodley's reaction to this costume is overwhelmingly positive, even as she knows that the men of the house will disapprove. As she enters the dressing room, she sees Miss Milner "and [is] struck with astonishment at the elegance of the habit, and the beautiful effect it had upon her graceful person," even though she is "astonished at [Miss Milner's] venturing on such a character—for it was the representative of the goddess of Chastity, yet from the buskins, and the petticoat made to festoon far above the ankle, it had, on the first glance, the appearance of a female much less virtuous."[121] Miss Woodley attempts to be the voice of reason, reminding Miss Milner, "[Your guardian] has desired you not [to go]—and you used always to obey his commands," she cannot help but "admir[e] the dress" even as she "object[s] to it; but as she admired first, her objections after had no weight."[122] Miss Woodley is in the privileged position throughout the novel of being allowed behind closed doors with the beautiful and youthful Miss Milner—just as Belinda has greater access to Lady Delacour and her body than Lady Delacour's own husband in Edgeworth's novel. Miss Woodley's flattery and her participation in the masquerade "without reluctance" as "a wood-nymph" very clearly align her not only on Miss Milner's "side," but also on the side of same-sex desires and bonds.[123] The choice of Diana and wood nymph also connects Miss Milner and Miss Woodley to nature, in opposition to the culture and social customs embodied by Sandford and Lord Elmwood. It is her eye that surveys Miss Milner in the guise of Diana; like Diana, who would allow only other women around her, so Miss Woodley is of the privileged gender in this scene.[124] As a "wood nymph," Miss Woodley is cast as Miss Milner's follower and admirer.

The masquerade scene establishes the importance of the legs as a sexualized and gendered body part, but it also alludes to sexual transgression and sapphic possibilities. Castle remarks that "Miss Milner's costume is at once ambiguously sexual and sexually ambiguous."[125] The gender-ambiguity, its nonbinary nature, is part of what makes the costume so objectionable in the eyes of Sandford and Lord Elmwood. Conversely, the ambiguity and the bodily exposure of the legs of this costume are precisely what make Miss Milner so attractive to the gaze of Miss Woodley. Although Miss Woodley expresses strict disapproval when Miss Milner exposes her feelings for Lord Elmwood while he is still "Dorriforth" and under religious orders, this is one of the only instances in which Miss Woodley treats Miss Milner with anything less than tenderness and indulgence. The two women are constant companions—or "bosom friends," to use the language of *Belinda*—and Miss Milner's revelation to Miss Woodley binds the two women together more closely than before. Miss Milner's marriage and later expulsion from the marital home as Lady Elmwood do not end her relationship with Miss Woodley, either. When, as Lady Elmwood, Miss Milner leaves her home for a "most dreary retreat," she refuses all company "but the still unremitting friendship of Miss Woodley."[126] For the next fifteen years, the two of them live together, bringing up Lord and Lady Elmwood's daughter, Matilda.[127] While other critics have read Miss Milner's acquiescence to patriarchal regulation and a silence bordering on the abject after her marriage to Lord Elmwood (Dorriforth) negatively, I propose that her relationship with Miss Woodley is a strong, dedicated one full of sapphic possibilities.[128] Their relationship spans the entire novel, visible even in the love Miss Woodley bears Miss Milner's daughter, Matilda, but these possibilities appear the most clearly as erotic in the moment when Miss Woodley admires her friend's exposed legs. She admires her friend even as she acknowledges the transgression against patriarchal norms that the costume suggests, accepting this transgression and even serving as "nymph" to Miss Milner's Diana. The transgressive legs of the ambiguously gendered costume elicit sapphic desires just as the legs of actresses—like Charke's, Woffington's, or even Inchbald's—do on (and off) the stage. Inchbald herself performed breeches roles onstage, and the masquerade incident in the novel was considered by some to be inspired by her own life. According to James Boaden's *Memoirs of Mrs. Inchbald* (1833), "As a frolic, she, who had acted Bellario on the public stage, as every other fine woman in the profession had done, probably appeared there [at a masquerade] in the male habit; for she was outrageously assailed on this subject, and charged with having captivated the affections of sundry witless admirers of her own sex."[129] Boaden's comments echo the comments made about Woffington and her appeal to women—though how "witless" they are of the cross-dressing actress's true gender is debatable. Yet again we see how transgender and nonbinary forms of gender performance put gender binaries into question and open up opportunities for reading sapphic possibilities.

In *Belinda*, Harriet Freke's legs are also at the center of debates over female power and acquiescence. Mrs. Freke and Lady Delacour are linked through (bosom) friendship, cross-dressing, the wounded breast, and Belinda, as I discuss at length in chapter 2. The sapphic possibilities produced through these interrelationships and exposed through the breast are further solidified through the legs. Mrs. Freke's transgressive legs are wounded, perhaps even mangled, toward the end of the novel, just as Lady Delacour learns that she is not really dying from breast cancer. Earlier in the novel, however, Lady Delacour's own leg is hurt: when her carriage overturns, she twists her ankle. Wounded legs signify a curtailing of mobility while also figuratively disabling the transgressive appendage of power. In *Belinda*, as in *A Simple Story*, this normative reading of legs is challenged by the body logic of the novel. The legs come to figure as appendages whose power and ability can make female desires legible through increased female mobility, as they also function in the autobiography of Charlotte Charke. At the same time, wounded legs, fatigue, and debilitating illnesses surface in all three of these texts as the disabling power of heteropatriarchy exerts itself to curtail these women's desires or economic possibilities. Sociosexual heteronormative hierarchies intersect in these texts in ways that urge the reader to understand that cross-dressing is effective for gaining feminine independence only as long as the cross-dresser is healthy and strong in body and minded—that is, able-bodied and able-minded. These texts thus critique the emphasis on able-bodiedness in the second half of the eighteenth century and tie it directly to critiques of heterocisnormativity and patriarchal power structures.

For Mrs. Freke, cross-dressing is an activity through which she shocks those around her while also facilitating easy movement between places and milieux. She mentions in passing to Lady Delacour that she used her disguise to enter the House of Commons, thus asserting masculine prerogative. She also encourages such unfeminine behavior in others. Belinda learns from the Percivals that Mrs. Freke's new friend Miss Moreton has been "persuaded by Mrs Freke to lay aside her half boots, and to equip herself in men's whole boots; and thus she rode about the country, to the amazement of all the world."[130] As in *A Simple Story,* the innocent Miss Moreton's wearing of men's boots exposes her to social disapproval, just as half-boots do for Miss Milner. Miss Moreton's appropriation of men's boots aligns her with all the dangerous sapphic intentions of Mrs. Freke, to say nothing of her gender non-normativity. Mrs. Freke's cross-dressing explicitly combines the two meanings of exposed legs: the pursuit of mobility and independence and the pursuit of sapphic desires and liaisons. Mrs. Freke's legs are so dangerous that they must be wounded at the end of the novel, and she is told by the doctors that she may never again be able to cross-dress as a result of the damage done to her legs.

Mrs. Freke's legs are most visible in the novel when they are caught in the gardener's trap at the home of Lord and Lady Delacour. Her leg, caught in the trap, is "much cut and bruised," and she complains of intense pain and lack of mobility. She asks "how long it was probable, that she should be confined by this accident; and she grew quite outrageous when it was hinted, that the beauty of her legs would be spoiled, and that she would never more be able to appear to advantage in man's apparel."[131] Mrs. Freke's legs and their connection to male prerogatives, masculine beauty, and mobility imply that she is metaphorically castrated and rendered powerless. The doctor's pronouncement that Mrs. Freke's legs will no longer "appear to advantage" in men's clothes, however, attempts to curtail only one of the transgressive possibilities of the legs—the sexual, not the mobile. From one perspective, it may seem that this mangling will forever end Mrs. Freke's ability to seduce other women with her legs; given her betrayal of Lady Delacour before the start of the novel, however, this mangling may be Mrs. Freke's punishment for deserting her bosom friend and betraying their sapphic bond.[132] The mangling of her legs at just the moment that Lady Delacour's breast is declared healthy further marks Mrs. Freke's legs as implicated in the novel's sapphic love triangle among these two formerly bosom friends and Belinda. Legs draw our attention to the sapphic possibilities of the novel; Lady Delacour's sprained ankle cements her love of Belinda, while Mrs. Freke's legs are punished for the wound she inflicts on Lady Delacour's heart. The reason for Mrs. Freke's spying on Lady Delacour is to ascertain whether she has a new male lover, suggesting jealousy on Mrs. Freke's part. Thus, the novel offers an economy of body parts in which the wounded legs function as symbolic of female desires, as the doctor's pronouncement emphasizes the seductive potential of exposed legs while leaving open the possibility of wearing men's clothes for other reasons, such as mobility, comfort, protection, or independence. *Belinda*, like *A Simple Story*, plays with gender binaries while subtly critiquing ableist and heterosexist discourses that can imagine only one possible outcome for these women: chastisement and a return to the safety of the domestic scene and cisgendered heterosexuality. Like the false tableau that ends the novel, which I discuss in chapter 2, Mrs. Freke's wounded legs are a sexual red herring, for we know by now in *Belinda* that the pronouncements of doctors can be wrong; that men's clothing is more than simply about "appearing to advantage"; and, most important, that wounds between women can heal and become stronger.

In *Belinda* and *A Simple Story*, legs, like the breast, symbolize female power and connections between women. Like breasts, legs are suggestive and sexual; the exposed leg signals desire for mobility and independence through transgender embodiments while also engendering and displaying same-sex desires. By contrast, though, the legs are explicitly rendered as body parts written about and used to perform for others. Men's legs and the female cross-dresser's legs are public appendages whose gender play and desirability bring sapphic desires into the public sphere for public consumption. While many scholars have discussed the importance of gesture and the body in eighteenth-century novels, it is necessary to go beyond the idea of gesture to fully understand the represented body in these works. Juliet McMaster, writing of gesture in *A Simple Story*, argues that "it seems the passion of the soul must be communicated to the limbs, so that the limbs can deliver back the signal the soul needs in order to take cognizance of its own passion. These are the necessary negotiations between consciousness and the unconscious, as the eighteenth century typically presented them."[133] But it is not usually legs that gesture; the gesturing is left to the hands. Legs, however, can still seduce, as we have seen in these two novels, connecting women together through the promise of shared female independence—and shared desires and companionship. Legs elicit and reveal other's desires; displaying her legs in breeches, the cross-dressed woman accesses male privileges, including the ability to seduce other women who then become her metaphorical beards. The legs of Mrs. Freke and Miss Milner come to symbolize the independence these women desire while also revealing to readers the titillating possibilities of sapphic connections mediated through a well-turned leg.

In eighteenth-century England, visible legs were associated with masculine appearance and dress. Yet male legs were often explicitly sexualized, especially those of macaronis and fops, as well as those of some women, for whom exposed legs were often equated with sex work and moral laxity. The difference between what was acceptable onstage compared with offstage points to the ambivalent attitude that eighteenth-century society had toward the practice of female cross-dressing—thus, "Gender-changing play had become a part of the culture [onstage]," and "women impersonating men proved an erotic attraction because they could show their legs and figures in ways that ordinary women could not."[134] The ability of women to show their legs onstage indicates that, to eighteenth-century audiences, the elements of performance and pleasure both had to be present for cross-dressing to be accepted. The tenuous social acceptance of this practice is evident when we consider how actresses were often praised for their performances in male parts and, like Woffington, even lauded for their ability to perform maleness, yet actresses' portraitists often depicted them from the waist up, cutting off the transgressive legs.[135] The mediation of actresses' bodies via art divulges, as close readings of actress memoirs do, that women's legs had a powerful erotic potential in the eighteenth century.

The legs of the female cross-dresser draw on this erotic potential, even as they confound any simple reading of it. The legs of actresses become a site for reading male and female, and heterosexual and homosexual desires, as well as transgender and nonbinary embodiments. In the novels, the exposed legs of cross-dressed women symbolize female independence, in terms of both freedom of movement and the appropriation of masculine prerogatives, while also questioning women's ability to truly hold on to this independence for any length of time. Like the legs of actresses, the legs of the female cross-dressing characters in *A Simple Story* and *Belinda* become the appendages through which same-sex desires are represented and mediated. The female cross-dresser's body, always marked as feminine even as it performs the masculine, disrupts boundaries of gender and sexuality, and the legs more than any other part explicitly suggest a body in transition or that is gender-fluid. The legs link women together through various desires—desire for mobility, desire for power, and desire for one another—while wounded, exhausted, or mangled legs focus readers' attention on the ways that independence is predicated on gender, social position, and physical and emotional strength.[136] As Lennard Davis notes, in the eighteenth century, "Virtually no major protagonist in a novel . . . is in some way physically marked with a disability," yet the stories of cross-dressing women often represent characters such as Lady Delacour, who suffers from a breast wound, or Charlotte Charke, whose fatigue and exhaustion are linked to her poverty and who survive and thrive due to the same-sex relationships they cultivate.[137]

The actress who performs in breeches exposes her legs to solicit male and female desires as a means to greater financial gain, and the appeal to both sexes—or even the possibility of same-sex desire—inherent to her transgender performance is a marker of the female cross-dresser's erotic power. Novels such as *Belinda* and *A Simple Story* punish their cross-dressers, though whether this punishment is a critique of how heteropatriarchy effectively disables women physically, emotionally, and financially or a critique of the cross-dresser herself is likewise ambiguous. The ambiguity of legs also reminds us that body parts are desirable not necessarily because of the gender to which they belong; thus, legs thematize the ambiguousness of gender and the desirability of trans bodies that we saw in earlier chapters. Even so, these texts emphasize the femaleness of the cross-dresser, creating a moment in which readers and spectators are invited to consider the power and pleasure of sapphic possibilities.

CODA

▸◂

FUTURE CROSSINGS

At the Battle of Pondicherry in 1748, the brave female soldier Hannah Snell sustains a dangerous groin wound, whose treatment by a surgeon would surely lead to the revelation that she is a woman. Determined not to allow this discovery to come to pass, Snell extracts the bullet herself. Readers learn the groin wound is so painful that Snell even considers divulging her secret to the surgeons; however, "She resolved to run all Risques, even at the hazard of Life, rather than that her Sex should be known. Confirmed in this Resolution, she communicated her Design to a black Woman, who attended upon her."[1] With the help of the "black woman," Snell is able to procure bandages and salves that allow her to extract the bullet on her own. She affirms her masculine valor through this brave act, even as she is forced to this dire resort as a passing woman. The episode functions to reaffirm Snell's courage and physical stamina, resourcefulness, and fearlessness, yet it is impossible to ignore the imperial values inherent in the situation. The Battle of Pondicherry was, after all, a battle between the British and the French for control of an Indian port city and, therefore, a site through which the imperial contest for power played out. European invaders and colonizers sought to keep and maintain power over a subjugated terrain and claim primacy for themselves. Snell's story of unexpected martial heroism in a woman plays out explicitly against this backdrop.

The appearance of the nonwhite woman who helps Snell survive seems at first nothing but a *deus ex machina* contrivance through which to save her from having to reveal her gender to male surgeons. Examined more closely, however, we see that this nonwhite person, whether ethnically Indian or African is unclear, serves as a willing accessory to Snell's passing. The description of this moment finds Snell enmeshed within imperial and patriarchal vectors of power that have everything to do with race and nationality. Snell "communicated her Design to a black Woman, who attended upon her, and could get at the Surgeons Medicines. . . . But not withstanding she [Snell] discovered her Pain and Resolution to this Black, yet she did not let her know that she was a Woman. The black readily came, and afforded her all the Assistance she could."[2] The nonwhite woman appears only too happy to serve this wounded British soldier, whom we assume to be white. This nonwhite woman "readily came" and gave "Assistance" and yet, this woman (apparently) never learns that Snell "was a woman." Scarlett Bowen has already persuasively argued that the valorous female soldier "possesses her own brand of female masculinity that she uses in order to cajole other male characters in the memoirs into being 'real men'" for the purposes of recruitment to the imperial army and navy.[3] Bowen's argument, as well as the arguments of Dianne Dugaw and Julie Wheelwright, highlights just how often the stories of female soldiers were co-opted for projects of nation building and imperialism. But Snell's valorous female masculinity, situated within constructions of race and nationality but also imbued with sapphic possibilities, plays with sexuality and sexual desires between women, as we have already seen. Snell's previous interactions with women, such as her beards in Lisbon, Portugal, and Portsmouth, England, suggest that these femme women are more than simply "helpers" in keeping Snell's sex a secret; they fulfill complex roles within the text that potently suggest to readers the importance of same-sex relationships. Significantly, though, there is no wooing of the "black" woman—or, at least, none that is explicitly alluded to by the narrator. According to him, Snell needs this woman only for her ability to procure materials and medicine. She functions as a subordinate, a servant, an objectified accessory to Snell's passing, and as a willing accomplice to the imperial project, thus legitimizing the narrative's role within eighteenth-century imperial discourses.

What does it mean, though, to read such a scene or person queerly while also paying close attention to imperial histories and nationalist representations? Histories of sexuality and postcolonial readings of the eighteenth century have often been mutually exclusive. Scholarship by Srinivas Aravamudan, Declan Kavanagh, Greta LaFleur, Sasha Turner, Kathleen Wilson, and others have begun to change the conversation, but much remains to be done. My project here only briefly touches on how constructions of whiteness and racial purity haunt the stories of cross-dressing women and gendered embodiments. Like the unidentified black woman who obligingly assists Snell in her cross-dressing project and quickly fades into the background, issues of racial difference arise in these narratives sporadically but persistently. As I discussed in chapter 2, Mary Read's breasts are legible as "feminine" in large part due to their whiteness, a color signifier that registers as part of the rise of racial categories predicated on skin color. In the case of Read and Bonny, sapphic possibilities are based on bodily ideals of whiteness, a concept that is problematically present in many cross-dressing texts. The cross-dresser and her beards are consistently marked as European and implicitly, by extension, white. Beyond this limitation, the cross-dresser at times also has encounters with nonwhite characters that are, at the very least, problematic, if not overtly racist. For example, Mrs. Freke's feud with Juba, a black servant of Mr. Vincent in *Belinda,* as well as the stereotyped representation of Mr. Vincent himself as a lethargic West Indian creole, implicate Maria Edgeworth's cross-dressing characters by association in current debates about slavery. And while the 1801 edition of Edgeworth's novel contains a mixed-race wedding between Juba and an Englishwoman, this relationship is erased from later editions. Thus, while narratives of female cross-dressing have already been actively read and discussed with an eye to nationality and national pride, issues of race remain to be discussed in more depth and attention as to how such readings connect to sexual orientation, desires, and embodiments. On the surface, at least, sapphic possibilities appear to be predicated on whiteness and Europeanness—an issue of representation that persists in popular culture representations of lesbians and lesbian desire in the twenty-first century.

At the same time, though, I would argue that these texts offer fascinating depths that we have not yet fully explored when it comes to the crossing of critical race studies and queer studies of eighteenth-century texts.

For example, an imaginative queer reading of the scene in which Hannah Snell asks for salves and assistance in extracting the bullet from her groin wound might encompass the other woman somehow helping in this procedure. The narrator of *The Female Soldier* presents Snell as being in a difficult condition with a very serious wound: she "probed the Wound with her Finger till she came where the Ball lay, and then upon feeling it, thrust in both her Finger and Thumb, and pulled it out. This was a very rough Way of proceeding with ones own Flesh; but of two Evils, as she thought, this was the least."[4] The phrase "a rough Way of proceeding with . . . Flesh" is suggestive, while the presence of the other woman draws our attention to a queer moment in the text, grounded in our earlier readings of Snell's wooing of various women during her travels. Like the women who flirt with Snell in Portugal and aid her in her passing, this "black woman" functions as a beard: a helpmeet to her project of passing. The parallels between these "femme" women allow for reading sapphic possibilities as one woman helps another keep her gender concealed. According to the text, Snell remains undiscovered as a woman due to her desire for female self-preservation against male aggression, as well as male-coded valor and resourcefulness. Although Snell does not court this woman as she does the European women in her story, she is still somehow able to induce this woman to help her. Such a reading that goes against the grain—or reads aslant, as Sarah Ahmed suggests—might figure moments of resistance to imperial and racial hierarchies, ever so subtly challenging the limits of race, gender, and sexuality.[5]

How might we understand other texts in which gender, sexuality, and race cross and recross one another? Aphra Behn's *The Widow Ranter* (1689) and Frances Burney's *The Wanderer* (1814) are useful bookends to this project and jumping-off points for additional consideration. In *The Widow Ranter,* the Widow, an Englishwoman, and Semernia, the Indian Queen, both dress in men's clothes to suit their needs and desires, yet the Widow prospers and finds love while Semernia's disguise brings about her death. In both cases, the women use men's clothing to facilitate covert relationships with men, rather than women, with the Widow's story echoing that of Viola in *Twelfth Night*. The queer courtship that ensues between the Widow and Daring while the Widow masquerades in men's clothes is complete when Daring acknowledges the Widow's ability to be a good wife to a soldier through her own display of masculine bravado that functions as a comic counterpoint to Semernia's tragic love story. Here, female masculinity functions to seduce a man, discursively a part of a long-standing tradition of cross-dressing to pursue heterosexual liaisons, but also implicitly underscoring the importance of national and racial continuity and homogeneity. By contrast, the tragic story of Semernia and Bacon suggests the oddity or "queerness" of the imperial project and how a romance that crosses national and racial lines leads to insubordination, rebellion, and martyr-like death. Behn's play provides an early example of onstage female cross-dressing that actively separates the fate of white women in the transatlantic world from those of nonwhite women, gesturing toward the same racial hierarchies that make Mary Read's white breasts legible as both feminine and desirable in this same transatlantic context while offering also the opportunity to read queer desires and transgender embodiments as explicit outcomes of the imperial project.

Coming at the other end of the long eighteenth century, Frances Burney's last novel begins with a fraught English Channel crossing during the French Revolution made by an incognita heroine, Juliet Granville, who disguises herself through brownface make up. She later comes to be the companion, dependent, and romantic rival of Elinor Joddrel, who in a crucial moment of the novel dresses as a man and attempts to stab herself in the breast during a public concert. Burney's novel capitalizes on earlier tropes of gender and racial crossing, deploying them in unexpected ways. Juliet's use of brownface marks her as Other, relying on racialized markers of Otherness in ways that undoubtedly make contemporary readers uncomfortable—and may have made early nineteenth-century readers uncomfortable, as well, though for different reasons. By contrast, Elinor as antagonist uses gender crossing to make her unrequited love for Harleigh and jealousy of Juliet visible to the public in an astonishing and shocking scene. Her love for, and desire for, Harleigh are excessive, however, and the Sedgwickian triangle formed by her, Juliet, and Harleigh is in no way satisfactorily resolved by the marriage of Juliet and Harleigh. As Margaret Anne Doody explains, "Burney gives us the 'happy ending' of course, but not until after she has made sure that we see it is just a formality, and by no means a solution."[6] Elinor's and Juliet's cross-dressing thus draw on eighteenth-century modes for expressing gender subversion and female courage while overlaying these notions with nascent nineteenth-century ideas about gender and racial Otherness. The ending that posits a return to safe and happy heterosexual domestic harmony that is somehow inadequate echoes the end of *Belinda* and the tableau that overtly positions heterosexuality as "just for show." Reading across texts that were informed by the stories and narratives of cross-dressing women highlights how authors and thinkers grappled with categories of gender, race, and sexuality that they found insufficient to their understanding of the world—and yet through which they always somehow structure their creative works. From one perspective, it may seem that Burney's novel reflects the increasingly negative social attitudes toward female cross-dressing off stage while implicitly condoning Juliet's use of racial crossing. In this way, the novel participates in a pattern in many eighteenth-century texts that give white women, and white women only, the opportunity to experiment with gender and sexual crossing. But what other perspectives might be found for reading cross-dressing in the novel? If moments of cross-dressing function as sites through which to explore same-sex desires, then how does *The Wanderer* fit into that pattern of representation? It is my hope that this book will open up such texts and encourage such questions for further commentary and interpretation in scholarship that considers gender crossing, racial passing, as well as queer desires.

In addition to crossing categories of being and Otherness, this book urges us to consider crossing time periods and national boundaries. The project has focused on the British context primarily, but also draws on Italian, transatlantic, and Irish histories of cross-dressing. But to look at such representations is, to an extent, to work in a vacuum. The stories of German, French, Spanish, American, Caribbean, and other cross-dressers inevitably were translated into English and circulated around Europe, and the translation histories alone deserve far more attention than they have been given.[7] Beyond this, it is worth considering how representations of the female cross-dresser mutated and developed when crossing the Atlantic and into the American context. The story of Deborah Sampson, which

Greta LaFleur analyzes so carefully in *The Natural History of Sexuality in North America,* deserves a second look for just how complex her representation really is. Cross-dressing women are not easily recuperable as feminist icons when we study their stories cautiously and with an eye toward categories of Otherness—even as these women's stories did, indeed, inspire future feminists, as well as lesbian, bisexual, and trans activists. The story of Christian Davies, for example, was retold and reprinted with illustrations throughout the nineteenth century, and the English suffragist and actress Cicely Hamilton dressed as Christian Davies for women's suffrage marches in the early twentieth century. Thus, the image of the martial woman was co-opted for women's rights, and her history of involvement in questionable world conflicts and imperial projects, to say nothing of her self-interested seduction of other women, is erased by the image of a courageous and strong woman holding a gun.

How do these stories collect and accrue meaning, and what does it mean to excavate their origins, tease out new understandings, and cross through time to look at their representations? What can we learn from how these women's legends changed, grew, and eventually diminished? Why have some of these women, such as the pirate Anne Bonny, the American Revolutionary soldier Deborah Sampson, or the surgeon James Barry, née Margaret Ann Bulkley, resurfaced? At the moment of this writing, Anne Lister is at the top of the list of gender-bending historical celebrities, and her home, Shibden Hall, is experiencing record numbers of tourists who wish to visit her home after watching the HBO miniseries about her life, *Gentleman Jack* (2019). Many viewers have also expressed outrage at the portrayal of Lister as an upper-class landowner Tory with little sympathy for her renters and a preternatural enthusiasm for exploiting the coal on her land. Beyond these issues, as I note in the introduction, the debate continues to rage as to whether we should consider Lister a (butch) lesbian, a trans person, gender-nonbinary, gender-fluid, or some combination of these, and whether the women who loved her were themselves lesbians, straight, or bisexual. The same questions could be posed about many of the women I write about in this project. While the debates continue and LGBTQ rights are still being brokered, questioned, or denied, the cultural capital of such texts continues to rise. Our personal investments often

Christian Davies reimagined for the nineteenth-century reader as "Christiana Davies," from *World of Wonders: A Record of Things Wonderful in Nature, Science, and Art,* 1873, page 9. (Wellcome Collection; Creative Commons Attribution 4.0 International License)

play out in our critical ones, and histories of sexuality and queer studies in academia are often connected to personal identifications as much as to institutional politics. To look at the female cross-dresser as a transhistorical figure is not to lose sight of her cultural meaning in the eighteenth century but, rather, as I hope I have shown here, to understand the many different possibilities of understanding her both then and now and to understand embodied histories of gender and sexuality as crucial to understanding these representations.

In many ways, the female cross-dresser can be understood as an artifact of embodied gender—a figure whose presence invites speculation about her body and how that body expresses, directs, and suggests possibilities for touch, desire, attraction, and sex. The cross-dresser engages in both passing as a man and performing masculinity, and these texts are fascinated explicitly by how such modes of being interfere with how we tend to view the world. Beyond passing and performance, though, the cross-dresser represents a mode of living within a body that has meaning beyond the performative. The transgender studies scholar Gayle Salamon argues that "the perceptual truth of the body is not necessarily what we see, and the traditional binary of sexual difference might have less purchase on the body's truth than other ways of apprehending lived reality."[8] The female cross-dresser illustrates these failures of perception and their effects on lived reality, figuring moments in which readers and "beards" can enjoy the cross-dresser's body from outside the confines of gender binaries. For Salamon, "The desire that houses itself in my body becomes my body itself. . . . If I can be said to have desire, this is only so to the extent that I find it as my body."[9] Desires and bodies need not have a gender to manifest, and Salamon's notion of transposition suggests a very personal, embodied form of desire, one that might, perhaps, challenge the primacy not only of gender and sexual hierarchies, but also of nationalist, imperialist, and capitalist hierarchies of desire and capital. Even as the cross-dresser is drafted for projects of nation building, her body and the desires of other women directed toward the cross-dresser, their moments of shared intimacy, may offer possibilities for disrupting such hegemonic histories. I imagine here future projects that build on this work to more fully consider how such disruptions play out in other texts and in new configurations.

Throughout this project, I have endeavored to demonstrate the crucial role that cross-dressing narratives played in the eighteenth-century imaginary and how the portrayals of queer desires and trans bodies are inextricably a part of eighteenth-century discussions about what constitutes masculinity, whiteness, heterosexuality, and disability, as well as how these categories are at different times mutually constitutive of one another. If, indeed, it is the function of histories of sexuality to bring to light the way our world today and in the past is structured through desire, bodies, and orientations, then this work intends to add to that discussion—but also to point out where we have yet to go. Histories of sexuality have yet to fully grapple with the haunting of texts by imperial, racial, and disabled Others, just as studies of gender outlaws such as Snell also potently suggest transhistorical concepts of lesbian, bisexual, and transgendered embodiments and the ways in which those embodiments attract and fascinate the rest of us.

NOTES

Introduction

1. Fielding, *The Female Husband and Other Writings*.
2. Garber, *Vested Interests*, 11.
3. Several scholars have argued that without concrete evidence of sex between the cross-dresser and her female admirers, it is difficult to argue for a lesbian identity. Such observations occur in Bullough and Bullough, *Cross Dressing, Sex, and Gender;* Dekker and van de Pol, *The Tradition of Female Transvestism in Early Modern Europe;* Faderman, *Surpassing the Love of Men*. Many other scholars have argued persuasively that descriptions of sexual intimacy need not be the benchmark for locating female intimacies and same-sex desires between women. Notable examples include Castle, *The Apparitional Lesbian;* Donoghue, *Passions between Women;* Lanser, *The Sexuality of History;* Traub, *The Renaissance of Lesbianism in Early Modern England*.
4. Braunschneider, "Acting the Lover," 214. See also Dugaw, *Warrior Women and Popular Balladry;* Friedli, "Passing Women"; Straub, *Sexual Suspects*.
5. For a closer reading of the "femme" women in eighteenth-century representations of sapphism, see O'Driscoll, "The Lesbian and the Passionless Woman."
6. Thomas Laqueur's work established and described the movement from a one-sex to a two-sex model of sexual difference in the eighteenth century, but his arguments have been complicated and challenged by a number of other scholars, including Karen Harvey and Susan Lanser: see Laqueur, *Making Sex;* Harvey, *Reading Sex in the Eighteenth Century;* Lanser, *The Sexuality of History*.
7. Much criticism on the female cross-dresser has followed this division. See Binhammer, "The 'Singular Propensity' of Sensibility's Extremities"; Braunschneider, "Acting the Lover."
8. Moore, *Dangerous Intimacies*, 3.
9. Lanser, *The Sexuality of History*, 39.
10. Ibid., 162.
11. Traub, *Thinking Sex with the Early Moderns*, 4.
12. Lanser, *The Sexuality of History*, 16.
13. Dinshaw, *How Soon Is Now?* 4.

14. Fradenburg and Freccero, "Introduction," xxvii.
15. Vicinus, *Intimate Friends,* 176.
16. Stryker, *Transgender History,* 1.
17. Stryker, "Foreword," xii.
18. Zigarovich, "Introduction," 7.
19. LaFleur, *The Natural History of Sexuality in Early America,* 141.
20. Saxton et al., "Teaching Eighteenth-Century Literature in a Transgendered Classroom."
21. Ibid., 168.
22. Marshall, "Beyond Queer Gothic," 27.
23. Butler, *Undoing Gender,* 43.
24. Garber, *Vested Interests,* 11.
25. Brideoake, *The Ladies of Llangollen,* xix.
26. Ibid.
27. Debates as to whether Anne Lister should be considered a trans person, gender nonconforming, or a butch lesbian have received increasing attention in the media since the filming of the show and the decision by the city of York to post a blue plaque about Lister in the city. Caroline Gonda presented on this issue in the session "Crisis of Queer Identities," International Society for Eighteenth-Century Studies Congress, Edinburgh, July 2019, and Chris Roulston presented on Anne Lister and transgender identification in the session "Transgender Studies and the Eighteenth Century," Annual Meeting of the American Society for Eighteenth-Century Studies. Los Angeles, 2015.
28. Fradenburg and Freccero, "Introduction," xvii–xix.
29. See Foucault, *The History of Sexuality.*
30. Goldberg and Menon, "Queering History," 1609.
31. Kavanagh, *Effeminate Years,* xxi–xxii.
32. Klein and Kugler, "Introduction to 'Eighteenth-Century Camp,'" 4.
33. Traub, "The New Unhistoricism in Queer Studies," 35.
34. Roulston, "New Approaches to the Queer 18th Century," 765–66.
35. The cross-dressing actress Charlotte Charke herself uses this term "to pass" in her autobiography in reference to a childhood exploit wherein she dressed in her father's clothing so as to "pass for him": Charke, *A Narrative of the Life of Mrs. Charlotte Charke,* 11. The use of "pass" in this way was not unusual in the eighteenth century, although the more racialized meaning of the term was not yet developed.
36. *The Female Soldier,* 7.
37. Fielding, *The Female Husband and Other Writings,* 33.
38. *The Female Soldier,* 19.
39. Fielding, *The Female Husband and Other Writings,* 47.
40. Ibid., 49.
41. Ahmed, *Queer Phenomenology,* 96.
42. Catherine Craft-Fairchild has argued that the stories of female warriors were considered in a much more positive light than the cross-dressing characters in novels: see Craft-Fairchild, "Cross-Dressing and the Novel."
43. Dianne Dugaw notes that Hannah Snell's story was published in two different for-

mats, the larger and more expensive of which suggests a wealthier readership. The extended length of the second printing further suggests an attempt to "novelize" Snell's experiences to an extent: see Dugaw, "Introduction [*The Female Soldier*]."

44. Butler, *Gender Trouble*, 187.

45. Traub, *The Renaissance of Lesbianism in Early Modern England*, 359. I am grateful to Kristina Straub for her suggestion that I consider Traub's concept for this project.

46. Ibid.

47. Ibid.

48. Nestle, "The Femme Question," 143. I am grateful to Kristina Straub yet again for pointing me to such an important text in the study of lesbian identity and desire.

49. Ibid., 138.

50. Nestle, "Flamboyance and Fortitude," 15–16.

51. Traub, *The Renaissance of Lesbianism in Early Modern England*, 358.

52. Rich, "Compulsory Heterosexuality and Lesbian Existence."

53. See, e.g., Brideoake, *The Ladies of Llangollen*; Marcus, *Between Women*; Rohy, *Impossible Women*; Vicinus, *Intimate Friends*.

1. Eighteenth-Century Female Cross-Dressers and Their Beards

1. Early modern narratives about intersex people (then called "hermaphrodites") often "explained away" a young woman's desire for another woman by having her suddenly become male. For more on this, see Laqueur, *Making Sex*.

2. *The Female Soldier*, 19.

3. Scott, *A Journey through Every Stage of Life*, 20.

4. Defoe, *Moll Flanders*, 281.

5. The slang definition of "beard" in the *Oxford English Dictionary* (listed as part of American slang, specifically) is "a person who pretends publicly to be involved in a heterosexual relationship with a homosexual person in order to help to conceal that person's homosexuality." The earliest published example provided by the *OED* is from the 1970s.

6. Valerie Traub has suggested the notion of a "cycle of salience" in which certain terms and phrases that show up in sexual discourse but with changing meanings reveal "recurrent explanatory logics [that] seem to underlie the organization, and reorganization, of erotic life": Traub, *The Renaissance of Lesbianism in Early Modern England*, 359. "Beard" is one of these terms that functions differently in different times but is almost always connected to notions of sexuality and gender difference.

7. For more on the discursive legibility of sapphism and same-sex desires in the eighteenth century, see Donoghue, *Passions between Women*; Lanser, *The Sexuality of History*; Moore, *Dangerous Intimacies*.

8. For a closer reading of the "femme" women in eighteenth-century representations of sapphism, see O'Driscoll, "The Lesbian and the Passionless Woman."

9. Braunschneider, "Acting the Lover," 220.

10. Dugaw, "Introduction [*Memoirs of Scandalous Women*]", 1–4.

11. O'Driscoll, "The Pirate's Breasts," 360.

12. Perry, "Colonizing the Breast," 210.

13. Lanser, *The Sexuality of History*, 39.

14. Craft-Fairchild, "Cross-Dressing and the Novel," 171. Fraser Easton notes that, although cross-dressing was not uncommon for plebeian women, at the same time they "were caught up . . . with both shifting notions of lesbian identity and the paternalistic regulation of women's work and sexuality": Easton, "Gender's Two Bodies," 132.

15. In addition, all of these pamphlets were republished throughout the century and into the nineteenth century, often in expanded versions with illustrations. The cost of such more expensive editions suggests that they were intended for a more genteel audience. For more information, see Baker, "Henry Fielding's *The Female Husband*"; Dugaw, "Introduction [*The Female Soldier*]."

16. Easton, "Covering Sexual Disguise," 98.

17. In the same article, Easton discusses the circulation and readership of the main eighteenth-century newspapers that published the stories of plebeian female cross-dressers: ibid.

18. O'Driscoll, "A Crisis of Femininity," 47.

19. In this approach, I am inspired in part by Lisa Moore's treatment of novels in *Dangerous Intimacies* She writes, "These readings [of novels] explore the textual and cultural unconscious of the novels discussed; their unintentional effects, excesses, and contradictions; their moments of ironic loss of control; and their resistances to their own conventions of realist representation and formal closure": Moore, *Dangerous Intimacies*, 20.

20. Fisher, "The Renaissance Beard," 156–57.

21. Fisher characterizes the beard as a prosthetic marker of sex and argues that facial hair must be accounted for when discussing the gendered body—something, he notes, that is missing in Thomas Laqueur's historical study: see ibid., 166; Laqueur, *Making Sex*.

22. Johnson, "Bearded Women in Early Modern England,"1.

23. Senelick, *The Changing Room*, 139.

24. Withey, "Shaving and Masculinity in Eighteenth-Century Britain," 226. Ann Charles and Roger DeAnfrasio note that facial hair regained its popularity in England starting in the 1830s: Charles and DeAnfrasio, *The History of Hair*, 155. However, as Wendy Cooper writes, some forms of facial hair were always present among military men: Cooper, *Hair*, 43. This is a significant point for me with regard to Hannah Snell, as I discuss later. Similarly, although, as William Andrews points out in his 1904 treatise on "hirsute history," the Van Dyke beard resurged in popularity at the time of the Restoration, "it did not remain popular for any length of time, the razor everywhere keeping down its growth": Andrews, *At the Sign of the Barber's Pole*, 47.

25. See, e.g., Jonathan Richardson's portrait of Pope, circa 1736; Swift's portrait by Charles Jervas, circa 1718; Johnson's portrait by Sir Joshua Reynolds, circa 1756–57; Richardson's portrait by Joseph Highmore, circa 1747; King George I's portrait from the studio of Sir Godfrey Kneller, 1714; King George II's portrait from the studio of Charles Jervas, circa 1727; and King George III's portrait from the studio of Alan Ramsey, 1761–62.

26. Fisher, "The Renaissance Beard," is an excellent source for information on the popularity of the beard in the early modern period and includes several illustrations.

27. "Richard Corson, in his monumental *Fashions in Hair,* emphasizes—perhaps too broadly, but significantly—that the eighteenth century is 'one of the few times in history that almost total beardlessness was ever practiced'": Rosenthal, "Raising Hair," 2.

28. Military men were urged to keep shaving as frequently as possible, and they often paid as much attention to their appearance as civilians. The artist's beard is thought to have started with the French portraitist Jean-Étienne Liotard, who not only grew and wore a long beard for significant periods of his life but also painted himself bearded (see *Self-Portrait with Beard,* circa 1749, Musée d'Art et d'Histoire, Geneva). Julianna Bark notes that "Liotard's beard often caused a stir and sometimes drew the artist negative publicity during his career": Bark, "The Spectacular Self," 2. Reginald Reynolds suggest that Liotard "was perhaps the originator of the Artist's Beard as a distinctive part of a uniform still observable": Reynolds, *Beards,* 249.

29. Although it might be relevant to note that Henry VIII and Elizabeth I also levied beard taxes.

30. Schiebinger, *Nature's Body,* 125.

31. Rosenthal, "Raising Hair," 3.

32. Withey, "Shaving and Masculinity in Eighteenth-Century Britain," 229.

33. Rosenthal, "Raising Hair," 2.

34. Schiebinger, *Nature's Body,* 120.

35. According to Schiebinger, "By the middle of the eighteenth century, however, a number of natural historians took the absence of a beard in native American males to be a sign that they belonged to a lower class of humans; some even argued that this absence of hair follicles on the chin proved them a separate species": ibid., 123.

36. Ibid., 125.

37. For more on the cultural significance of hair, shaving, and wigs in the eighteenth century, see *Eighteenth-Century Studies* 38, no. 1 (2004), a special issue on hair.

38. Kavanagh, *Effeminate Years,* xii.

39. Harvey, *Reading Sex in the Eighteenth Century,* 96.

40. Ibid.

41. Ibid.

42. Ibid., 150.

43. In the Middle Ages, many stories circulated of female saints who miraculously grew beards to avoid marriage, the beard being one of the simplest ways for women to disguise themselves and their beauty. Bullough and Bullough describe some of these stories, including the case of Paula of Avila, who "implored Jesus to disfigure her. She immediately grew a beard, and her suitor passed by without noticing her": Bullough and Bullough, *Cross Dressing, Sex, and Gender,* 55. A female facial beard functions as "disfigurement" in this case; it confers male power but also eradicates the threat of male attraction. Laurence Senelick notes that in many early European folk cultures, "The capture or taming of the wild (or hairy or green) man was an important feature of European folk festivals . . . and would seem an obvious trope for the progress of civilization." Similarly, there also existed "the aggressive figure of the wild woman who lurks beneath women's skirts, a phantasm of deranged male appetite": Senelick, *The Changing Room,* 163. Hairiness in these earlier times was always connected to

baser instincts, sexual appetites, or, in the case of female saints, to patriarchal power and male attributes.

44. Johnson provides an example of this phenomenon in the painting *Magdalena Ventura with Her Husband and Son,* by Jusepe de Ribera, 1631: see Johnson, "Bearded Women in Early Modern England."

45. Ibid., 2.

46. Quoted in Schiebinger, *Nature's Body,* 125.

47. "Beards even lent dignity to certain animals in the eighteenth century. The Scottish Lord Monboddo reported that the 'barris' (probably an orangutan) husbanded a long white beard. Monboddo went so far as to attribute to these apes the wisdom associated with the philosopher's beard, stating that they excelled in judgment and intelligence": ibid., 121–22.

48. "Beards were associated with catamenia in the minds of eighteenth-century natural historians through the outmoded, though still influential, theory of humors which taught that, in men, vital heat processed excess bodily fluids into sweat, semen, and beards (beard growth resulting from the reabsorbed semen) and, in women, into catamenia (which explained the hair that sometimes appeared after menopause)": ibid., 124–25.

49. At the other side of the spectrum of androgynous beauty in the eighteenth century was the castrato singer whose voice, "lacking exact gender colouration, was widely praised for its seraphic enchantment" and whose appearance contained an "erotic charisma of the androgynous": Senelick, *The Changing Room,* 195–96. The castrato, like the cross-dressed actress, came under increasing attack as the century wore on, indicating the increasing transgressive quality of gender ambiguity.

50. Friedli, "Passing Women," 250.

51. Straub, *Sexual Suspects,* 129.

52. Garber, *Vested Interests,* 11.

53. Butler, *Gender Trouble,* 187.

54. See, e.g., Andrews, *At the Sign of the Barber's Pole,* 47. Similarly, Charles and DeAnfrasio note that "beards were out [in the eighteenth century, and] shaving was in": Charles and DeAnfrasio, *The History of Hair,* 113. See also Alun Withey's more recent article on shaving, which discusses the "gentlemanliness" of shaving in the eighteenth century and the material history of razor technology in this time period: Withey, "Shaving and Masculinity in Eighteenth-Century Britain."

55. Dulaure, *Pogonologia,* 52.

56. Ibid.

57. Reynolds, *Beards,* 221.

58. Dugaw points that the more commonly found version is the shorter one, with forty-six original pages. The longer, illustrated version was printed the same year, but with expanded descriptions of Snell's adventures and illustrations that would have made it more novelistic, more expensive, and hence less available to the working classes: Dugaw, "Introduction [*The Female Soldier*]," v. For more on Snell's narratives, see Bowen, *The Politics of Custom in Eighteenth-Century British Fiction;* Braunschneider, "Acting the Lover"; Easton, "Gender's Two Bodies"; Locke and Worrall, "Cross-Dressed Per-

formance at the Theatrical Margins." See also Dugaw, "Introduction [*Memoirs of Scandalous Women*]; Dugaw, *Warrior Women and Popular Balladry*.

59. *The Female Soldier*, 17–18.
60. Scott's Leonora also goes on to cross-dress as a foreign artist and as a schoolmaster. It is as a clergyman, however, that her feminine appearance garners the most attention in the narrative. For more on Scott's novel, see Gonda, "The Odd Women," 111–26.
61. Scott, *A Journey through Every Stage of Life*, 15. This particular element of the novel's plot is reminiscent of Samuel Richardson's novel *Clarissa* (1748).
62. *The Female Soldier*, 19.
63. Ibid., 20.
64. Scott, *A Journey through Every Stage of Life*, 18.
65. Dugaw, *Warrior Women and Popular Balladry*, 149.
66. Interestingly, Louisa's face is made more feminine as part of the disguise. Louisa uses rouge to add "by Art a Colour to her Cheeks which even in Health Nature had denied her": Scott, *A Journey through Every Stage of Life*, 18.
67. Ibid., 20.
68. It is noteworthy that Snell is judged too feminine by other men, whereas Leonora is judged too feminine by older women who, themselves, are physically bearded. The ability to grow a beard oneself, not necessarily one's gender, draws these characters' attention to the cross-dresser's comparative lack of beard.
69. Scott, *A Journey through Every Stage of Life*, 20.
70. *The Female Soldier*, 19–20.
71. Scott, *A Journey through Every Stage of Life*, 20.
72. The question of whether women do or do not desire men with beards appears in other novels in the eighteenth century. Fielding's *Tom Jones*, for example, suggests that Bridget Allworthy desires Captain Blifil because her desires are more mature, and she is therefore more able to accept a heavily bearded, masculine man like him: see Fielding, *Tom Jones*, chap. 11. The chapter is titled, "Containing Many Rules, and Some Examples, Concerning Falling in Love: Descriptions of Beauty, and Other More Prudential Inducements to Matrimony."
73. Easton notes that for most of the eighteenth century, there was a distinction between working-class women who cross-dressed for mobility and work and those who cross-dressed to pursue other women. "Women warriors, like the majority of passing-women workers, were generally viewed as properly subordinate and industrious individuals, and were well tolerated," Easton writes, "whereas female husbands were seen as loose and disorderly, and were ostracized and sometimes criminalized": Easton, "Gender's Two Bodies," 133. The article argues, however, that such distinctions are less significant when considering the way that both kinds of cross-dressers manage to attract other women not as an archetypal plot device but, rather, through the specifics of her body and its textual mutability.
74. For more on this, see Castle, "Matters Not Fit to Be Mentioned."
75. Fielding, *The Female Husband and Other Writings*, 29.
76. Ibid., 33.
77. Ibid., 35–36.

78. Ibid., 42.
79. Ibid., 38.
80. Ibid.
81. Scott, *A Journey through Every Stage of Life*, 21.
82. For more on beards and maturity, see Fisher, "The Renaissance Beard."
83. Scott, *A Journey through Every Stage of Life*, 20–21.
84. Fielding's story and the stories of Hannah Snell and Leonora posit a type of "female masculinity," as described by Jack Halberstam, that is both feminine *and* masculine and capable of attracting other women. Halberstam's term suggests a way of understanding the contributions that women throughout history have made to the Western conception of masculinity, as well as, specifically, queer interventions into masculinity. "A sustained examination of female masculinity can make crucial interventions within gender studies . . . [and] queer studies": Halberstam, *Female Masculinity*, 2.
85. The author of *The Female Soldier*, in emphasizing Snell's virtue and honor as a woman, may have been reacting to the representations of less virtuous passing women, such as Mary Hamilton in *The Female Husband* (published only four years before *The Female Soldier*) or the representations of the female pirates Anne Bonny and Mary Read in Captain Charles Johnson's *A General History of the Robberies and Murders of the Most Notorious Pyrates* (once attributed to Daniel Defoe, but that attribution has come under scrutiny).
86. *The Female Soldier*, 28.
87. For differing notions of intimacy between women in the eighteenth century, see Moore, *Dangerous Intimacies;* Wahl, *Invisible Relations.*
88. Scott, *A Journey through Every Stage of Life*, 26.
89. Braunschneider notes that in the stories of passing women, it is a common trope for other women to fall passionately in love with the cross-dresser, to the point that readers may come to expect such a plot twist. She writes, "The consistency with which these texts turn to narratives of courtship or erotic mistaken-identity plots leads readers to expect such plots whenever we encounter a female character who dons men's clothing": Braunschneider, "Acting the Lover," 214.
90. Scott, *A Journey through Every Stage of Life*, 21.
91. Fielding, *The Female Husband and Other Writings*, 42.
92. Ibid., 47.
93. Ibid., 48.
94. Ibid., 50.
95. Ibid., 49.
96. Sally O'Driscoll situates *The Female Husband* as part of a short-lived trend in the mid-eighteenth century in which dildos were portrayed as morally transgressive usurpations of masculine prerogative rather than as instruments of pleasure: see O'Driscoll, "A Crisis of Femininity." I would argue that the two ideas are intimately connected, and both are apparent in Fielding's narrative of Mary Hamilton. For more on the dildo and the cross-dresser, see chapter 3.
97. Castle, "Matters Not Fit to Be Mentioned," 604.
98. For a detailed discussion of the publication history of this text, see Dugaw, "Introduction [*Memoirs of Scandalous Women*]."

99. *The Life and Adventures of Mrs. Christian Davies,* 36.

100. Ibid., 36–37.

101. Ibid., 27.

102. Ibid.

103. Ibid.

104. Dugaw, "Introduction [*Memoirs of Scandalous Women*]," 4.

105. Many scholars have written about Charlotte Charke's autobiography and its representation of Charke's identity, especially Charke's vacillation between traditionally "masculine" qualities of independence and forthrightness and her more stereotypically "feminine" qualities of virtue and daughterly affection. The porousness of her narrative and its contradictory representations leaves ample room for reading cross-gender performances and same-sex desire.

106. I discuss Charke's relationship with the mysterious Mrs. Brown more extensively in chapter 4.

107. Charke, *A Narrative of the Life of Mrs. Charlotte Charke,* 56.

108. Ibid., 27–28.

109. Lanser, *The Sexuality of History,* 252.

110. Braunschneider, "Acting the Lover," 224.

111. Traub, "Afterword," 293.

112. Donoghue, *Passions between Women,* 108.

2. Sapphic Breasts and Bosom Friends

1. *The Female Soldier,* 34.

2. See Perry, "Colonizing the Breast."

3. Angela Rosenthal notes that, at this time, "not only could hair, by virtue of its fashioning, mark (or dangerously blur) the seemingly natural differences between the sexes, but it also was perceived as registering ethnic divides, separating the controlled hair of the 'superior' European from, on the one hand, the alleged unkempt hairiness of Africans, or, on the other hand, the 'beardless' men of the Americas and Asia": Rosenthal, "Raising Hair," 2.

4. See Rediker, "Liberty beneath the Jolly Roger"; Yalom, *A History of the Breast.* The ideal of the exposed breasts of liberty, epitomized in Eugène Delacroix's painting *Le 28 juillet: La Liberté guidant le peuple (July 28: Liberty Leading the People),* suggests how the female breast became transformed from an embodied marker of sex or even a sexualized appendage of pleasure into a rhetorical marker of liberty and freedom, completing the transformation of the breast from a private body part to a fetishized marker of national sentiment and nativist ideals.

5. Even within her own discussion of breastfeeding mothers of the Napoleonic era and the fashion for loose, uncorseted breasts and gauzy dresses, Yalom concludes that, while "the breasts had been separated during the Renaissance into two groups, one for nursing, the other for sexual gratification[, they] were now reunited into one multipurpose bosom. Lactating breasts had become sexy": Yalom, *A History of the Breast,* 120. Gillray satirizes both the fashion for loose, gauzy dresses for women at the end of the century and the fashion for all women to breastfeed their children in

the cartoon "A Fashionable Mama; or, The Convenience of Modern Dress" (1796). The cartoon represents a very fashionable lady dressed as though she is about to go to an evening ball while her maid holds a child to her breast to suckle.

6. Simon Richter critiques the notion that the sexual breast was colonized completely and turned into a maternal breast, as "certainly eros is involved even in the biological constructions of sexuality, as it undoubtedly is in the construction of motherhood and the maternal breast. How can we possibly keep separate the erotic voyeurism of the male gaze . . . the many fantasies, male and female, private and collective, relating to the breast?": Richter, "Wet-Nursing, Onanism and the Breast in Eighteenth-Century Germany," 4. Richter also challenges the notion that breastfeeding is exclusively the domain of women, alluding to male lactation, which also suggests a one-sex model understanding of sex and gender.

7. O'Driscoll, "The Pirate's Breasts," 368.

8. See Fildes, *Breasts, Bottles, and Babies;* Schiebinger, *Nature's Body;* Warner, *Monuments and Maidens;* Yalom, *A History of the Breast.*

9. Schiebinger points out that Linnaeus had a variety of other words he could use to name our particular class of animals, yet he chose to focus on the breast, despite the fact that "the *mammae* are 'functional' in only half of this group of animals (the females)": Shiebinger, *Nature's Body,* 41. She focuses on this fact as the jumping-off point for a discussion of the gender politics inherent in Linnaeus's classification and what it meant for the cultural significance of the breast.

10. Yalom argues that "a virulent outcry against wet nursing began to be heard through-out Europe in the mid-eighteenth century from the ranks of moralists, philosophers, physicians and scientists. Speaking in the name of Nature, they set out to prove that what was natural in the human body was basically good for the body politic": Yalom, *A History of the Breast,* 106. She differentiates this pro-republic argument against wet-nursing from the earlier, less-virulent arguments against it in the earlier eighteenth and seventeenth centuries that focused on the infant's possibly imbibing negative qualities via a wet-nurse's milk: ibid., 106–10). Instead, the ideological focus of mater-nal breastfeeding is on its connection to "good mothers" who will raise strong citizens and represent a nation that "feeds" its people and its metaphorical mother.

11. Perry, "Colonizing the Breast."

12. Perry's argument is that "motherhood was a colonial form—the domestic, familial counterpart to land enclosure at home and imperialism abroad. . . . The invention of childhood and the invention of motherhood . . . can be seen as adaptations of an existing social system to the new political and economic imperatives of an expanding English empire": ibid., 206.

13. Yalom, *A History of the Breast,* 120.

14. Richter, "Wet-Nursing, Onanism and the Breast in Eighteenth-Century Germany," 1.

15. For a further discussion of the challenges that have been made against Laqueur's argument, see Karen Harvey's review essay "The Century of Sex? Gender, Bodies, and Sexuality in the Long Eighteenth Century." In it, she discusses how investigations of earlier and later sexualities problematize Laqueur's claim that the eighteenth century was a pivotal moment in this change. Similarly, she notes that it may not be possible to argue for how people understood their own sex in the eighteenth century, and

Laqueur's argument rests primarily on medical texts that did not have a wide circulation at the time: Harvey, "The Century of Sex?" 913–15.

16. Richter, "Wet-Nursing, Onanism and the Breast in Eighteenth-Century Germany," 4.

17. Richter, "Wieland and the Phallic Breast," 137.

18. Prytula, "Great-Breasted and Fierce," 175.

19. Prytula uses the example of Miss Tishy Snap and Blear-Eyed Moll in *Jonathan Wild*, in which Fielding's placement of their breasts as "a little below the girdle' graphically parodies [these women's] own trespasses into what he considered to be exclusively male preserves of thought and behavior: just as their minds assume masculine characteristics, so their breasts—the most conspicuous sign of their sex—abandon their proper feminine sphere to hang suspended instead at the groin in grotesque imitation of the phallus.": Prytula, "Great-Breasted and Fierce," 178.

20. Schiebinger points out that the breast and its association with women links women with the bestial: like female animals, women also suckle their young. "Within Linnaean terminology," she writes, "a female characteristic (the lactating mamma) ties humans to brutes": Shiebinger, *Nature's Body*, 55. The lactating breast is, of course, larger usually than a "virginal" breast, thus again linking large breasts to a negative value, though not quite the same in meaning as the "phallic" breast that threatens with female power.

21. Barker-Benfield, *The Culture of Sensibility*, 351–96.

22. Wahrman, *The Making of the Modern Self*, 8.

23. Shiebinger, *Nature's Body*, 64.

24. Wilson, *The Island Race*, 178.

25. Ibid., 179.

26. Given the interests in female cross-dressing, hermaphrodites, and ambiguously gendered celebrities like the Chevalier d'Éon, it is unsurprising that certain androgynous characteristics would be considered fashionable and appealing in the eighteenth century.

27. Warner, *Monuments and Maidens*, 278.

28. Wahrman, *The Making of the Modern Self*, discusses female cross-dressers such as Hannah Snell and Christian Davies in the context of the term "Amazon" and how it changed over the course of the eighteenth century, but he does not discuss the breasted element of the Amazon.

29. O'Driscoll, "The Pirate's Breasts," 360.

30. *The Life and Adventures of Mrs. Christian Davies* has been attributed in the past to Daniel Defoe (see Donoghue, *Passions between Women*, 94). The text was published in the nineteenth century as a part of Defoe's works—for example, in *De Foe's Works: Roxana, The Fortunate Mistress and Mother Ross*, Bohn's Standard Library, vol. 4 (London, 1883). I have not found anything that substantiates this claim, however, especially since *The Life and Adventures of Mrs. Christian Davies* was published in 1741 and Defoe died in 1731. Similarly, biographies of and monographs on Defoe, such as Backscheider, *Daniel Defoe*, and Novak, *Daniel Defoe*, do not mention it (though both mention, at least in passing, *A General History of the Robberies and Murders of the Most Notorious Pyrates*, in which the stories of Anne Bonny and Mary Read appear).

31. Davies's narrative has received somewhat less attention than Snell's, although Emma

Donoghue, Dianne Dugaw, Dror Wahrman, and Julie Wheelwright all mention it. The discussion of Davies's narratives tends in two primary directions, similar to the discussions of Snell's narrative and those of other female cross-dressers such as Deborah Sampson and Mary Ann Talbot: looking at how these women's narratives were co-opted either for discussions of national valor and character or as signs of acceptable gender-bending among the plebeian classes in Britain.

32. *The Life and Adventures of Mrs. Christian Davies,* 373. The idea of preserving the breasts from being hurt foreshadows, possibly, the diseased breast in *Belinda,* suggesting perhaps that femininity is defined by the pure, unharmed breast. Conversely, the desire to preserve the breasts from harm might simply be a precaution against being exposed as a woman. If the breasts are wounded, then sex might be revealed by the army medics—as eventually happens in her story.

33. Ibid., 415–16.

34. For a more detailed account of the role of skin color and race in the narrative of Mary Read, see Klein, "Busty Buccaneers and Sapphic Swashbucklers."

35. *A General History of the Pyrates* was at one time attributed to Daniel Defoe—as was the story of Mrs. Christian Davies. Both attributions have been, at the time of this writing, deattributed. For more on the deattribution of *The Life and Adventures of Mrs. Christian Davies,* see n. 31.

36. Very little of these women's lives remains in the public record, and my analysis focuses exclusively on their representation in print culture of the time. Their fame in England was made through their inclusion in Johnson's *A General History,* which, though first published in 1724, went through a number of issues and reprints throughout the eighteenth century and, in increasingly fictionalized and edited versions, in the nineteenth century. Many scholars have identified the elements of literary romance in the stories of Bonny and Read, further affirming the notion that their narratives function separately from the women's lived reality, much in the same way as do the stories of Snell, Davies, and other female cross-dressers.

37. It was not uncommon for stories of cross-dressing women to attribute their behavior to earlier cross-dressing tendencies in their childhood, as in Charlotte Charke's autobiography.

38. Johnson, *A General History of the Robberies and Murders of the Most Notorious Pyrates,* 154.

39. Ibid.

40. Ibid., 157.

41. This example echoes Prytula's argument about hierarchies of breasts in Fielding's works, in which she marks the contrast between white and brown breasts, white ones naturally being more feminine and less "Amazonian": Prytula, "'Great-Breasted and Fierce,'" 188–89. Significantly, Prytula's argument is that in a closer reading, though Fielding's narrator appears to prefer white, small breasts, the descriptions of the "virtuous" women and the "Amazonian" ones are actually more similar than different.

42. While I assume that the whiteness of Read's breast indicates her femininity because a woman's breasts are never exposed to the sun in the way a laboring-class man's might be, several problematic points arise here. An aristocratic or middle-class man

might also have a very white chest, for example. Second—and more to the point, perhaps—is the indication of racial preference that echoes Wiseman's and Perry's discussions of colonial/colonized breasts. For a more detailed discussion of Read's white breasts, see Klein, "Busty Buccaneers and Sapphic Swashbucklers."

43. O'Driscoll, "The Pirate's Breast," 365.

44. See Klein, "Eighteenth-Century Female Cross-Dressers and Their Beards"; Lanser, *The Sexuality of History*.

45. Johnson, *A General History of the Robberies and Murders of the Most Notorious Pyrates*, 156–57.

46. Both Londa Schiebinger and Kathleen Wilson have noted how the size and shape of women's breasts took on added importance in the transnational eighteenth century. Schiebinger writes that the eighteenth-century ideal breast was a "virginal" one. The qualities of the virginal breast—small and rounded—were thought to exemplify a civilized society. Schiebinger points out that the colonial enterprise contributed to this classification, writing, "The ideal breast—for all races—was once again young and virginal. Europeans preferred the compact 'hemispherical type,' found, it was said, only among whites and Asians": Schiebinger, *Nature's Body*, 64. Similarly, Kathleen Wilson finds evidence for such emphasis on small-breastedness in the eighteenth century. She argues that British historians and writers on the Cook voyages to the Pacific frequently cite the size and shape of native women's breasts to determine the level of civilization in that society. According to Wilson, the ideal eighteenth-century mother had "round and moderately sized breasts with well-formed nipples": Wilson, *The Island Race*, 178.

47. See Perry, "Colonizing the Breast."

48. Joseph Roach argues that whiteness held multiple resonances in the eighteenth century, which pointed to its superiority not only racially but as a skin tonality—for example, as a skin tone aligned with Neoclassical ideas, emotional sensibility, purity, and so on. For more, see Roach, *It*, 146–73.

49. Ibid., 122.

50. Ibid., 123.

51. O'Driscoll, "The Pirate's Breasts," 365.

52. *The Female Soldier*, 31.

53. Ibid., 32.

54. Ibid., 32–33.

55. I explore the implications of depicting or discovering a missing body part in chapter 3 in this volume.

56. *The Female Soldier*, 7.

57. Bowen uses this phrase as a way to discuss how stories of female soldiers "rall[ied] both men and women's support for the ensuing war": Bowen, "The Real Soul of a Man in Her Breast," 21. This is a similar argument to the one apparent in the epilogue "The Female Volunteer; or, An Attempt to Make Our Men Stand," read by the actress Margaret Woffington in drag. A pamphlet version with a full-length portrait of Woffington in drag along with the epilogue was printed in 1746. Bowen herself remarks on the similarity of ideology between Snell's account as brave soldier and Woffington's

epilogue, exhorting British men to volunteer: ibid., 29. On the more performative aspects of women in regimentals used to solicit volunteers for the British army, see Dugaw, *Warrior Women and Popular Balladry*, 52.

58. Warner, *Monuments and Maidens*, 278.

59. Within the confines of the one-sex model of human sexuality, we can understand that although Snell is burdened by the frailties of the female frame, her soul aspires to a "higher" humanity, which in this model, is masculine. At the same time, however, I wish to suggest that this is not the only way to read Snell's narrative, which is so full of openings and slippages on the part of the narrator that it is possible to read it several ways.

60. *The Life and Adventures of Mrs. Christian Davies*, 378–79.

61. Ibid.

62. Ibid., 381.

63. Castle has pointed out that "Mary Hamilton is indeed both 'Villain' and 'Heroe' for Fielding; she is the object of both 'Contempt' and 'Admiration.' From one part of him, she elicits anxiety, but from another, she draws engagement and identification—for the purity of her daring, the beauty of her sham": Castle, "Matters Not Fit to Be Mentioned," 619.

64. In this case, it is clear that Hamilton fears the discovery of her biological sex, but the text never explicitly mentions Hamilton's own sense of gender. Her story, like that of Catherine Vizzani, the Italian female husband, can thus be read as a proto-transgender representation. I discuss Vizzani's story at length in chapter 3.

65. Fielding, *The Female Husband and Other Writings*, 31. In Fielding's satire, the Methodists are responsible for seducing all the members of their sect, whether men or women. Misty Anderson further explores Fielding's use of Methodism in *The Female Husband*, suggesting that "the broad joke of the story, that Hamilton has become the 'new man' of Methodism, reveals Fielding's fears about the indeterminacy of gender and the flexibility within the emerging sex gender system in the face of an evangelical discourse of spiritual *jouissance*": Anderson, *Imagining Methodism*, 72.

66. "Rogers," as slang for sex, like the Isle of "Man," is another satirical play on words that Fielding deploys in the text.

67. Fielding, *The Female Husband and Other Writings*, 31.

68. Ibid., 46–47.

69. Ibid., 47.

70. Ibid., 49.

71. Fielding's use of "every body" rather than "everyone" suggests another playful use of language that implicates the bodies of the townspeople as well as of Hamilton in the text's gender ambiguities.

72. Fielding, *The Female Husband and Other Writings*, 50.

73. Ibid., 46. Emily Finlay suggests that Mary Price's lack of reaction to Hamilton's breasts and her commitment to defending her "husband" shows us that "Price's desire for Hamilton suggests that female desire for female form may be indigenous." Finlay contrasts Price's desire with Hamilton's, arguing that Hamilton had to be seduced by Anne Johnson into loving women, while Price's desire is naturally geared toward women. I would question this assertion by saying that, first of all, Price was also

seduced by a woman (Hamilton), and second, if we believe that Price believed Hamilton was a man, then she might not recognize Hamilton's female body in that moment of revelation: Finlay, "So Lovely a Skin Scarified with Rods," 165.

74. For more on "middling class" texts, see O'Driscoll, "A Crisis of Femininity," 47. Craft-Fairchild compares what she calls the more positive representations of working-class cross-dressing women such as Hannah Snell, Charlotte Charke, Christian Davies, and Maria Knowles with the "whimsical" dramatic interpretations of the Restoration comedy and the condemnatory, pathetic renderings of such women in eighteenth-century novels. "Plays and novels depicted cross-dressing as either a whimsical or a vicious activity of the well-to-do," she writes, "often undertaken to advance various sexual or political intrigues": Craft-Fairchild, "Cross-Dressing and the Novel," 171.

75. Susan Greenfield writes, "The cure constructs her as a domestic woman, whose internal femininity proves her fitness to serve the interior space of the home": Greenfield, "Abroad and at Home," 218. Teresa Michals continues this argument in "Like a Spoiled Actress off the Stage," 191–214.

76. Ty, "Freke in Men's Clothes," 164.

77. Perry, "Colonizing the Breast," 232.

78. "Edgeworth dispels one of sensibility's key tenets, 'unhealthy soul equals an unhealthy body', or she suggests that Lady Delacour's dissentious behavior is salutary": Montwieler, "Reading Disease," 348.

79. Edgeworth, *Belinda*, 32.

80. Ibid.

81. Tita Chico notes that "Lady Delacour's dressing room evokes the context of privacy, a relation that we have seen regularly associated with illicit models of femininity": Chico, *Designing Women*, 223. In Chico's analysis, however, the dressing room symbolizes the negative association of Lady Delacour's dressing room with her behavior that transgresses and rejects domestic ideals.

82. Edgeworth, *Belinda*, 43.

83. Warner, *Monuments and Maidens*, 278.

84. Moore also notes that for a novel bent on distinguishing between the "good" Belinda and the "evil" Mrs. Freke, the two women end up functioning very similarly in relation to Lady Delacour. She writes, "The rivalry and the comparison set up here between Harriot and Belinda suggest a troubling equation between two characters who are supposed to represent moral opposites": Moore, *Dangerous Intimacies*, 93.

85. Edgeworth, *Belinda*, 43.

86. Ibid., 47.

87. Ibid., 65.

88. Ibid., 62. Significantly, Mrs. Luttridge is the woman with whom Mrs. Freke replaces Lady Delacour. Lady Delacour is betrayed by Mrs. Freke when Mrs. Freke befriends Mrs. Luttridge, Lady Delacour's sworn enemy, thus exacerbating the wound to her bosom.

89. Ibid., 66.

90. The character of Mrs. Luttridge and her rigged faro table may have been based on the case of Lady Buckinghamshire and three of her friends whose illegal gaming tables were the ruin of many gamblers. Although the women were only fined, various carica-

turists depicted them in the stocks or even being flogged for their cheating: see, e.g., the cartoons *Faro's Daughters*, by Isaac Cruikshank (1796), and *Discipline à la Kenyon*, by James Gillray (1797). One of the women involved was Lady Elizabeth Luttrell, whose last name sounds quite a bit like "Luttridge."

91. Edgeworth, *Belinda*, 56.
92. Ibid., 60.
93. Ibid., 57–58.
94. Ibid., 54.
95. Ibid., 43.
96. Moore, *Dangerous Intimacies*, 96.
97. See Bobker, "The Literature and Culture of the Closet"; Chico, *Designing Women*.
98. Edgeworth, *Belinda*, 127.
99. Ibid., 128.
100. Once we begin to consider the role of female intimacies in *Belinda*, we may notice the importance of other relationships, such as Lady Delacour's to her maid Marriot, who is both companion and dictatorial nurse.
101. Edgeworth, *Belinda*, 43.
102. Ibid.
103. Ibid., 45–46. The incident is possibly based on the real-life version of such events. In 1793, Eglantine, Lady Wallace, did indeed cross-dress as a man and sneak into the upper galleries in the House of Commons: see Chalus, *Elite Women in English Political Life*, 50–51.
104. Ibid., 47.
105. Ibid.
106. At the same time, Mrs. Freke's preference for masculine clothing and pursuits suggests an opportunity for a trans reading of this character. Jason Farr explicitly reads Mrs. Freke as a transgender character in *Novel Bodies*, 152.
107. Ibid., 204. While Lady Delacour seems to suggest that she is angry at Belinda for scheming to take away her husband, her accusations also illustrate her pain at the idea that Belinda would prefer someone else to her.
108. Ibid., 225. The inclusion of Mrs. Luttridge in her speech suggests that if Belinda left Lady Delacour for the company of Harriet Freke, she would be immediately plunged into yet another sapphic triangle.
109. The novel is unclear about Mrs. Freke's motives in this scene. While it is obvious she wishes to have Belinda as a battle prize in the war between herself and Lady Delacour, there is nothing explicitly stating that she is not interested in Belinda in and of herself.
110. Edgeworth, *Belinda*, 229.
111. Ibid.
112. Weiss, "The Extraordinary Ordinary Belinda," 446.
113. Weiss discusses the influence of Wollstonecraft's work on *Belinda* more extensively in her article. Her argument, however, focuses much more on Belinda as a "female philosopher," with Freke as her antithesis: ibid.
114. Edgeworth, *Belinda*, 183.
115. Ibid., 93.

116. Significantly, in early drafts of the novel, Lady Delacour was drawn with many of Mrs. Freke's traits. Kathryn Kirkpatrick, the editor of the edition of *Belinda* cited here, notes in an appendix that in later drafts, "Edgeworth displaced many of Lady Delacour's offending qualities on to a foil, Harriet Freke": Edgeworth, *Belinda*, 479. The two characters remain linked through theme as well as plot.

117. Sedgwick, *Between Men*.

118. Edgeworth, *Belinda*, 75.

119. Ibid., 76.

120. Edgeworth, *Belinda*, 314.

121. Clarence's cultivation of a "perfect wife" in "Virginia" serves a similar purpose in *Belinda*, as it also emphasizes that perfection is unappealing because it is boring.

122. Edgeworth, *Belinda*, 478.

123. Harvey, *Reading Sex in the Eighteenth Century*, 95.

3. Penetrating Discourse and Sapphic Dildos

1. Norton, *Mother Clap's Molly House*, 194.

2. Rubin, "Of Catamites and Kings," 472.

3. Ibid., 479.

4. Bianchi, *An Historical and Physical Dissertation on the Case of Catherine Vizzani*.

5. Cleland, *Fanny Hill*.

6. Laqueur, *Making Sex*, 135. He adds that "biological sex, which we generally take to serve as the basis of gender, was just as much in the domain of culture and meaning as was gender"; that "sex is a shaky foundation"; and that legal and social categories of sex were often determined by "gender distinctions—active/passive, hot/cold, formed/unformed, informing/formable—of which an external or an internal penis was only the diagnostic sign. Maleness and femaleness did not reside in anything particular."

7. The eighteenth-century use of the word "hermaphrodite" needs more consideration for its connection to neoclassical ideals and interests in ancient Greek and Roman mythology. Beyond this cultural fascination with people who do not conform to the norm, intersex people inhabited an ambiguous position at this time from a legal standpoint. They could be considered male for legal purposes, such as inheritance, if their bodies tended more toward the masculine according to physicians who examined them. For more on this, see Fausto-Sterling, "The Five Sexes"; Friedli, "'Passing Women,'" 246–49; Laqueur, *Making Sex*, 135.

8. Donoghue, *Passions between Women*, 27.

9. Laqueur, *Making Sex*, 126. Bullough and Bullough also comment on Marie's story. They conclude that, "regardless of biology . . . , gender was not immutable, and there was a real fear that too much masculine behavior might actually transform a female into a male." In the same section, they go on to say, "Though males could not change their sex, feminization could change their gender identity, and there was fear that this might lead to homosexuality": Bullough and Bullough, *Cross Dressing, Sex, and Gender*, 90.

10. According to Tim Hitchcock, stories of female tribades—women with enlarged clitorises, such as one of the women referenced in the *Onania* (London, 1718)—"the

existence of the possibility of the 'clitoris as penis', or tribady, allowed for a further biological explanation of how two women could have sex, and how women could come to find other women attractive": Hitchcock, *English Sexualities*, 80.

11. Lignac, *A Physical View of Man and Woman in a State of Marriage*, 92; Venette, *Conjugal Love Reveal'd*, 20. Lignac's text, like Venette's, appeared in English translation and was widely available. There were, of course, examples of such discourses written by Englishmen—for example, Thomas Gibson's textbook for medical students, *The Anatomy of Humane Bodies Epitomized* (1682), which Donoghue mentions. According to Donoghue, Venette's text, however, was "very popular in eighteenth-century England": Donoghue, *Passions between Women*, 37.

12. Lignac suggests that "the largeness of the clitoris, which sometimes equals, and even surpasses, that of the penis, has impelled some women to abuse this part with others of their sex," while Venette argues that "this part [the clitoris], lascivious Women, often abuse. The *Lesbian Sappho* would never have acquired such indifferent Reputation, if this part of hers had been less": Lignac, *A Physical View of Man and Woman in a State of Marriage*, 92; Venette, *Conjugal Love Reveal'd*, 21.

13. Brandon Teena's tragic story was portrayed in the 1999 film *Boys Don't Cry*, based on the documentary film *The Brandon Teena Story*. Teena was a transgender man who was raped and murdered in a transphobic hate crime that was spurred in part by Teena's attempts to pass as male with his cisgendered girlfriend. In *Female Masculinity*, Halberstam discusses how public bathrooms becomes sites of gender policing, especially for butch or gender nonconforming/androgynous women: see Halberstam, *Female Masculinity*, 20–29.

14. Donoghue, *Passions between Women*, 206.

15. Only two years after *The Female Husband*, another dildo-centered story appears in England entitled *A Spy on Mother Midnight*. Each of these examples is discussed in more detail in Donoghue, *Passions between Women*. I do not linger over them because they do not feature a female cross-dresser.

16. Caulfield, *Blackguardiana*, 96.

17. For a more detailed reading of how dildos came to function as material markers of sapphism in the eighteenth century, see Klein, "Dildos and Material Sapphism in the Eighteenth Century."

18. In his discussion of sexual practices and the dildo poems of the eighteenth century, Wagner notes that "the view that buggery and sodomy were 'unnatural' and of foreign origin . . . was quite common among English writers until well into the nineteenth century." Similarly, "It was an eighteenth-century English myth that everything perverse or 'unnatural' could only have its origin in such immoral and sexually corrupt countries as Bulgaria, France, and Italy": Wagner, "The Discourse on Sex," 50, 53.

19. Wilmot, "Signior Dildoe," ll. 81–84.

20. Rochester's poem also alludes to elements of male homoeroticism by portraying the penises as waiting for Signior Dildo to "come" and then "falling" on him. At the end, Signior Dildo, as he is running away from the attacking penises, is saved by his own "Ballocks," which come "wobbling after" and whose weight "retarded the Foe" or else, the poem tells us, it would have "gone hard with Signior Dildo": Wilmot, "Signior Dildoe," ll. 90–92.

21. "Seignior D—o," as he is called in this poem, was "born" in France, moved to London, took lodgings, and received visitors. Through his extraordinary talents, he eventually "became an Englishman": *Monsieur Thing's Origin*, 8–12.

22. Ibid., ll. 18–19.

23. Ibid., l. 19. The poem is unclear as to how the milliners continue to pleasure each other without Seignior Dildo.

24. Donoghue notes that in the case of the milliners, "The dildo is not an accessory to a masculine identity, but a flexible toy which the women use turn by turn to give each other pleasure": Donoghue, *Passions between Women*, 211.

25. The end of *Monsieur Thing's Origin* also contains a not-so-veiled condemnation of sex between men: "No doubt but this Uncouth contriv'd New Fashion / Was to destroy the End of the Creation; / Like that foul Sin which is as bad in Men, For which God did the Eastern World condemn": *Monsieur Thing's Origin*, 23. Wagner interprets the ending as the author's "succumbing to one of the main obsessions of his age, the fear of depopulation": Wagner, "The Discourse on Sex," 54.

26. As Carellin Brooks remarks, "The dildo's enactment of a penis-like economy only reminds the observer that, no matter how close the dildo comes to the penis, it can never come close enough to be one": Brooks, *Every Inch a Woman*, 149.

27. Caulfield's definition also suggests that women who use the dildo do so only because they cannot access a penis for whatever reason. He writes, "Dildo, an implement resembling the virile member, for which it is said to be substituted, by nuns, boarding school misses, and others obliged to celibacy, or fearful of pregnancy": Caulfield, *Blackguardiana*, 96.

28. Brooks remarks that "an actual penis . . . is hardly necessary to phallic possession by women. . . . The textual woman who appropriates masculine presentation or masculine desire or who sports a penile substitute addresses, however obliquely, her own phallic investiture": Brooks, *Every Inch a Woman*, 115.

29. Donoghue, among others, notes that the vagina in eighteenth-century slang, was a "flat." "The game of (or at) flats is an interesting slang phrase for lesbian sex," she writes. "'Flat' or 'flatt' could mean a 'foolish fellow', and 'flat cock' referred to a woman": Donoghue, *Passions between Women*, 261.

30. She adds, "Given the rudimentary hygiene and the various illnesses, menstruation could easily have been taken for a symptom of venereal disease unless amenorrhea was brought on by a deficient diet or psychological constraints": Leduc, "The Adventure of Cross-Dressing," 150.

31. Dekker and van de Pol recount the story of the Dutch female soldier Martigen Jans, who managed to hide her lack despite a wound in the backside and the fact that she was nursing at the time. "Nursing and medical treatments could involve disrobing," they write. "The 'Stout-Hearted Heroine' relates how she was wounded in the backside in battle, but was nonetheless successful in keeping her real sex hidden throughout two months of nursing. When gangrene threatened, however, the surgeon brought in another doctor to cut out the wound," at which point Jans was found to be a woman: Dekker and van de Pol, *The Tradition of Female Transvestism in Early Modern Europe*, 21.

32. Hollander examines how the male crotch was not prominently displayed in eighteenth-century fashion. Between about 1650 and 1780, according to Hollander, men's fash-

ions emphasized a pear shape that not only would have helped conceal a woman's wide hips but also kept the crotch area rather baggy: Hollander, *Sex and Suits*, 83.

33. Dekker and van de Pol, *The Tradition of Female Transvestism in Early Modern Europe*, 23. They point out, however, that in some documented cases children were able to figure out the "true" gender of the cross-dresser. "Modern psychological research shows that children are less easily fooled by cross-dressing than grown-ups," they write. In one case, a woman was discovered when she landed in Tahiti: "She was immediately indicated as a woman by the natives. They made no automatic assumptions related to trousers and other outward accoutrements of a European male person": ibid. What is most significant here, however, is how much adults of the period in England and Europe relied on clothing and outward markers of gender to judge a person's gender.

34. The crossover between medical and erotic texts of the eighteenth century is discussed in Harvey, "The Century of Sex?"; Hitchcock, *English Sexualities*; Wagner, "The Discourse on Sex."

35. *The Life and Adventures of Mrs. Christian Davies*, 2.

36. Ibid.

37. Ibid.

38. Norton, *Mother Clap's Molly House*, 194. There is no mention whatsoever of this tube in the body of Christian's text, or even of the other female captain whose is supposed to be mentioned on page 6 but is not. However, the bookseller's attempt to explain how she passed despite not having the physical parts necessary to urinate standing up emphasizes both Christian's physical lack and the desire of the text to explain how and why cross-dressing women passed.

39. Donoghue, *Passions between Women*, 94.

40. Ibid.

41. Unlike the female pirates Mary Read and Anne Bonny and the female soldier Jenny Cameron in Archibald Arbuthnot's biography. Arbuthnot's "biography" describes Jenny Cameron as a young woman who, before she even ventured out in men's clothes, had many escapades with young men. She later uses men's clothes to accompany her male lover in the army. For more, see Arbuthnot, *Memoirs of the Remarkable Life and Surprizing Adventures of Miss Jenny Cameron*.

42. Brooks, *Every Inch a Woman*, 160–61.

43. Ibid., 163.

44. Faderman, *Surpassing the Love of Men*, 52.

45. Linck cross-dressed as a man and fought as a soldier in a variety of Central European armies, only to leave and marry another woman. Faderman writes about Linck, "According to her trial transcript, she fashioned a dildo from leather and fastened on it a bag of pigs' bladders and two stuffed leather testicles. This was strapped to her pubis in order to perform coitus. When, after an altercation, her 'wife' confessed to her mother that Linck was a woman, the outraged mother brought her before the law and she was imprisoned and tried. Her 'mother-in-law' produced the dildo as evidence against her. She was executed in 1721": Faderman, *Surpassing the Love of Men*, 51–52. Faderman does note, however, that not in all cases of female husbands, even among those who used dildos, were the women put to death or even punished very severely.

She notes that there is no record, for example, of any female cross-dressers having been put to death in England or America.

46. Fielding, *The Female Husband and Other Writings*, 49. For more about the legal implications of the charges of vagrancy, specifically, see Nicolazzo, "Henry Fielding's *The Female Husband*," 335–53.

47. Norton notes that "female cross-dressing was often classed as fraud, and a scattering of cases can be found in the House of Correction lists": Norton, *Mother Clap's Molly House*, 395.

48. Fielding expresses a similar view in his satirical *An Apology for the Life of Mrs. Shamela Andrews* (1741).

49. Fielding, *The Female Husband and Other Writings*, 34–35.

50. Norton, *Mother Clap's Molly House*, 404.

51. Easton, "Covering Sexual Disguise."

52. Ibid., 99–100.

53. The report of Hamilton's arrest and trial for fraud was published in a variety of newspapers in 1746. However, the differences between those reports and Fielding's tale are quite vast, especially given that the original newspaper reports were hardly more than a paragraph or two. For the exact differences, see Baker, "Henry Fielding's *The Female Husband*."

54. See Castle, "Matters Not Fit to Be Mentioned," 602.

55. Braunschneider, "Acting the Lover," 221.

56. Castle, "Matters Not Fit to Be Mentioned," 615, 618.

57. "On one level, he is afraid of her and what she represents; on another, he delights in speaking of her," Castle, "Matters Not Fit to Be Mentioned," 608. Castle makes a convincing argument for the rereading of Fielding's text as one that allows for a reevaluation of Hamilton's story as both a natural part of Fielding's oeuvre and an important contribution to the eighteenth-century discussion of gender and masquerade.

58. Jill Campbell has also written about the uncertainty of attitude toward gender play in Fielding's other works, such as his satirical poems and plays. "The stock jokes about gender in Fielding's plays show not only a satiric interest in men who abdicate their masculinity and all it is imagined to entail," she writes, "but an apocalyptic vision of women's appropriation of that masculine power": Campbell, "When Men Women Turn," 59.

59. Misty Anderson analyzes the use of Methodism and its relationship to sapphism and gender fluidity in Fielding's text, noting that, "for Fielding, Methodism functions like a sexuality, explaining Hamilton's same-sex 'conversion,' shaping her subsequent cross-gender identity, and driving the picaresque narrative": Anderson, *Imagining Methodism in Eighteenth-Century Britain*, 71. For more on her reading, see ibid., 70–99.

60. Fielding, *The Female Husband and Other Writings*, 39. Please note that in most places, I use the feminine pronoun when referring to Mary Hamilton, though this usage is not meant to foreclose readings of Hamilton as transgender. Fielding's narrator uses both at different times, but his ironic outrage is directed toward the sapphic elements of the narrative, making Hamilton's femaleness an important element of my analysis. Throughout the chapter, as in previous chapters, I mark the moment in which the text

cannot support a singular understanding of Hamilton's gender and where transgender subjectivity and bodies can be read.

61. Donoghue, *Passions between Women*, 77.

62. Ibid.

63. Blackwell, "An Infallible Nostrum," 69. "Greensickness" was thought to be an illness afflicting virgins; now it is commonly thought to be anemia. In the case of the widow Rushford, of course, the problem of reproduction does not exist. At sixty-eight, she is unlikely to conceive, despite her own insistence at the wedding that the parson "not omi[t] the prayer in the matrimonial service for fruitfulness." In a sense, Hamilton underestimates the widow's sexual appetites, which are what end up undoing Hamilton's charade. This particular marriage is significant in the ways in which Fielding satirizes lusty widows and Hamilton's inability to keep up with her appetites: Fielding, *The Female Husband and Other Writings*, 38.

64. Fielding, *The Female Husband and Other Writings*, 42.

65. Craft-Fairchild, "Sexual and Textual Indeterminacy," 420.

66. Donoghue, *Passions between Women*, 77.

67. Fielding, *The Female Husband and Other Writings*, 48.

68. Anderson, *Imagining Methodism in Eighteenth-Century Britain*, 97.

69. Fielding, *The Female Husband and Other Writings*, 29–31.

70. Ibid., 37, 49.

71. Ibid., 51.

72. Castle, "'Matters Not Fit to Be Mentioned,'" 610.

73. Braunschneider, "Acting the Lover," 222.

74. Ahmed, *Queer Phenomenology*, 106. For more on the "fleeting" representations of lesbian orientations, see ibid., chap. 2.

75. Ibid., 106.

76. Fielding, *The Female Husband and Other Writings*, 49.

77. Braunschneider, "Acting the Lover," 222.

78. Ibid.

79. Blackwell, "An Infallible Nostrum," 59.

80. Donoghue, *Passions between Women*, 78.

81. Braunschneider, "Acting the Lover," 222.

82. Blackwell, "An Infallible Nostrum," 73.

83. Fielding, *The Female Husband and Other Writings*, 50.

84. Traub, *The Renaissance of Lesbianism in Early Modern England*, 197.

85. Fielding, *The Female Husband and Other Writings*, 51.

86. Ibid.

87. Ibid., 39.

88. As with Hamilton in *The Female Husband*, I tend to refer to Vizzani using the feminine pronoun, a fraught choice for a person who eventually comes to live as a man and is at times referred to using the masculine pronoun in the text—as well as the feminine pronoun. My choice reflects my primary interest in the text's fears of lesbian sexuality and its investment in proving that Vizzani was physically female, but I acknowledge that the masculine pronoun is just as appropriate as the feminine one,

and transgender readings of Vizzani, like those by other scholars, will help develop the discourse on transness and gender fluidity in the past.

89. Roger Lonsdale identifies Cleland as the translator of the Italian text and the author of the translator's note: see Lonsdale, "New Attributions to John Cleland."

90. Lanser has identified both of these narratives as part of a growing body of literature in the eighteenth century that she terms "sapphic picaresques." For more on this concept, see Lanser, *The Sexuality of History*, 157–69, and also Lanser, "Sapphic Picaresque, Sexual Difference, and the Challenges of Homo-Adventuring."

91. Bianchi, *An Historical and Physical Dissertation on the Case of Catherine Vizzani*, 37.

92. Ibid., 43–44.

93. For more on the perceived link between lesbians and monstrous clitorises, see Lanser, *The Sexuality of History;* Findlen, "Anatomy of a Lesbian"; Traub, *The Renaissance of Lesbianism in Early Modern England*.

94. Bianchi, *An Historical and Physical Dissertation on the Case of Catherine Vizzani*, 3–4.

95. Ibid., 10.

96. Ibid., 10–11.

97. Ibid., 11.

98. Ibid.

99. Ibid., 34–35.

100. Donoghue, *Passions between Women*, 83. See also the frontispiece in Bianchi, *An Historical and Physical Dissertation on the Case of Catherine Vizzani*.

101. Bianchi, *An Historical and Physical Dissertation on the Case of Catherine Vizzani*, 39.

102. For more on the material aspects of the dildo, see Klein, "Dildos and Material Sapphism in the Eighteenth Century."

103. Bianchi, *An Historical and Physical Dissertation on the Case of Catherine Vizzani*, 12, 21. In *The Female Husband*, Hamilton's wives do not know that Hamilton is a woman, suggesting that the same-sex attraction is only on the side of Hamilton. I argue elsewhere, however, that the women Hamilton seduces are, in fact, attracted to her feminine or gender-neutral qualities—something that is evident in Vizzani's narrative, as well: see Klein, "Eighteenth-Century Female Cross-Dressers and Their Beards."

104. Just as the English dildo poems attribute dildos to France and Italy.

105. Bianchi, *An Historical and Physical Dissertation on the Case of Catherine Vizzani*, 55.

106. Ibid., 53.

107. Ibid., 54.

108. Lonsdale surmises that Cleland's editorial comments condemning Vizzani's behavior had one main function: "to give some air of respectability to the publication": Lonsdale, "New Attributions to John Cleland," 278. However, I contend that the reasons Cleland provides for his condemnation of her behavior as specifically coming from the mind rather than the body (i.e., nature) complicates our understanding of motivations and attraction in *Fanny Hill*: ibid.

109. Ibid.

110. Gladfelder, *Fanny Hill in Bombay*, 168.

111. Ibid.

112. A term coined in Marcus, *The Other Victorians*, 268, to describe a pornographic fantasy.

113. Lanser, *The Sexuality of History*, 176.

114. Ibid., 177.

115. Cleland, *Fanny Hill*, 15.

116. Ibid., 40.

117. Ibid., 180.

118. Miller, "The 'I's' in Drag," 54.

119. Epstein, "Fanny's Fanny," 139, 149.

120. Moore argues that "Fanny's sexual agency, which is supposed to guarantee her insatiable desire for men, intersects with the conventions of memoir form and heroine description to produce a female homosexual gaze": Moore, *Dangerous Intimacies*, 66.

121. Ibid., 60.

122. Many queer and feminist literary scholars have noted that there is a strong case to be made for the centrality of anal sex and homosexual male economies of desire in the novel: see, e.g., Haggerty, "Keyhole Testimony"; Mitchell, "Dreadful Necessities."

123. See Beynon, "Traffic in More Precious Commodities"; Gladfelder, *Fanny Hill in Bombay*; Moore, *Dangerous Intimacies*.

124. It appears ten times over the course of the text.

125. Cleland, *Fanny Hill*, 39 ("weapon of pleasure"), 47 ("the engine of love-assaults"), 74 ("truncheon"), 84 ("a may-pole"), 86 ("engine"), 87 ("pick-lock" and "delicious stretcher"), 97 ("superb piece of furniture"), 140 ("pleasure-pivot"), 160 ("a splitter"), 173 ("instrument").

126. Cleland frequently refers to the head of the penis and its color, as well as to pubic hair and other elements of the flesh that make up the genitalia, but he never uses the word "penis."

127. Bordo, *The Male Body*, 48.

128. Ibid., 48, 64.

129. Previous scholarship on the penises of *Fanny Hill; or, The Memoirs of a Woman of Pleasure* includes Blackwell, "It Stood an Object of Terror and Delight"; Kubek, "The Man Machine"; McCracken, "A Burkean Analysis of the Sublimity and the Beauty of the Phallus in John Cleland's *Fanny Hill*," 138–41.

130. Cleland, *Fanny Hill*, 176.

131. Ibid., 177. Danielle Bobker suggests that Cleland constructs male-female anal sex in terms of "mis-direction," a much less condemnatory logic than that which he uses to discuss male-male anal sex, thus implying a certain acceptance of the former: Bobker, "Sodomy, Geography, and Misdirection in *Memoirs of a Woman of Pleasure*," 1036–45.

132. Cleland, *Fanny Hill*, 143.

133. Ibid., 160.

134. Ibid.

135. Ibid., 176.

136. Fanny notes that "nothing in nature could represent a prettier boy than [Emily] did; being so extremely fair and well limb'd": ibid., 175.

137. Bobker, "Sodomy, Geography, and Misdirection in *Memoirs of a Woman of Pleasure*," 144.

138. Cleland, *Fanny Hill*, 176.

139. Ibid., 179.

140. Ibid., 15.

141. Nussbaum, "One Part of Womankind," 26.

142. Mengay, "The Sodomitical Muse," 191.

143. Nussbaum, "One Part of Womankind," 32.

144. Gladfelder, *Fanny Hill in Bombay*, 99.

145. For more on the representation of flagellation in the novel, see Anderson, "Mr. Barvile's Discipline," 199–220.

146. This moment in the novel is reminiscent of Rochester's poem *The Disabled Debauchee*, in which the narrator admonishes "Chloris" to remember "our love-fits . . . / When each the well-looked linkboy strove t'enjoy, / And the best kiss was the deciding lot / Whether the boy used you, or I the boy" (ll. 33–36): Wilmot, *The Poems of John Wilmot*, 97–99.

147. Faderman has noted that "nontransvestite women had a great latitude in the affection they could show toward other women," while "transvestite lesbians do not seem to have been let off as easily." The difference, according to Faderman, was that the transvestite women more obviously "impersonated men" and thus "the claim of male prerogative combined with the presumed commission . . . of certain sexual acts, especially if a dildo was used, seem to have been necessary to arouse extreme societal anger." She also notes that "eighteenth-century French and German transvestite lesbians who wore men's clothes for the freedom they symbolized and did not seriously attempt to pass, or whose transvestism could be explained as an 'honest mistake,' were also treated less harshly under the law." Faderman, *Surpassing the Love of Men*, 50–53.

4. Putting on Gender, One Leg at a Time

1. Freeman, *Character's Theater*, 162.

2. Brooks, *Actresses, Gender, and the Eighteenth-Century Stage*, 70.

3. The dandies and macaronis of the Augustan period were often satirized for the height of the boot heels, the care they took in choosing their tights, and the unnecessary tightness of their breeches.

4. Mandeville, *The Fable of the Bees*, 146.

5. Nearly all fashion historians note that in the first half of the eighteenth century, men's coats were long, and the bottom half often jutted out, reinforced with whalebone, in imitation of women's skirts: see, e.g., Cunnington and Cunnington, *Handbook of English Costume in the Eighteenth Century*, 44–45.

6. Hollander notes that in the eighteenth century, women did not even wear bifurcated underwear. Similarly, the petticoat "became the one defining female garment, along with the veil for the head. To dress as a woman, in such a way as to be wholly transformed and disguised, all a man needed was a skirt and a kerchief": Hollander, *Sex and Suits*, 26, 53.

7. Ibid., 47, 53.

8. Ibid., 53, 47.

9. DeRitter, *The Embodiment of Characters*, 79. Similarly, Dianne Dugaw writes, "The fashion for women in male attire in Restoration plays is usually attributed to audi-

ence interest in seeing the female actresses in form-revealing attire. Thus, Pepys' remarks on Nell Gwynn 'in her boy's clothes, mighty pretty' lead critics to conclude, as does Robert Hume, that 'females in male dress [were] a favourite for showing off legs'": Dugaw, *Warrior Women and Popular Balladry*, 176n29. See also Hume, *The Development of English Drama in the Seventeenth Century*, 137.

10. Marion Jones notes some of the reasons for putting women in breeches onstage. "More than one excuse," she writes, "served to get actresses into breeches for the delectation of a predominantly male audience. . . . Revivals of old plays with parts written for boys playing women, where the plot demanded assumption of male disguises at times during the action; with the advent of actresses, titillating denouements with bared bosoms and flowing tresses became popular, and new plays were written to exploit this 'disguise penetrated' motif. Next . . . came the 'roaring-girl' type of part, where the heroine adopted men's clothes as a free expression of her vivacious nature: prologues and epilogues were sometimes given by favourite actresses in men's clothes with no other apparent reason than to provide the same arbitrary thrill. Something akin to this was the practice by which an actress took the part of a male character just to amuse the audience. . . . Occasionally a whole play would be performed by women": Jones, quoted in Bullough and Bullough, *Cross Dressing, Sex, and Gender*, 137.

11. Nussbaum, *Rival Queens*, 195.

12. Ibid.

13. Hollander, *Sex and Suits*, 53.

14. Travesty roles were originally men's roles that were often played by women, as opposed to breeches parts, which were female characters who appeared at some point during the play in the disguise of a man. Viola in *Twelfth Night* would be considered a breeches part, while Peg Woffington's or Anne Barry's performance as the character Sir Harry Wildair in Farquhar's *The Constant Couple* would be considered a travesty part. Significantly, the breeches role casts the actress as "obviously" cross-dressing, while travesty roles were meant to be more serious male impersonations. For more on the differences between these two different kinds of cross-dressing parts, see Friedman-Rommell, "Breaking the Code."

15. See, e.g., John Gillray's caricature *A Corner, near the Bank; or, An Example for Fathers* (1797), in which a hunched over man, dressed in Quaker clothes, observes with interest two streetwalkers, one of whom expertly flourishes an exposed leg from underneath her petticoats while gesturing suggestively with her fingers.

16. *Hic Mulier; Haec-Vir*.

17. Scott, *A Journey through Every Stage of Life*, 18–19.

18. The legs of ballet dancers became increasingly exposed toward the end of the eighteenth century, as well, due partly to changes in choreography. The shortening of ballet dancers' skirts in the last decades of the eighteenth century caused an outcry, most notably by the Bishop of Durham, regarding the immorality of these depictions. Isaac Cruikshank satirizes the debate in caricatures. One caricature, of the famed French ballerina Mlle. Parisot, *A Peep at Parisot! With Q in the Corner!* (1796), depicts Parisot lifting up one leg while audience members crane their necks to see up her skirts. Another, *Durham Mustard Too Powerfull for Italian Capers; or, The Opera in an*

Uproar (1807), depicts the bishop climbing the stage, outraged, as several ballerinas lift up their exposed legs while dancing.

19. Farr, *Novel Bodies,* 1.

20. Harvey, "Men of Parts," 806.

21. DiGangi, *The Homoerotics of Early Modern Drama,* 85; Vincent, *The Anatomy of Fashion,* 98.

22. Vincent, *The Anatomy of Fashion,* 98.

23. Ibid., 106.

24. The long coats of the seventeenth century began to shorten, and "breeches, almost invisible at the beginning of the century, were gradually revealed by the shortening of the waistcoat and the backward movement of the coat, and were cut high to meet the rising line of the waistcoat": Buck, *Dress in Eighteenth-Century England,* 31.

25. Buck goes on to say that, after the 1770s, the "breeches, closely moulding the leg above the knee, extended this display. Fine buckles which fastened the straps of the shoe over the tongue gave the final touch of costly elegance to the leg": Buck, *Dress in Eighteenth-Century England,* 31. The male leg, then, was clearly on display and expected to be ornamented, if one could afford it.

26. "By about 1670, however, the amount of material in the petticoat breeches being too inconvenient when worn with a long coat, narrower breeches fastening below the knee became the modes, and the doublet was replaced with a waistcoat. This three-piece suit was to remain the basis of male attire for the foreseeable future; for the next hundred years there was relatively little change in its essential cut apart from fairly minor elements like pocket flap and cuffs, and a gradual shortening of the waistcoat": Ribeiro, *Dress and Morality,* 87.

27. Of course, one could always go "too far" with these fashions. Many considered the bold colors and expensive fabrics worn by fops and macaronis to be an example of such excesses. For more on the censuring of fops, macaronis, and end-of-century "Jessamies," see ibid., 95–118.

28. By contrast, the full-length trousers that started to come into fashion at the end of the century "did not require a perfect body": Hollander, *Sex and Suits,* 54.

29. "In the 1770s, the stock character that came to embody gender-indeterminate male fashions was the 'Macaroni,' an exaggerated type drawing on the contemporary penchant for oversize wigs, brightly colored tight-fitting coats, and impractical accessories." According to Wahrman, the Macaroni was "an easy target for jokes" in the eighteenth century: Wahrman, *The Making of the Modern Self,* 60–61. See also Gowrley, "Representing Camp."

30. Fisher, "Wantoning with the Thighs," 1.

31. Other prints reveal how legs signify social class or good breeding. Excessively thin legs signify masculine weakness or poverty; excessively fat ones indicate a lack of good breeding, greediness, or bourgeois wealth. For examples, see Gillray's *French Liberty and British Slavery* (1792), *John Bull Taking a Luncheon* (1798), and *Britannia between Death and the Doctors* (1804), in which men's incompetence is equally divided between excessively thin and excessively fat male legs.

32. Brooks, *Actresses, Gender, and the Eighteenth-Century Stage,* 67.

33. Dekker and van de Pol, *The Tradition of Female Transvestism in Early Modern Europe*, 94.

34. For discussions of female cross-dressing on the stage in the nineteenth century, see, e.g., Allen, "The Leg Business"; Buckley, "The Culture of 'Leg Work'"; Bullough and Bullough, *Cross Dressing, Sex and Gender*, chap. 10; Garafola, "The Travesty Dancer in Nineteenth-Century Ballet"; Senelick, "Boys and Girls Together"; Senelick, *The Changing Room*, 262–82. As the titles of these texts indicate, while many eighteenth-century scholars claim that female cross-dressing onstage came under heavy censure at the end of the century and was consequently discouraged, the practice persisted well into the nineteenth century.

35. Dugaw comments on the popularity of travesty roles for women in the eighteenth century, saying, "Nor was the theatrical preoccupation with women-in-trousers restricted to the texts. In the eighteenth century it extended beyond the fictional realm of the plays and manifested itself as well in the casting of parts: eighteenth-century actresses played male parts in both operas and spoken plays, serious works and comic. Shakespearean roles often take by women included 'Hamlet' and 'Romeo.' Peg Woffington, Ann Barry, Dorothy Jordan, Margaret Farrell, and many other actresses were regularly featured in the role of 'Sir Harry Wildair' in Farquhar's *The Constant Couple*. Charlotte Charke—who masqueraded as a man in real life—is known to have routinely played male stage roles: 'Macheath' in *The Beggar's Opera*, 'Archer' in *The Beaux Stratagem*": Dugaw, *Women Warriors and Popular Balladry*, 177. She continues, "Through the century women frequently acted the part of 'Macheath' in *The Beggar's Opera*—indeed, in more than one eighteenth-century production of this enormously popular play, *all* the roles were performed *en travestie*, the women playing the men, the men playing the women": ibid., 179.

36. Wahrman, *The Making of the Modern Self*, 49.

37. Ibid., 50. Wahrman attributes this change in ideology as part of the late eighteenth-century turn away from gender play to a more rigid idea of gender difference. With regard to cultural critics of the 1770s and 1780s in England, he writes, "What these commentators on theatrical cross-dressing registered most of all, as they marshaled one by one their belief in the unbridgeable difference between the sexes, was their own unbridgeable difference from their forebears. They could only view this formerly popular practice through a glass darkened by pooh-poohing incredulity . . . and sniggering incomprehension. . . . Here, in sum, is another instance of an eighteenth-century cultural form that appears to have derived its resonance from the *ancien régime* of gender, but then lost its cultural intelligibility as understandings of gender changed": ibid.

38. Lanser, "Of Closed Doors," 283.

39. Senelick, *The Changing Room*, 260.

40. Robert Folkenflick notes also that Charke's performances at the Haymarket often "featured her (frequently cross-dressed) in farces whose satire was sometimes aimed at Colley Cibber. . . . These performances led to a rift [between them]": Folkenflick, "Gender, Genre, and Theatricality in the Autobiography of Charlotte Charke," 99.

41. Higa, "Charlotte Charke's Gun," 2.

42. An unauthorized, anonymously written, and highly fictionalized scandalous biography of Woffington appeared after her death, *Memoirs of the Celebrated Mrs. Woffington*

(1760), that detailed many sexual encounters with men. The biography mostly ignores her cross-dressing and same-sex appeal, focusing instead on her sexual liaisons with various men.

43. Nussbaum, *Rival Queens*, 191.

44. The rift between Charke and her father was quite public, as both were still in the limelight at the time of the quarrel.

45. In addition to Fidelis's biography, *The Well-Known Trouble-maker;* Friedli, "Passing Women"; Mackie, "Desperate Measures"; Rogers, "The Breeches Part"; Straub, *Sexual Suspects*, chap. 7; and a collection of essays on Charke (Baruth, *Introducing Charlotte Charke*), a newer biography of the actress has appeared in recent years (Shevelow, *Charlotte*), as well as essays and book chapters, including Cloud, "The Chameleon"; Redher, "Introduction"; Wanko, *Roles of Authority*, chap. 3.

46. Cheryl Wanko likewise comments on the irregularity of the narrative. She notes, "On one page she's a waiter; on the next she's a mother. With breathtaking rapidity, Charke's shifting roles change her relations to her eighteenth-century reader. . . . Sometimes she addresses the reader directly; sometimes she narrates her adventures in the third person": Wanko, *Roles of Authority*, 81–82. Similarly, Folkenflick writes that "her theatricality and her autobiography consist at once of exposing and hiding": Folkenflick, "Gender, Genre, and Theatricality in the Autobiography of Charlotte Charke," 103.

47. Brian Glover comments on this aspect of her cross-dressing, as well, writing, "First of all, she avoids directly mentioning the topic until the hat episode . . . (ninety pages into the book). When she finally does mention the fact that she has been living in masculine attire, it is only as a hasty aside, buried in the middle of the sentence": Glover, "Charlotte Charke Is Not Her Job," 99.

48. See, e.g., Mackie, "Desperate Measures"; Marsden, "Charlotte Charke and the Cibbers"; Redher, "Introduction"; Smith, *A Poetics of Women's Autobiography*, chap. 4; Wanko, *Roles of Authority*, chap. 3.

49. For more on this usage, see Faderman, *Odd Girls and Twilight Lovers*.

50. Charke, *A Narrative of the Life of Mrs. Charlotte Charke*, 10.

51. Ibid., 11.

52. Ibid.

53. Ibid., 56.

54. Ibid., 10.

55. It is possible, of course, to interpret the young lady's reaction as a way to cover up her shame for falling in love with a woman. After all, undoubtedly very few dissatisfied suitors used the excuse, "Well, actually I'm a woman," and Charke gestures toward this unlikelihood, as well, saying, "[I] desired her to consider, whether 'twas likely an indigent young Fellow must not have thought it an unbounded Happiness, to possess as once so agreeable a Lady and immense a Fortune": Charke, *A Narrative of the Life of Mrs. Charlotte Charke*, 58. Charke's focus on the lady's fortune may also be a commentary on the stories of female husbands who married unsuspecting young women for their dowries, only to leave them—like Mary Hamilton.

56. Charke, *A Narrative of the Life of Mrs. Charlotte Charke*, 58.

57. Ibid., 59.

58. Straub, *Sexual Suspects*, 147.
59. Glover, "Charlotte Charke Is Not Her Job," 99.
60. Much existing scholarship on Charke's *Narrative* focuses on how to interpret her sexuality. In *The Well-Known Trouble-maker*, Fidelis downplays the possibility of same-sex attraction, while Robert Redher, in his introduction to the 1999 edition of *Narrative*, acknowledges the possibility of Charke's bisexuality: Redher, "Introduction." By contrast, Pat Rogers argues that Charke "was in all probability homosexual" but qualifies this statement by saying, "It is a lesbianism which might be described as part-cultural [*sic*], in that Charke seeks a more active and dynamic role outside bed as well as in it": Rogers, "The Breeches Part," 252. Folkenflick and Jade Higa both argue persuasively that Charke's sexuality is ambiguous and open to interpretation, while Marilyn Morris cites Charke's autobiography as an example of "the difficulties of categorizing premodern figures according to the modern notion of sexual orientation": Morris, "Objects of Desire, Identity, and Eros in the Writings of Lord Hervey and Charlotte Charke," 91. See also Folkenflick, "Gender, Genre, and Theatricality in the Autobiography of Charlotte Charke"; Higa, "Charlotte Charke's Gun."
61. Donoghue, *Passions between Women*, 164.
62. Ibid., 166.
63. Craft-Fairchild, "Sexual and Textual Indeterminacy," 429.
64. Donoghue, *Passions between Women*, 164.
65. Charke, *A Narrative of the Life of Mrs. Charlotte Charke*, 96.
66. Ibid., 97.
67. Ibid.
68. It is somewhat unclear as to whether Mrs. Brown actually goes by this appellation or this is just the way Charke refers to her in the text.
69. Charke bemoans her own failed business attempts and squandering of money because of the trials she has put her companion through. She writes, "If every Shilling had been a Guinea, I had made but a reasonable Acknowledgement, after having immers'd her [Mrs. Brown] in Difficulties which nothing but real Friendship and a tender regard to my Health . . . could have made her blindly inconsistent with her own Interest to give into, and so patiently endure": ibid., 124.
70. Ibid., 118.
71. Ibid., 120.
72. Ibid., 135.
73. Ibid., 53.
74. For detailed information on Woffington's life from birth to death, as well as information about life in the theaters where she worked, see Dunbar, *Peg Woffington and Her World*.
75. Those scenes are preceded by descriptions that border on the semi-pornographic and strongly hark back to Cleland's *Fanny Hill*. The moment of intercourse is marked by a series of asterisks, interspersed with phrases indicating consummation of the union, such as "Oh happy Bob!"; "again they plunge"; and "Love's *Elysium*": *Memoirs of the Celebrated Mrs. Woffington*, 15, 55–56.
76. Nussbaum, "The Nation in Breeches," 297.

77. A reference to Woffington's debut role as Polly in John Gay's *Beggar's Opera*.

78. Hitchcock, *An Historical View of the Irish Stage*, 107.

79. Wahrman remarks that the reference to "nature" here suggests that "Woffington's ability to step into a man's boots was seen . . . as a triumph of nature itself" rather than an affront to it. Later in the century, Wahrman argues, attitudes toward cross-dressing actresses became more severe, though, as mentioned earlier, I question this assertion: Warhman, *The Making of the Modern Self*, 49.

80. Nussbaum, *Rival Queens*, 198.

81. Bowen, *The Politics of Custom in Eighteenth-Century British Fiction*.

82. Quin, *The Life of Mr. James Quin, Comedian*, 68.

83. Nussbaum, *Rival Queens*, 218.

84. All subsequent scholarly sources cite Dunbar, and Dunbar's book does not explicitly state which newspaper in Dublin this appeared in, or even its date: Dunbar, *Peg Woffington and Her World*, 39. Hitchcock's *An Historical View of the Irish Stage* cites Woffington's debut in Aungier Street as Wildair in April 1740, so reasonably, these verses must have appeared in one of the Dublin newspapers in the same month.

85. Quin, *The Life of Mr. James Quin, Comedian*, 67.

86. Ibid., 68.

87. As quoted in Rogers, "The Breeches Part," 246.

88. Prosser, *Second Skins*, 5–6.

89. Rogers, "The Breeches Part," 248.

90. Craft-Fairchild, "Cross-Dressing and the Novel," 178.

91. Much scholarly criticism has already been devoted to the discussion of this unusual break in the novel's plot: See, e.g., Castle, *Masquerade and Civilization*, chap. 4; Craft-Fairchild, *Masquerade and Gender*, chap. 4; Parker, "Complicating *A Simple Story*"; Schofield, *Masking and Unmasking the Female Mind*, 175–87; Ty, *Unsex'd Revolutionaries*, chap. 5. Many of these scholars base their critique of the unity of the novel on the comments of Inchbald's biographer, James Boaden, who notes that the two sections were probably unrelated initially and that Inchbald's inclusion of the mourning ring at the end of the second volume was probably an afterthought: see Boaden, *Memoirs of Mrs. Inchbald*.

92. This complexity is in contrast to the often negative portrayal of Catholics in other English novels. One example from the end of the eighteenth century would be Matthew Lewis's *The Monk*, in which Catholicism is explicitly constructed as a debased and vicious religion, and it provides the opportunity for exploring Monk's gothic motifs.

93. With the term "sentimental masculinity" I am thinking of the trope of the "man of feeling" and the novel of sensibility. Some critics have suggested that *A Simple Story* has elements of the novel of sensibility, and certainly Rushbrook appears to embody a form of the sentimental hero, one who, in Patricia Meyer Spacks's description, enjoys a "lavish indulgence in the pleasures of sympathy. . . . The hero of sensibility allows himself to feel": Spacks, "Oscillations of Sensibility," 506.

94. Inchbald, *A Simple Story*, 4–5.

95. Ibid., 337.

96. Ibid., 338.

97. Gary Kelly argues expressly for the second interpretation, writing, "Like most women writers Mrs. Inchbald blamed the degraded condition of women on their education": Kelly, *The English Jacobin Novel*, 71.

98. The critical reception of *A Simple Story* has been varied, and the novel has received much attention, especially with regard to its feminist viewpoint. Various other critics also read the novel as showing that female empowerment is not possible at this time.

99. Castle, *Masquerade and Civilization*, 292.

100. Spacks challenges Castle's stance explicitly, writing that "taking a rather less rosy view than Castle's, I find in Matilda's career not a narrative of female freedom and power but one of necessary acceptance and limited reconciliation": Spacks, *Desire and Truth*, 199. Craft-Fairchild agrees with Spacks's point of view in part, arguing that "Inchbald's work cannot be defined as an unambiguously feminist masquerade text in the way that Castle wishes to define it. Inchbald's presentation is complicated and ambivalent; it is often vehement in its denial of the possibility of female power and equally vehement in its portrayal of male violence directed at women": Craft-Fairchild, *Masquerade and Gender*, 76.

101. Craft-Fairchild, *Masquerade and Gender*, 77.

102. Ibid., 77–78.

103. Inchbald, *A Simple Story*, 154.

104. Inchbald, *A Simple Story*, 142.

105. Pawl, "Only a Girl?" 113.

106. Castle argues that "Inchbald invokes the masquerade quite explicitly as an emblem of liberation": Castle, *Masquerade and Civilization*, 294. Other scholars have also noted the importance of the masquerade to the representation of the power struggle between Miss Milner and Lord Elmwood. Kelly notes, for example, that "the conclusive engagement in the battle for power in love between Miss Milner and her guardian Dorriforth takes place over that classic *locus* for exposition of the theme of liberty and libertinism in fiction and drama, the masquerade": Kelly, *The English Jacobin Novel*, 68.

107. It is doubly significant that Miss Milner initially jokes that she might go in the habit of a nun, later rejecting that idea in favor of Diana. The habit of a nun, while certainly blasphemous when used as a costume, would cover all of Miss Milner's body while still, undoubtedly, referencing pornographic descriptions of nuns circulating throughout the eighteenth century in pamphlet form. Miss Milner's change in costume seems less incendiary from a religious perspective, though it retains the transgressive elements I discuss earlier.

108. Inchbald, *A Simple Story*, 159.

109. Ibid.

110. Ibid., 160.

111. Ribeiro, *Dress in Eighteenth-Century Europe*, 99.

112. Ibid., 230.

113. Ibid., 232.

114. Inchbald, *A Simple Story*, 7.

115. Ibid., 8.

116. Ibid.

117. Schofield, *Masking and Unmasking the Female Mind*, 177.
118. Ibid., 178.
119. It is generally accepted in the criticism of the novel that the relationship between Miss Milner and Lord Elmwood is suggestive of incest, as Lord Elmwood is meant to be a father to Miss Milner rather than a love object. George Haggerty discusses the incestuous implications of the relationship, as do Catherine Craft-Fairchild, Candace Ward, and John Morillo, among others. Most critics discuss the incestuous aspects of Miss Milner's relationship with Dorriforth to make a thematic connection to the incestuous love of Matilda for her actual father (also Lord Elmwood): see Craft-Fairchild, *Masquerade and Gender*, 89; Haggerty, "Female Abjection in Inchbald's *A Simple Story*," 657; Morillo, "Editing Eve," 217; Ward, "Inordinate Desire," 7.
120. Castle, *Masquerade and Civilization*, 312.
121. Inchbald, *A Simple Story*, 154–55.
122. Ibid.
123. Ibid., 156.
124. And as in the story of Diana, who would not allow any men to see her naked, Miss Milner agrees to dress at home only when she learns that Dorriforth and Sandford have gone to Windsor for a hunt. The story of Diana is reversed when Miss Milner returns from the masquerade, however. Instead of Diana punishing the man who crosses her boundary, Miss Milner is punished by men for transgressing the boundaries of propriety. In this way, to return to Castle, we see how "as a narrative event Inchbald's masquerade has only one real purpose: to disclose relations of power, of dominance and submission": Castle, *Masquerade and Civilization*, 309. The exertion of men's power over women, however, does not negate the power of women to love, support, and comfort one another.
125. Castle, *Masquerade and Civilization*, 311.
126. Inchbald, *A Simple Story*, 197.
127. It has been noted, of course, that Matilda is also educated by Sandford. Jo Alyson Parker goes as far as to argue that "Matilda . . . is essentially male-authored, owing her moral authority to a male mentor. Just as Clarissa has her Dr. Lewen, Amelia her Dr. Harrison, and Cecilia her Dean, Matilda has her priest Sandford, her virtue thus regulated by the text's most fervent upholder of patriarchal values": Parker, "Complicating *A Simple Story*," 262. I would argue, however, that such a conclusion overlooks the role of Miss Woodley as friend, companion, and mother figure. There is little indication that Miss Woodley has less influence on Matilda than Sandford, and by the time Lady Elmwood dies, Sandford and Miss Woodley are both dependent on Lord Elmwood.
128. Both Haggerty and Craft-Fairchild discuss Miss Milner and her daughter, Matilda, in terms of the abject. Haggerty argues that "Inchbald's double narrative insists, moreover, on abjection as implicit in the position of the female in a patriarchal culture," while Craft-Fairchild emphasizes that Matilda is "completely abject" when she "has (like her mother) lost access to language. She speaks with looks and gestures, with tears and illness. As was the case with Lady Elmwood, Matilda's mental anguish results in physical impairment": Haggerty, "Female Abjection in Inchbald's *A Simple Story*," 656; Craft-Fairchild, *Masquerade and Gender*, 115.
129. Boaden, *Memoirs of Mrs. Inchbald*, 140.

130. Edgeworth, *Belinda*, 252.
131. Ibid., 312.
132. Reading the wounded legs, Lisa Moore suggests that "Harriot Freke's clothing, then, is linked . . . to her freedom of movement and her opposition to the 'slavery' of women," and "although she is later brutally mangled, as we will see, such violence aims not to recuperate her into the domestic space inhabited by virtuous women but rather finally to do away with the threat of her deviance by severing her completely from that space": Moore, *Dangerous Intimacies*, 91, 97.
133. McMaster, *Reading the Body in the Eighteenth-Century Novel*, 132.
134. Bullough and Bullough, *Cross-Dressing, Sex, and Gender*, 85.
135. Perry notes, for example, that portraits of Dora Jordan, another comic actress known for her breeches roles, "reveal a carefully mediated representation of those erotic and flirtatious possibilities" inherent to breeches parts, and they were "usually half or three-quarter-length rather than full-length portraits, thus avoiding representation of the lower legs and ankles," rendering "the erotic potential of Jordan's legs and ankles . . . absent." Perry argues that "the actress could be re-presented as masculinised yet acceptably feminine and flirtatious" in paintings: Perry, "Ambiguity and Desire," 74.
136. My argument challenges, to an extent, Craft-Fairchild's, in which she argues that novelists "condemn 'benign' forms of cross-dressing" as opposed to the positive portrayals in print culture of working-class cross-dressers: Craft-Fairchild, "Cross-Dressing and the Novel," 171. While it is true that portrayals of cross-dressing novels are often cast negatively, the same-sex desires that emerge from these representations are often cast in a positive or merely ambiguous light. Craft-Fairchild, "Cross-Dressing and the Novel," 171.
137. Davis, "Who Put the 'The' in 'The Novel'?" 328.

Coda

1. *The Female Soldier*, 36.
2. Ibid.
3. Bowen, "The Real Soul of a Man in Her Breast," 26.
4. *The Female Soldier*, 36.
5. Ahmed, *Queer Phenomenology*, 96.
6. Doody, "Introduction," xxxiv.
7. Lanser's *The Sexuality of History* looks extensively at the French context, especially in regard to the text *The Travels and Adventures of Mademoiselle de Richelieu*.
8. Salamon, *Assuming a Body*, 62.
9. Ibid., 52.

BIBLIOGRAPHY

Ahmed, Sarah. *Queer Phenomenology: Orientations, Objects, Others*. Durham, NC: Duke University Press, 2006.

Allen, Robert C. "'The Leg Business': Transgression and Containment in American Burlesque." *Camera Obscura*, no. 23 (1990): 43–68.

Anderson, Misty G. "Mr. Barvile's Discipline: Habit, Passion, and Methodism in the Eighteenth-Century English Imagination." In *Launching Fanny Hill: Essays on the Novel and Its Influences*, edited by Patsy S. Fowler and Alan Jackson, 199–220. AMS Studies in the Eighteenth Century no. 41. New York: AMS, 2003.

———. *Imagining Methodism in Eighteenth-Century Britain: Enthusiasm, Belief, and the Borders of the Self*. Baltimore: Johns Hopkins University Press, 2012.

Andrews, William. *At the Sign of the Barber's Pole: Studies in Hirsute History*, reprint ed. Detroit: Singing Tree, (1904) 1969.

Arbuthnot, Archibald. *Memoirs of the Remarkable Life and Surprizing Adventures of Miss Jenny Cameron*. New York: Garland, 1974.

Backscheider, Paula R. *Daniel Defoe: Ambition and Innovation*. Lexington: University of Kentucky Press, 1986.

Baker, Sheridan. "Henry Fielding's *The Female Husband*: Fact and Fiction." *PMLA* 74, no. 3 (1959): 213–24.

Bark, Julianna M. "The Spectacular Self: Jean-Etienne Liotard's *Self-Portrait Laughing*." *Inferno Journal of Art History* 12, art. 5 (2007–8): 1–6.

Barker-Benfield, J.G. *The Culture of Sensibility: Sex and Society in Eighteenth-Century Britain*. Chicago: University of Chicago Press, 1992.

Baruth, Philip, ed. *Introducing Charlotte Charke: Actress, Author, Enigma*. Springfield: University of Illinois Press, 1998.

Beynon, John C. "'Traffic in More Precious Commodities': Sapphic Erotics and Economics in *Memoirs of a Woman of Pleasure*." In *Launching Fanny Hill: Essays on the Novel and Its Influences*, edited by Patsy S. Fowler and Alan Jackson, 3–26. AMS Studies in the Eighteenth Century no. 41. New York: AMS, 2003.

Bianchi, Giovanni. *An Historical and Physical Dissertation on the Case of Catherine Vizzani*. Translated by John Cleland. London, 1751.

Binhammer, Katherine. "The 'Singular Propensity' of Sensibility's Extremities: Female Same-Sex Desire and the Eroticization of Pain in Late-Eighteenth-Century British Culture." *GLQ* 9, no. 4 (2003): 471–98.

Blackwell, Bonnie. "'An Infallible Nostrum': Female Husbands and Greensick Girls in Eighteenth-Century England." *Literature and Medicine* 21, no. 1 (2002): 56–77. DOI: 10.1353/lm.2002.0004.

Blackwell, Mark. "'It Stood an Object of Terror and Delight': Sublime Masculinity and the Aesthetics of Disproportion in John Cleland's Memoirs of a Woman of Pleasure." *Eighteenth-Century Novel* 3 (2003): 39–63.

Boaden, James. *Memoirs of Mrs. Inchbald: Volumes One and Two.* London: Richard Bentley, 1833.

Bobker, Danielle. "The Literature and Culture of the Closet of the Eighteenth Century." *Digital Defoe* 6, no. 1 (2014): 70–94.

———. "Sodomy, Geography, and Misdirection in *Memoirs of a Woman of Pleasure*." *University of Toronto Quarterly* 79, no. 4 (2010): 1036–45.

Bordo, Susan. *The Male Body: A New Look at Men in Public and Private.* New York: Farrar, Straus, and Giroux, 1999.

Bowen, Scarlet. *The Politics of Custom in Eighteenth-Century British Fiction.* New York: Palgrave Macmillan, 2010.

———. "'The Real Soul of a Man in Her Breast': Popular Opposition and British Nationalism in Memoirs of Female Soldiers, 1740–1750." *Eighteenth-Century Life* 28, no. 3 (2004): 20–45.

Braunschneider, Theresa. "Acting the Lover: Gender and Desire in Narratives of Passing Women." *Eighteenth Century: Theory and Interpretation* 45, no. 3 (2004): 211–29.

Brideoake, Fiona. *The Ladies of Llangollen: Desire, Indeterminacy, and the Legacies of Criticism.* Lanham, MD: Bucknell University Press and Rowman and Littlefield, 2017.

Brooks, Carellin. *Every Inch a Woman: Phallic Possession, Femininity, and the Text.* Vancouver: University of British Columbia Press, 2006.

Brooks, Helen. *Actresses, Gender, and the Eighteenth-Century Stage: Playing Women.* New York: Palgrave Macmillan, 2015.

Bullough, Vern L., and Bonnie Bullough. *Cross Dressing, Sex, and Gender.* Philadelphia: University of Pennsylvania Press, 1993.

Buck, Anne. *Dress in Eighteenth-Century England.* New York: Homes and Meier, 1979.

Buckley, Peter. "The Culture of 'Leg Work': The Transformation of Burlesque after the Civil War." In *The Mythmaking Frame of Mind: Social Imagination and American Culture,* edited by A. J. Gilbert, D. Scott Gilman, and J. Scott, 113–34. Belmont, CA: Wadsworth, 1993.

Butler, Judith. *Gender Trouble.* New York: Routledge, 1990.

———. *Undoing Gender.* New York: Routledge, 2004.

Butler, Samuel. *Dildoides, a Burlesque Poem. By Samuel Butler, Gent. With a Key Explaining Several Names and Characters in Hudibras. Never before Printed.* London, 1706.

Campbell, Jill. "'When Men Women Turn': Gender Reversals in Fielding's Plays." In *Crossing the Stage: Controversies on Cross-Dressing,* edited by Lesley Ferris, 58–79. New York: Routledge, 1993.

Castle, Terry. *The Apparitional Lesbian: Female Homosexuality and Modern Culture.* Columbia University Press, 1993.

——. *Masquerade and Civilization: The Carnivalesque in Eighteenth-Century Culture and Fiction*. Stanford, CA: Stanford University Press, 1986.

——. "Matters Not Fit to Be Mentioned: Fielding's *The Female Husband*." *ELH* 49, no. 3 (1982): 602–22.

Caulfield, James. *Blackguardiana; or, A Dictionary of Rogues, Bawds, Pimps, Whores, Pickpockets, Shoplifters, . . . Illustrated with Eighteen Portraits of the Most Remarkable Professors in Every Species of Villainy. Interspersed with Many Curious Anecdotes, Cant Terms, Flash Songs, etc. The Whole Intended to Put society on Their Guard against Depredators*. London, 1795.

Chalus, Elaine. *Elite Women in English Political Life, circa 1754–1790*. Oxford: Clarendon, 2005.

Charke, Charlotte. *A Narrative of the Life of Mrs. Charlotte Charke* (1755). Edited by Robert Rehder. London: Pickering and Chatto, 1999.

Charles, Ann, and Roger DeAnfrasio. *The History of Hair: An Illustrated Review of Hair Fashions for Men throughout the Ages, plus a Complete Guide to Hair Care for Men*. New York: Bonanza, 1970.

Chico, Tita. *Designing Women: The Dressing Room in Eighteenth-Century English Literature*. Lewisburg, PA: Bucknell University Press, 2005.

Cleland, John. *Fanny Hill; or, The Memoirs of a Woman of Pleasure* (1749). New York: Modern Library Paperback, 2001.

Cloud, Christine. "The Chameleon, Cross-Dressed Autobiography of Charlotte Charke (1713–60)." *Women's Studies* 38, no. 8 (2009): 857–71. DOI: 10.1080/00497870903238448.

Cooper, Wendy. *Hair: Sex, Society, Symbolism*. New York: Stein and Day, 1971.

Craft-Fairchild, Catherine. "Cross-Dressing and the Novel: Women Warriors and Domestic Femininity." *Eighteenth-Century Fiction* 10, no. 2 (1998): 171–202.

——. *Masquerade and Gender: Disguise and Female Identity in Eighteenth-Century Fictions by Women*. University Park: Pennsylvania State University Press, 1993.

——. "Sexual and Textual Indeterminacy: Eighteenth-Century English Representations of Sapphism." *Journal of the History of Sexuality* 15, no. 3 (2006): 408–31. DOI: 10.1353 /sex.2007.0025.

Cunnington, C. Willett, and Phillis Cunnington. *Handbook of English Costume in the Eighteenth Century*. Waukesha, WI: Kalmbach, 1972.

Davis, Lennard. "Who Put the 'The' in 'The Novel'? Identity Politics and Disability in Novel Studies." *Novel: A Forum on Fiction* 31, no. 3 (1998): 317–34.

Defoe, Daniel. *Moll Flanders* New York: Penguin, [1722] 1989.

Dekker, Rudolf, and Lotte van de Pol. *The Tradition of Female Transvestism in Early Modern Europe*. New York: St. Martin's, 1989.

DeRitter, Jones. *The Embodiment of Characters: The Representation of Physical Experience on Stage and in Print, 1728–1749*. Philadelphia: University of Pennsylvania Press, 1994.

DiGangi, Mario. *The Homoerotics of Early Modern Drama*. Cambridge: Cambridge University Press, 1997.

Dinshaw, Carolyn. *How Soon Is Now? Medieval Texts, Amateur Readers, and the Queerness of Time*. Durham, NC: Duke University Press, 2012.

Donoghue, Emma. *Passions between Women: British Lesbian Culture, 1668–1801*. London: Scarlet, 1993.

Doody, Margaret Anne. "Introduction." In *The Wanderer*, by Frances Burney, edited by Margaret Anne Doody, Robert L. Mack, and Peter Sabor, vii–xxxvii. Oxford: Oxford University Press, 2001.

Dugaw, Dianne. "Introduction." In *The Female Soldier; or, The Surprising Life and Adventures of Hannah Snell* (1750), edited by Dianne Dugaw, v–xiii. Augustan Reprint Society Publication no. 257. Los Angeles: William Andrews Clark Memorial Library, 1989.

———. "Christian Davies." In *Memoirs of Scandalous Women*, edited by Dianne Dugaw, 1–5. Chawton House Library Series: Women's Memoirs, vol. 5. London: Pickering and Chatto, 2011.

———. *Warrior Women and Popular Balladry, 1650–1850*. Cambridge: Cambridge University Press, 1989.

Dulaure, Jacques-Antoine. *Pogonologia; or, A Philosophical and Historical Essay on Beards, Translated from the French*. Exeter: R. Thorn, 1786.

Dunbar, Janet. *Peg Woffington and Her World*. New York: Houghton Mifflin, 1968.

Easton, Fraser. "Covering Sexual Disguise: Passing Women and Generic Constraint." *Studies in Eighteenth-Century Culture* 35 (2006): 95–125.

———. "Gender's Two Bodies: Women Warriors, Female Husbands, and Plebeian Life." *Past and Present* 180 (2003): 131–74.

Edgeworth, Maria. *Belinda* (1801). Edited by Kathryn J. Kirkpatrick. Oxford: Oxford University Press, 1999.

Epstein, Julia. "Fanny's Fanny: Epistolary, Eroticism, and the Transsexual Text." In *Writing the Female Voice: Essays on Epistolary Literature*, edited by Elizabeth C. Goldsmith, 135–53. Boston: Northeastern University Press, 1989.

Faderman, Lillian. *Odd Girls and Twilight Lovers: A History of Lesbian Life in Twentieth-Century America*. New York: Columbia University Press, 1991.

———. *Surpassing the Love of Men: Romantic Friendship and Love between Women from the Renaissance to the Present*. New York: Harper Collins, 1981.

Farr, Jason S. *Novel Bodies: Disability and Sexuality in Eighteenth-Century British Literature*. Lewisburg, PA: Bucknell University Press, 2019.

Fausto-Sterling, Anne. "The Five Sexes: Why Male and Female Are Not Enough." *The Sciences* (1993): 20–24.

The Female Soldier; or, The Surprising Life and Adventures of Hannah Snell (1750). Edited by Dianne Dugaw. Augustan Reprint Society Publication no. 257. Los Angeles: William Andrews Clark Memorial Library, 1989.

Fidelis, Morgan. *The Well-Known Trouble-maker: A Life of Charlotte Charke*. New York: Faber, 1988.

Fielding, Henry. *The Female Husband and Other Writings*. English Reprints Series no. 17. Liverpool: Liverpool University Press, 1960.

———. *The History of Tom Jones, A Foundling*. 1749. Edited by John Bender, Oxford: Oxford University Press, 1996.

Fildes, Valerie. *Breasts, Bottles, and Babies: A History of Infant Feeding*. Edinburgh: Edinburgh University Press, 1989.

Findlen, Paula. "Anatomy of a Lesbian: Medicine, Pornography, and Culture in Eighteenth-Century Italy." In *Italy's Eighteenth Century: Gender and Culture in the Age of the Grand Tour*, edited by Paula Findlen, Wendy Roworth, and Catherine Sama, 216–50. Stanford, CA: Stanford University Press, 2008.

Finlay, Emily. "'So Lovely a Skin Scarified with Rods': Modern Notions in Fielding's *The Female Husband*." *Antithesis* 17 (2007): 154–70.

Fisher, Will. "The Renaissance Beard: Masculinity in Early Modern England." *Renaissance Quarterly* 54, no. 1 (2001): 155–87. DOI: 10.2307/1262223.

———. "'Wantoning with the Thighs': The Socialization of Thigh Sex in England, 1590–1730." *Journal of the History of Sexuality* 24, no. 1 (2015): 1–24.

Folkenflick, Robert. "Gender, Genre, and Theatricality in the Autobiography of Charlotte Charke." In *Representations of the Self from the Renaissance to Romanticism*, edited by Patrick Coleman, Jayne Lewis, and Jill Kowalik, 97–116. Cambridge: Cambridge University Press, 2000.

Foucault, Michel. *The History of Sexuality, Volume 1: An Introduction.* New York: Vintage, 1990.

Fradenburg, Louise, and Carla Freccero. "Introduction." In *Premodern Sexualities*, edited by Louise Fradenburg and Carla Freccero, xiii–xxiv. New York: Routledge, 1996.

Freeman, Lisa A. *Character's Theater: Genre and Identity on the Eighteenth-Century English Stage.* Philadelphia: University of Pennsylvania Press, 2001.

Friedli, Lynne. "'Passing Women'—A Study of Gender Boundaries in the Eighteenth Century." In *Sexual Underworlds of the Enlightenment*, edited by Roy Porter and George Rousseau, 234–60. Chapel Hill: University of North Carolina Press, 1988.

Friedman-Rommell, Beth. "Breaking the Code: Towards a Reception Theory of Theatrical Cross-Dressing in Eighteenth-Century London." *Theatre Journal* 47, no. 4 (1995): 459–79.

Garafola, Lynn. "The Travesty Dancer in Nineteenth-Century Ballet." In *Crossing the Stage: Controversies in Cross-Dressing*, edited by Lesley Ferris, 96–106. New York: Routledge, 1993.

Garber, Marjorie. *Vested Interests: Cross-Dressing and Cultural Anxiety.* New York: HarperCollins, 1993.

Gladfelder, Hal. *Fanny Hill in Bombay: The Making and Unmaking of John Cleland.* Baltimore: Johns Hopkins University Press, 2012.

Glover, Brian. "Charlotte Charke Is Not Her Job: The Visual Imagery of Class and Profession in Charke's Narrative." In *Mapping the Self: Space, Identity, Discourse in British Auto/Biography*, edited by Frédéric Regard and Geoffrey Wall, 87–107. Saint-Etienne, France: Publications de l'Université de Saint-Etienne, 2003.

Goldberg, Jonathan, and Madhavi Menon. "Queering History." *PMLA* 120, no. 5 (2005): 1608–17.

Gonda, Caroline. "The Odd Women: Charlotte Charke, Sarah Scott and the Metamorphoses of Sex." In *Lesbian Dames: Sapphism in the Long Eighteenth Century*, edited by John Beynon and Caroline Gonda, 111–26. Farnham, UK: Ashgate, 2010.

Gowrley, Freya. "Representing Camp: Constructing Macaroni Masculinity in Eighteenth-Century Visual Satire," *ABO: Interactive Journal for Women in the Arts, 1640–1830* 9, no. 1, art. 4 (2019): 1–16. DOI: https://doi.org/10.5038/2157-7129.9.1.1171.

Greenfield, Susan C. "'Abroad and at Home': Sexual Ambiguity, Miscegenation, and Colonial Boundaries in Edgeworth's *Belinda*." *PMLA* 112, no. 2 (1997): 214–28.

Haec-Vir; or, The Womanish-Man: Being an Answere to a Late Booke Intituled Hic-Mulier. Exprest in a Briefe Dialogue betweene Haec-Vir the Womanish-Man, and Hic-Mulier the Man-Woman. London, 1620.

Haggerty, George. "Female Abjection in Inchbald's *A Simple Story*." *Studies in English Literature, 1500–1900* 36, no. 3 (1996): 655–71.

———. "Keyhole Testimony: Witnessing Sodomy in the Eighteenth Century." *Eighteenth Century* 44, nos. 2–3 (2003): 167–82.

Halberstam, Jack (Judith). *Female Masculinity*. Durham, NC: Duke University Press, 1998.

Harvey, Karen. "The Century of Sex? Gender, Bodies, and Sexuality in the Long Eighteenth Century." *Historical Journal* 45, no. 4 (2002): 899–916.

———. "Men of Parts: Masculine Embodiment and the Male Leg in Eighteenth-Century England." *Journal of British Studies* 54, no. 4 (2015): 797–821.

———. *Reading Sex in the Eighteenth Century: Bodies and Gender in English Erotic Culture.* Cambridge: Cambridge University Press, 2004.

Hic Mulier; or, The Man-Woman: Being a Medicine to Cure the Coltish Disease of the Staggers in the Masculine-Feminines of Our Times. Exprest in a Briefe Declamation. London, 1620.

Higa, Jade. "Charlotte Charke's Gun: Queering Material Culture and Gender Performance." *ABO: Interactive Journal for Women in the Arts, 1640–1830* 7, no. 1, art. 2 (2017): 1–12.

Hitchcock, Robert. *An Historical View of the Irish Stage, from the Earliest Period Down to the Close of the Season 1788,* 2 vols. Dublin, 1788–94.

Hitchcock, Tim. *English Sexualities, 1700–1800.* New York: St. Martin's, 1997.

Hollander, Anne. *Sex and Suits.* New York: Knopf, 1994.

Hume, Robert D. *The Development of English Drama in the Seventeenth Century.* Oxford: Clarendon, 1976.

Inchbald, Elizabeth. *A Simple Story* (1791). Edited by J. M. S. Tompkins. Oxford World's Classics. Oxford: Oxford University Press, 1988.

Johnson, Charles. *A General History of the Robberies and Murders of the Most Notorious Pyrates.* London, 1724.

———. *The History of the Pyrates: Containing the Lives of Captain Mission, Captain Bowen, Captain Kidd . . . and Their Several Crews.* London, 1728.

Johnson, Mark Albert. "Bearded Women in Early Modern England." *Studies in English Literature, 1500–1900* 27, no. 1 (2007): 1–28. doi: 10.1353/sel.2007.0004.

Kavanagh, Declan. *Effeminate Years: Literature, Politics, and Aesthetics in Mid-Eighteenth-Century Britain.* Lewisburg, PA: Bucknell University Press, 2017.

Kelly, Gary. *The English Jacobin Novel, 1780–1805.* Oxford: Clarendon, 1976.

Klein, Ula Lukszo. "Busty Buccaneers and Sapphic Swashbucklers." In *Transatlantic Women Travelers, 1688–1843,* edited by Misty Kreuger. Lewisburg, PA: Bucknell University Press, 2021.

———. "Dildos and Material Sapphism in the Eighteenth Century." *Eighteenth-Century Fiction* 31, no. 2 (2019): 395–412.

———. "Eighteenth-Century Female Cross-Dressers and Their Beards." *Journal for Early Modern Cultural Studies* 16, no. 4 (2016): 119–43.

Klein, Ula Lukszo, and Emily Kugler. "Introduction to 'Eighteenth-Century Camp' [Special Issue]." *ABO: Interactive Journal of Women in the Arts, 1640–1830* 9, no. 1 (2019).

Kubek, Elizabeth. "The Man Machine: Horror and the Phallus in *Memoirs of a Woman of Pleasure.*" In *Launching Fanny Hill: Essays on the Novel and Its Influences,* edited by Patsy S. Fowler and Alan Jackson, 173–97. AMS Studies in the Eighteenth Century no. 41. New York: AMS, 2003.

LaFleur, Greta. *The Natural History of Sexuality in Early America*. Baltimore: Johns Hopkins University Press, 2018.

Lanser, Susan S. "Of Closed Doors and Open Hatches: Heteronormative Plots in Eighteenth-Century (Women's) Studies." *ECTI* 53, no. 3 (Fall 2012): 273–90.

———. "Sapphic Picaresque, Sexual Difference, and the Challenges of Homo-Adventuring." *Textual Practice* 15, no. 2 (2001): 251–68. DOI: 10.1080/09502360110044087.

———. *The Sexuality of History: Modernity and the Sapphic, 1565–1830*. Chicago: University of Chicago Press, 2014.

Laqueur, Thomas Walter. *Making Sex: Body and Gender from the Greeks to Freud*. Cambridge, MA: Harvard University Press, 1990.

Leduc, Guyonne. "The Adventure of Cross-Dressing: Hannah Snell." In *Adventure: An Eighteenth-Century Idiom, Essays on the Daring and the Bold as Pre-modern Medium*, edited by Serge Soupel, Kevin L. Cope, and Alexander Pettit, 145–67. AMS Studies in the Eighteenth Century, no. 58. New York: AMS, 2009.

The Life and Adventures of Mrs. Christian Davies, the British Amazon, Commonly Called Mother Ross. 2d ed., London: R. Montagu, 1741.

Lignac, Louis Francois Luc de. *A Physical View of Man and Woman in a State of Marriage. With Anatomical Engravings. Translated from the Last French Edition of M. de Lignac*. London, 1798.

Locke, Georgina, and David Worrall. "Cross-Dressed Performance at the Theatrical Margins: Hannah Snell, the Manual Exercise, and the New Wells Spa Theater, 1750." *Huntington Library Quarterly* 77, no. 1 (2014): 17–36.

Lonsdale, Roger. "New Attributions to John Cleland." *Review of English Studies, New Series* 30, no. 119 (1979): 268–90.

Mackie, Erin. "Desperate Measures: The Narratives of the Life of Mrs. Charlotte Charke." *ELH* 54, no. 4 (1991): 841–65. DOI: 10.2307/2873284.

Mandeville, Bernard. *The Fable of the Bees; or, Private Vices Publick Benefits. Containing, Several Discourses, to Demonstrate, That Human Frailties, during the Degeneracy of Mankind, May Be Turn'd to the Advantage of the Civil Society, and Made to Supply the Place of Moral Virtues*. London, 1714.

Marcus, Sharon. *Between Women: Friendship, Desire, and Marriage in Victorian England*. Princeton, NJ: Princeton University Press, 2007.

Marcus, Steven. *The Other Victorians: A Study of Sexuality and Pornography in Mid-Nineteenth-Century England*. Reprint. New York: Routledge, (1964) 2009.

Marsden, Jean. "Charlotte Charke and the Cibbers: Private Life as Public Spectacle." In *Introducing Charlotte Charke: Actress, Author, Enigma*, edited by Philip Baruth, 65–83. Springfield: University of Illinois Press, 1998.

Marshall, Nowell. "Beyond Queer Gothic: Charting the Gothic History of the Trans Subject in Beckford, Lewis, Byron." In *TransGothic in Literature in Culture*, edited by Jolene Zigarovich, 25–52. New York: Routledge, 2018.

McCracken, David. "A Burkean Analysis of the Sublimity and the Beauty of the Phallus in John Cleland's *Fanny Hill*." *American Notes and Queries* 29, no. 3 (2016): 138–41.

McMaster, Juliet. *Reading the Body in the Eighteenth-Century Novel*. New York: Palgrave Macmillan, 2004.

Memoirs of the Celebrated Mrs. Woffington, Interspersed with Several Theatrical Anecdotes; the

Amours of Many Persons of the First Rank; and Some Interesting Characters Drawn from Real Life, 2d ed. London, 1760.

Mengay, Donald H. "The Sodomitical Muse: *Fanny Hill* and the Rhetoric of Crossdressing." In *Homosexuality in Renaissance and Enlightenment England: Literary Representations in Historical Context*, edited by Claude J. Summers, 185–98. Philadelphia: Haworth, 1992.

Michals, Teresa. "'Like a Spoiled Actress off the Stage': Anti-Theatricality, Nature, and the Novel." *Studies in Eighteenth-Century Culture* 39 (2010): 191–214.

Miller, Nancy K. "The 'I's' in Drag: The Sex of Recollection." *Eighteenth Century: Theory and Interpretation* 22, no.1 (1981): 47–57.

Mitchell, Margaret. "'Dreadful Necessities': Nature and the Performance of Gender in *Memoirs of a Woman of Pleasure*." *Women's Studies* 32, no. 3 (2003): 305–24.

Monsieur Thing's Origin; or, Seignior D—o's Adventures in Britain. London, 1722.

Montwieler, Katherine. "Reading Disease: The Corrupting Performance of Edgeworth's *Belinda*." *Women's Writing* 12, no. 3 (2005): 347–68.

Moore, Lisa L. *Dangerous Intimacies: Toward a Sapphic History of the British Novel*. Durham, NC: Duke University Press, 1997.

Morillo, John. "Editing Eve: Rewriting the Fall in Austen's *Persuasion* and Inchbald's *A Simple Story*." *Eighteenth-Century Fiction* 23, no. 1 (2010): 195–223. DOI: 10.3138/ecf.23.1.195.

Morris, Marilyn. "Objects of Desire, Identity, and Eros in the Writings of Lord Hervey and Charlotte Charke." In *Sexual Perversions, 1670–1890*, edited by Julie Peakman, 72–94. New York: Palgrave Macmillan, 2009.

Nestle, Joan. "The Femme Question." In *A Persistent Desire: A Butch-Femme Reader*, edited by Joan Nestle, 138–46. New York: Alyson, 1992.

———. "Flamboyance and Fortitude: An Introduction." In *The Persistent Desire: A Femme-Butch Reader*, edited by Joan Nestle, 13–22. New York: Alyson, 1992.

Nicolazzo, Sarah. "Henry Fielding's *The Female Husband* and the Sexuality of Vagrancy." *Eighteenth Century: Theory and Interpretation* 55, no. 4 (2014): 335–53.

Norton, Rictor. *Mother Clap's Molly House: The Gay Subculture in England, 1700–1830*. London: GMP, 1992.

Novak, Maximillian E. *Daniel Defoe: Master of Fictions, His Life and Ideas*. Oxford: Oxford University Press, 2001.

Nussbaum, Felicity. "The Nation in Breeches: Actress Margaret Woffington." In *"The Stage's Glory": John Rich, 1692–1761*, edited by Berta Joncus and Jeremy Barlow, 211–22. Newark: University of Delaware Press, 2011.

———. "One Part of Womankind: Prostitution and Sexual Geography in *Memoirs of a Woman of Pleasure*." *Differences* 7, no. 2 (1995): 16–40.

———. *Rival Queens: Actresses, Performance, and the Eighteenth-Century British Theater*. Philadelphia: University of Pennsylvania Press, 2010.

O'Driscoll, Sally. "A Crisis of Femininity: Remaking Gender in Popular Discourse." In *Lesbian Dames: Sapphism in the Long Eighteenth Century*, edited by Caroline Gonda and John Beynon, 45–60. Farnham, UK: Routledge, 2010.

———. "The Lesbian and the Passionless Woman: Femininity and Sexuality in Eighteenth-Century England." *Eighteenth Century: Theory and Interpretation* 44, nos. 2–3 (2003): 103–31.

———. "The Pirate's Breasts: Criminal Women and the Meanings of the Body." *Eighteenth Century* 53, no. 3 (2012): 357–79.

Parker, Jo Alyson. "Complicating *A Simple Story:* Inchbald's Two Versions of Female Power." *Eighteenth-Century Studies* 30, no. 3 (1997): 255–70. DOI: 10.1353/ecs.1997.0014.

Pawl, Amy J. "Only a Girl? Miss Milner, Matilda, and the Consolations of Filial Piety in *A Simple Story.*" In *Reflections on Sentiment: Essays in Honor of George Starr,* edited by Alessa Johns, 105–33. Newark: University of Delaware Press, 2016.

Perry, Gill. "Ambiguity and Desire: Metaphors of Sexuality in Late Eighteenth-Century Representation of the Actress." In *Notorious Muse: The Actress in British Art and Culture, 1776–1812,* edited by Robyn Aselson, 57–80. New Haven, CT: Yale University Press, 2003.

Perry, Ruth. "Colonizing the Breast: Sexuality and Maternity in Eighteenth-Century England." *Journal of the History of Sexuality* 2, no. 2 (1991): 204–34.

Prosser, Jay. *Second Skins: The Body Narratives of Transsexuality.* New York: Columbia University Press, 1998.

Prytula, Nina. "'Great-Breasted and Fierce': Fielding's Amazonian Heroines." *Eighteenth-Century Studies* 35, no 2 (2002): 173–93. DOI: 10.1353/ecs.2002.0015.

Quin, James. *The Life of Mr. James Quin, Comedian. With the History of the Stage from His Commencing Actor to His Retreat to Bath.* London, 1766.

Redher, Robert. "Introduction." In *A Narrative of the Life of Mrs. Charlotte Charke* (1755), by Charlotte Charke, ix–li. London: Pickering and Chatto, 1999.

Rediker, Marcus. "Liberty beneath the Jolly Roger: The Lives of Anne Bonny and Mary Read, Pirates." In *Iron Men, Wooden Women: Gender and the Seafaring in the Atlantic World, 1700–1920,* edited by Margaret S. Creighton and Lisa Norling, 1–33. Baltimore: Johns Hopkins University Press, 1996.

Reynolds, Reginald. *Beards: Their Social Standing, Religious Involvements, Decorative Possibilities, and Value, Offence, and Defence through the Ages.* New York: Harcourt, Brace, Jovanovich, 1949.

Ribeiro, Aileen. *Dress and Morality.* New York: Holmes and Meier, 1986.

———. *Dress in Eighteenth-Century Europe, 1715–1789.* New Haven, CT: Yale University Press, 1984.

Rich, Adrienne. "Compulsory Heterosexuality and Lesbian Existence," *Signs* 5, no. 4 (1980): 631–60.

Richter, Simon. "Wet-Nursing, Onanism and the Breast in Eighteenth-Century Germany." *Journal of the History of Sexuality* 7, no. 1 (1996): 1–22.

———. "Wieland and the Phallic Breast." *German Life and Letters* 52, no. 2 (1999): 136–50.

Roach, Joseph. *It.* Ann Arbor: University of Michigan Press, 2007.

Rogers, Pat. "The Breeches Part." In *Sexuality in Eighteenth-Century Britain,* edited by Paul-Gabriel Boucé, 244–57. Manchester, UK: Manchester University Press, 1982.

Rohy, Valerie. *Impossible Women: Lesbian Figures and American Literature.* Ithaca, NY: Cornell University Press, 2000.

Rosenthal, Angela. "Raising Hair." *Eighteenth-Century Studies* 38, no.1 (2004): 1–16.

Roulston, Chris. "New Approaches to the Queer 18th Century." *Literature Compass* 10, no. 10 (2013): 761–70.

Rubin, Gayle. "Of Catamites and Kings: Reflections on Butch, Gender, and Boundaries." In

The Transgender Studies Reader, edited by Susan Stryker and Stephen Whittle, 471–81. New York: Routledge, 2006.

Salamon, Gayle. *Assuming a Body: Transgender and Rhetorics of Materiality.* New York: Columbia University Press, 2010.

Saxton, Kirsten T., Ajuan Maria Mance, and Rebekah Edwards. "Teaching Eighteenth-Century Literature in a Transgendered Classroom." In *Heteronormativity in Eighteenth-Century Literature,* edited by Ana de Freitas Boe and Abby Coykendall, 167–86. New York: Routledge, 2014.

Schofield, Mary Anne. *Masking and Unmasking the Female Mind: Disguising Romances in Feminine Fiction, 1713–1799.* Newark: University of Delaware Press, 1990.

Scott, Sarah. *A Journey through Every Stage of Life, Described in a Variety of Interesting Scenes, Drawn from Real Characters. By a Person of Quality. In Two Volumes. Volume 1 of 2* (1754). Breiningsville, PA: Eighteenth Century Collections Online Print Editions, 2010.

Schiebinger, Londa. *Nature's Body: Gender in the Making of Modern Science.* Boston: Beacon, 1993.

Sedgwick, Eve Kosofsky. *Between Men: English Literature and Male Homosocial Desire.* New York: Columbia University Press, 1985.

Senelick, Laurence. "Boys and Girls Together: Subcultural Origins of Glamour Drag and Male Impersonation on the Nineteenth-Century Stage." In *Crossing the Stage: Controversies in Cross-Dressing,* edited by Lesley Ferris, 80–95. New York: Routledge, 1993.

———. *The Changing Room: Sex, Drag and Theatre.* New York: Routledge, 2000.

Shevelow, Kathryn. *Charlotte: Being a True Account of an Actress's Flamboyant Adventures in Eighteenth-Century London's Wild and Wicked Theatrical World.* New York: Henry Holt, 2005.

Smith, Sidonie. *A Poetics of Women's Autobiography: Marginality and the Fictions of Self-Representation.* Bloomington: Indiana University Press, 1987.

Spacks, Patricia Meyer. *Desire and Truth: Functions of Plot in Eighteenth-Century English Novels.* Chicago: University of Chicago Press, 1990.

———. "Oscillations of Sensibility." *New Literary History* 25, no. 3 (1994): 505–20. DOI: 10.2307/469464.

Straub, Kristina. *Sexual Suspects: Eighteenth-Century Players and Sexual Ideology.* Princeton, NJ: Princeton University Press, 1992.

Stryker, Susan. "Foreword." In *TransGothic in Literature and Culture,* edited by Jolene Zigarovich, xi–xvii. New York: Routledge, 2018.

———. *Transgender History.* Berkeley, CA: Seal, 2008.

Traub, Valerie. "Afterword." In *Sex before Sex: Figuring the Act in Early Modern England,* edited by James M. Bromley and Will Stockton, 291–303. Minneapolis: University of Minnesota Press, 2013.

———. "The New Unhistoricism in Queer Studies." *PMLA* 128, no. 1 (2013): 21–39.

———. *The Renaissance of Lesbianism in Early Modern England.* Cambridge: Cambridge University Press, 2002.

———. *Thinking Sex with the Early Moderns.* Philadelphia: University of Pennsylvania Press, 2015.

Ty, Eleanor. "Freke in Men's Clothes: Transgression and the Carnivalesque in Edgeworth's *Belinda.*" In *The Clothes That Wear Us: Essays on Dressing and Transgressing in Eighteenth-*

Century Culture, edited by Jessica Munns and Penny Richards, 157–73. London: Associated University Press, 1999.

———. *Unsex'd Revolutionaries: Five Women Novelists of the 1790s.* Toronto: University of Toronto Press, 1993.

Vicinus, Martha. *Intimate Friends: Women Who Loved Women, 1778–1928.* Chicago: University of Chicago Press, 2006.

Vincent, Susan. *The Anatomy of Fashion: Dressing the Body from the Renaissance to Today.* New York: Berg, 2009.

Venette, Nicholas. *Conjugal Love Reveal'd; in the Nightly Pleasures of the Marriage Bed, and the Advantages of That Happy State. In an Essay Concerning Humane Generation. Done from the French of Monsieur Venette by a Physician,* 7th ed. London, 1720.

Wagner, Peter. "The Discourse on Sex—or Sex as Discourse: Eighteenth-Century Medical and Paramedical Erotic." In *Sexual Underworlds of the Enlightenment,* edited by G. S. Rousseau and Roy Porter, 46–68. Chapel Hill: University of North Carolina Press, 1988.

Wahl, Elizabeth. *Invisible Relations: Representations of Female Intimacy in the Age of Enlightenment.* Stanford, CA: Stanford University Press, 1999.

Wahrman, Dror. *The Making of the Modern Self: Identity and Culture in Eighteenth-Century England.* New Haven, CT: Yale University Press, 2006.

Wanko, Cheryl. *Roles of Authority: Thespian Biography and Celebrity in Eighteenth-Century Britain.* Lubbock: Texas Tech University Press, 2003.

Ward, Candace. "Inordinate Desire: Schooling the Senses in Elizabeth Inchbald's *A Simple Story.*" *Studies in the Novel* 31, no. 1 (1999): 1–18.

Warner, Marina. *Monuments and Maidens: The Allegory of the Female Form.* Oakland: University of California Press, 2001.

Weiss, Deborah. "The Extraordinary Ordinary Belinda: Maria Edgeworth's Female Philosopher." *Eighteenth-Century Fiction* 19, no. 4 (2007): 441–61.

Wheelwright, Julie. *Amazons and Military Maids: Women Who Dressed as Men in the Pursuit of Life, Liberty and Happiness.* London: Pandora, 1989.

Wilmot, John, Second Earl of Rochester. *The Poems of John Wilmot, Earl of Rochester.* Edited by Keith Walker. Oxford: Basil Blackwell, 1984.

———. "Signior Dildo." In *Poems on Affairs of State, from the Reign of K. James the First, to This Present Year 1703. Written by the Greatest Wits of the Age, viz. The Duke of Buckingham. The Earl of Rochester. The Earl of D—t. Lord J—s. Mr. Milton. Mr. Marvel. Mr. St. J—n. Mr. John Dryden. Dr. G—th. Mr. Toland. Mr. Hughes. Mr. F—e. Mr. Finch. Mr. Harcourt. Mr. T—n, etc. Many of Which Never before Published,* vol. 2. London, 1703.

Wilson, Kathleen. *The Island Race: Englishness, Empire, and Gender in the Eighteenth Century.* New York: Routledge, 2003.

Withey, Alun. "Shaving and Masculinity in Eighteenth-Century Britain." *Journal for Eighteenth-Century Studies* 36, no. 2 (2013): 225–43.

Yalom, Marilyn. *A History of the Breast.* New York: Ballantine, 1998.

Zigarovich, Jolene. "Introduction." In *TransGothic in Literature and Culture,* edited by Jolene Zigarovich, 1–22. New York: Routledge, 2018.

INDEX